NECES

SETTLING MISSOURI
WITH A ROPE AND A GUN

JOE JOHNSTON

Missouri History Museum Press
St. Louis
Distributed by University of Chicago Press

Dedicated to Rebecca Asling Johnston. Never say never.

Unless otherwise noted, the photos in this book are from the author's private collection, and the maps were created by the author.

Library of Congress Cataloging-in-Publication Data

Johnston, Joe, 1948-
  Necessary evil : settling Missouri with a rope and a gun / Joe Johnston.
    pages cm
  Includes bibliographical references and index.
  ISBN 978-1-883982-81-2 (paperback)
1. Missouri--History--19th century. 2. Vigilance committees--Missouri--History--19th century. 3. Vigilantes--Missouri--History--19th century. 4. Frontier and pioneer life--Missouri. 5. Crime--Missouri--History--19th century. I. Title.
  F466.J65 2014
  977.8'03--dc23
                    2014021727

Cover art by Joe Johnston
Distributed by University of Chicago Press
Printed and bound in the United States by Thomson-Shore, Inc.

CONTENTS

Contents

Introduction

Every system of justice is imperfect. That's why in America we elect new sheriffs, the mayor chooses a new police chief, and the legislature makes new laws and strikes down old ones. Every president brings his own attorney general. Court decisions can be appealed to higher courts. We keep trying to make it better.

But there are some people, in some situations, who just can't wait for things to get better. While vigilantes have been active all over America, Missouri is unique with its long and consistent vigilante history. For decades, before Missouri was a state, residents needed protection from criminals. And since it was a land populated by independent, problem-solving pioneers, somebody was bound to step up and deliver what everybody needed. It was the only way to settle such a place. Vigilantism was a necessary evil.

"The right of the people to take care of themselves, if the law does not, is an indisputable right," said Professor Bigger, head of the normal school of Johnson County, Missouri, in 1867 (Ewing Cockrell, *History of Johnson County, Missouri*, Historical Publishing Company, Topeka, KS, 1918). He said that in a speech to inspire a vigilante mob of about four hundred men who then went out and lynched crooks for a couple of weeks. And Bigger wasn't the only public figure with such views. As reported in the Baltimore newspaper, *The Niles Register*, President Andrew Jackson commented on a Missouri lynching in 1834, "As law, emanates from the people, written or not . . . the unanimous decision among that people to put a man to death for the crime of murder, rendered the act legal." He knew that private violence by the American people is deeply woven into the democratic ideal. Our nation was born in blood when diplomacy failed. "We the people" believe we can and should run the show, one way or another.

Vigilantes have punished the bad and protected the good since the beginning of time. Europeans brought vigilantism with them to the New World, where vast territories opened to settlement long before there was any local government, law enforcement officers, or laws to be enforced. When evil struck, people had to make up laws and enforce them on the spot.

When the Louisiana Territory was under Spanish rule, Spain only granted land to settlers who would live at least 15 miles from the nearest settlement. Of course such courageous, isolated pioneers had to provide their own protection. The Louisiana Purchase brought all that land into America, and yet it was not all open to settlement. The government offered the land a bit at a time, which meant that for decades squatters moved in, built houses, fenced fields, and established entire towns, all without paying anything for the land they were on. Then when an area was opened by the government, squatters who were already there had the right to buy it first. If they couldn't afford it, and someone else could, the squatters had to move on. Of course, some of them had crops in the ground, and some of them just resented being kicked off the land they worked, so disagreements flared up. Squatters paid no taxes, while property owners did, and that too created hard feelings. Groups of immigrants would sometimes move in, bringing their own ways of life, which conflicted with the locals. And often, when there was trouble, there were neither laws on the books nor officials to enforce them.

It could be said that there were a few places in America where vigilantism found it hard to take root. East of the Mississippi River, and in the upper Midwest, law enforcement was solidly established by the early 1800s, with newspapers that were quick to scold anyone who took the law into their own hands. A vigilante group calling itself the Union Horse Company formed in 1869 in Keokuk County, Iowa, to combat a wave of thefts. Soon, however, it evolved into a more of a social club. It persisted into the 1900s with a healthy membership and in over thirty years never had any exploits that made the papers. It seems that forming the group was all it took to suppress crime around there.

In Wyoming, where livestock rustling was a problem, Tom Horn was a famous enforcer for the ranchers. But the very nature of the people who lived that far west was a strike against vigilantism; they moved out there to mind their own business. In fact, land was so plentiful in the western part of the Louisiana Purchase, including the future Iowa, Nebraska, and beyond, and it was so sparsely populated with poor farm families, there was little to fight about and little need for vigilantes.

In contrast, the Southwest, where water was scarce, gave rise to range wars and the legend of Billy the Kid. The mining camps of California, Arizona, Dakota, and Colorado were notorious for their instant justice in the absence of lawmen. Arkansas was a wild place where outlaws ran to disappear. After the war that made Texas a U.S. territory, it was a fiercely independent, dangerous place with its own style of vigilantism. Instead of mobs and regulator organizations, every Texan was his own vigilante, and violence was as swift and sure as a quick-drawn revolver.

Kansas vigilantes were bloodying their hands as early as Missouri vigilantes, but the action was mainly in the eastern part of Kansas. The flat grasslands out west offered nothing to interest the bad guys. Non-Indians weren't even supposed to be in Indian Territory, so it was a favored destination of outlaws. When the territory opened to white settlement with the land runs around 1890, violence swept through like a prairie fire. Then the territory became Oklahoma in 1907, and the vigilante fire went out.

As wild as young America could be, no place was home to such a long-lasting concentration of bristling, take-the-law-into-their-own-hands people as Missouri, where vigilantism was common, violent, and more enduring. It kept Missouri hot for most of the nineteenth century. The level of vigilante activity that explodes across the following pages, of this length and depth of depredation, happened only in Missouri.

Missouri was a foster child, passed from home to home, ruled by the Spanish, French, and American governments within a five-year period. Revolutionary War veterans flooded into Missouri after 1800 to claim land grants for war service. Then more veterans came after the War of 1812 and the Black Hawk War. They were all armed, hardened by battle, and ready to defend the rights of their neighbors. Along with those earnest settlers, the worst kind of men flowed into the territory. Not just grifters and burglars who sneaked around in the dark, but the kind of rattlesnake who'd look a man in the eye while stabbing him in the back. Anyone who wanted to hide could do so in Missouri. There were deep, forested hollows and caves big enough to house people, livestock, and wagons. The Ozarks offered steep hills and outcroppings towering over a wilderness few white men had seen.

The Territory of Missouri was created on March 3, 1805, and it didn't get a U.S. marshal until 1822. He was the only law for all that land. Most men stayed in the job for only a year, if they survived that long, and there were periods of over a year when the job was vacant. Finally, in 1857, a second marshal was appointed, so there was one for the east and one for the west, but each still covered a vast area. Every town and county was supposed to have local lawmen in place, but enforcement was spotty at best.

Missouri was a slave state with hardly any slaves. It was the only divided state during the Civil War, not only furnishing her sons to both sides, but also living under martial law and a federally installed state government the people didn't elect. And St. Louis, with its riches, commerce, and international soul, contrasted with the wild western border, the Ozark hills, and the boundless grazing and farm land that spread west from the Mississippi River.

When Missouri became a state in 1821, there was little outside of St. Louis and Kansas City to suggest that anyone lived in the territory. The population amounted to only about one person per square mile. In the next ten years, settlers lined the two major waterways, the Mississippi and Missouri rivers, and then spread out to find game, pelts, timber, metal ore, and virgin farm land. Even in the 1830s, western Missouri was still the edge of the American West. Mormons were setting the Missouri frontier ablaze forty years before miners swarmed into the Dakota gold camps, and fifty years before the first tents were pitched in Tombstone, Arizona.

Surveying counties, electing sheriffs, appointing judges, and writing laws all took time. In some remote areas, it took years. Daviess County, for example, was established in 1836, but didn't have a prosecuting attorney until 1855. When the law fell short, the people administered justice. Settlers, farmers, and shopkeepers throughout Missouri secured their homes with guns, and without badges. Beautiful Missouri gave birth to one generation after another of threatening, property-destroying, gun-slinging enforcers of the law, as they understood the law.

Vigilantes rose up to defend themselves and their own property, or to take up the cause of the weaker ones in the community. They rode to restore justice or to reap revenge. Vigilantes could even be authorized lawmen who had to act illegally to do their jobs. The violence surprised and unnerved folks. It could be slow and painful, or it could be over in a heartbeat.

Lawmen were corralled by their jurisdiction, but vigilantes could go wherever they saw a need. Oliver P. Frakes, of Nevada, in Vernon County, was arrested for murder, then released for testifying against the bad men he rode with. He continued to steal horses and dabble in other crimes, always keeping on the move, disappearing into Texas, Arkansas, and Indian Territory. Finally, decent folks got fed up with him.

Frakes, who was living with a prostitute, was sleeping next to an open window on a balmy July night, 1874, when he was awakened by two men at the window pointing revolvers at him, while two more busted in the door. They took him out of town, and the woman went to Sheriff Taylor. Six miles east of town, the sheriff found Frakes hanged and shot under the right shoulder blade at such close range that the muzzle blast set his shirt on fire. The shirt burned completely off, a detail that was exciting enough to earn Frakes coverage in newspapers like *The Sedalia Democrat, St. Louis Dispatch,* and *New York Times.* Everybody knew the eight vigilantes were from Vernon and Cedar counties, the same men who'd already crossed county lines to hang three other crooks. Sheriff Taylor tracked them east to the Cedar County line, and that was as far as he could go, so he went home and ate breakfast.

Some vigilantes acted alone, and a loner had certain advantages over a mob. He could strike quickly and move undetected, and he didn't need anyone's approval. The mob, on the other hand, could bring more resources, like guns, ropes, and information, not to mention the overwhelming persuasive power of sheer numbers of people. Mobs might be organized as regulators, serving for years, and planning their moves and targets as carefully as the best military campaigns. Other mobs were frighteningly spontaneous, spilling out of bars into dusty streets, with no leadership, no direction, and no conscience.

The gun and the rope were the vigilante's most trusted weapons. In August 1874, the *St. Louis Dispatch* reported that Major T. B. Rummell, of Chapel Hill, had been found shot to death because he wrote "inappropriate letters" to women of the community. And the same issue described a man named Osborne found hanged in the woods near Aullville and decorated with a note reading, "This is the way we serve horse thieves." However, vigilantes could also be very creative in finding a punishment to fit the crime. The rope was used to torture, as when victims were strung up and released, sometimes repeatedly. And the rope, switches, and sticks were used in beatings. Self-appointed lawmen used knives, swords, and axes. And those who lived in wooden houses lived in fear of the vigilante riding in the night with a flaming torch to burn barns, tools, crops, and homes.

There's so much vigilante history in Missouri, I've omitted some aspects of it from this book. Racially motivated violence, especially leading to lynchings, reared its ugly head throughout America for many years. But I've avoided stories of racism. I've also included only an overview of the Civil War years, focusing on how the war's guerrillas and Bushwhackers gave birth to a new breed of Missouri vigilante.

There are familiar tales of men like James Butler Hickok, Wyatt Earp, William Quantrill, and Sam Hildebrand. But for the first time I'll tell their stories as vigilantes. Not as lawmen or criminals, but as men without badges, fighting for their communities.

The vigilante history of Missouri is a journey that spans a century and is relentlessly violent. And yet the overriding story of Missouri's vigilantes is the story of good people in good families, yearning for happiness and peace. Our ancestors blazed the trail where we now walk. They knew pain and joy, love and disgrace, the same emotions and adventures of life that we experience. In this state uniquely shaped by nature, immigration, war, division, slavery, paranoia, and violence, vigilantism was a fact of life. Missouri could not have been settled without its vigilantes.

NECESSARY EVIL

A note on historical accuracy

The facts of these stories have been thoroughly researched and verified. They're supported with relevant quotes from the written record, including books, newspapers, court records, government archives, and other credible sources. This is narrative history—flesh on the bones. I've mined oral histories and family legends, bolstered by the historical record. I've created fine points of place, time, dress, equipment, and other details. But everything that was added to a story was added around the framework of known and verified historical facts.

CHAPTER ONE

FIRST FLAMES:
THE MORMON WARS

Mason Cope used the reins to whip his galloping horse, knowing it was the slowest of the bunch. His father, two uncles, and eleven others were in the dark ahead of him, and they were all riding hell bent, their wool greatcoats flapping in the stinging autumn air, with fifty Mormon vigilantes on their tail. The horses' feet kicked up snowy plumes, and, though clouds hid the moon, sparkling reflections bathed the whole frantic scene in an eerie blue light. The creaking leather, the heavy breathing of horses, and the dozens of pounding hooves were all dampened by the snow, sounding thin, dry, and otherworldly. Above the clamor the pursuers' shouts were clear enough, warning that Mormons would be coming to invade the county seat, Gallatin, and everybody better get out before daylight.

Earlier that night, October 17, 1838, Cope and the other men had ridden out of Gallatin to the Mormon Road, which ran between the two Mormon towns, one to the north, and one south. The men were scouting, that's all. They just rode out to see if Mormon vigilantes were on the move, and they got their answer, never expecting to run into a band that big, and certainly never expecting the Mormons to come after them.

The frightened riders pulled up at Stallings's store on the south side of the Gallatin town square and looked back, thankful to see that the Mormons didn't follow all the way into town. Then everybody talked at once. Now that they'd been warned, all agreed that resistance was foolish in the face of such force. They'd rest, gather their belongings, and leave before first light. All except George Worthington. As postmaster, he was determined to stay.

His family was at home, a half-mile up the lane to the northeast. But the other women and children of Gallatin had already been sent to friends and kinfolk in other towns as far away as possible. They were able to take only some clothes and personal items, and of course they took their slaves. They hated to leave household goods for the Mormons to steal, but they weren't about to leave their human property to be liberated by the invaders.

Some of the men of the town, including Sheriff William Morgan, had already left too. Remaining behind to guard the little town as best they could were the Copes, James Bristow, county clerk James Turner, treasurer Elisha B. Creedmore, newly elected state representative John Williams, young tailor Joseph McGee, store clerk Patrick Lynch, and a few others, all of them townsmen and settlers from surrounding farms. Now they too were about to give up the village.

George Worthington had built the first cabin in town, a little twelve-by-fourteen-foot lean-to, where his family lived while he finished their combination home and tavern. Sixteen-year-old Joseph McGee came from Ohio with his family, who settled on a farm fifteen miles from town. McGee, who had been apprenticed to a tailor back east, boarded with the Worthingtons and rented their little lean-to for a tailor shop. Across the town square was Stallings's store, where Worthington kept the post office. That's why he couldn't leave. Surely, he thought, the Mormons would respect his position as postmaster.

Along toward midnight, Worthington, his friend Representative Williams, and the young boarder McGee bid the other men in the store goodnight and walked up the lane to sleep at Worthington's. The others turned the horses into the pen and stayed in the store that night, taking turns keeping watch. There was a lot of conversation but not much sleep. Finally, as a rosy glow touched the sky behind the trees east of town, they gave up on the idea of rest and made coffee. Bundled against the cold morning they saddled their horses at the rail out front, always keeping an eye up the road. They were busy, yet uncommonly quiet, and the mix of fear, tension, and bravery was thick enough to stir with a stick.

McGee walked down from the house to get breakfast at the store. As soon as he had a biscuit and coffee in hand, the men sent him back to tell Worthington and Williams the group was ready to ride, and they better get going. No sooner had McGee arrived back at the house than he heard loud voices and a thunder of hooves descending into the village, signaling that it was too late to escape. The Mormons, 150 strong, had swept in just that quickly.

McGee turned to see the men he left at the store, abandoning their horses at the rail, and running up the lane toward him, the Mormons riding hot on their heels. At the Worthington house the terrified little group turned and faced the angry Mormon vigilantes. Only young McGee was more mad than scared, and he shook his biscuit at the marauders, telling them they had no business in the town and to get out.

Worthington came out onto the porch beside McGee and put his hand on the boy's arm to quiet him. Then he boldly announced that he was a federal officer, the tiny post office in the store was federal property, and he would not surrender it to Mormons or anybody else. The aggressors laughed, and then several dismounted, tied McGee's and Worthington's hands and feet, then demanded to know who the county treasurer was. Creedmore identified himself and, like Worthington, proclaimed that he would never surrender the county's money. The Mormon spokesman told him they were going to find the money anyway, so he might as well cooperate. When they had the money, they'd turn the two prisoners loose. With that, the two bound men were rolled into the root cellar like sacks of potatoes. Then the dismounted Mormons grabbed Creedmore roughly and pushed him back down the lane toward town. The Mormons told the rest of the townsmen to head for the hills, which they did.

It was cold and dark in the cellar, and the two men were miserable. They couldn't hear anything except Worthington's wife pacing back and forth to the window upstairs. Two hours later, the cellar door swung open and they saw the Mormons' heavy boots descending the steps. With their bonds finally released, Worthington and McGee followed their captors out of the cellar and squinted, through the glare of sun on snow, at several mounted Mormons, their rifles at the ready. They told Worthington to get out, that he could return the next day for his household goods. Then they cantered down the lane. The defiant postmaster had no choice but to hitch up his two-wheeled cart and load his wife and children. They started for McGee's father's house fifteen miles away, the two men walking beside the wagon through the six-inch-deep snow.

Passing through their beloved village, they could hardly believe their eyes. Every non-Mormon, including Creedmore, was long gone. The Mormons had sent riders to bring wagons from their stronghold, the town of Adam-ondi-Ahman, which lay just three miles away. Now the raiders were like a line of industrious ants, marching in and out of Stallings's store and house, each one with a burden, depositing it in a wagon. They'd also been enjoying the whiskey and wine from Stallings's, and most of them were quite drunk by that time. It might have been funny, seeing the self-righteous Mormons laughing and stumbling as they attended to their dirty work. But they were heavily armed, known to be ruthless, and even more frightening with the liquor in them. If they'd steal everything in town in broad daylight, and do it in the name of the Lord, there was no telling what else they might do. Worthington led the little cart up the road and hurried away with young McGee following, looking back over his shoulder, his temper boiling.

The Mormon wagons were heavy with lard, lamp oil, bolts of cloth, yarn, tools, plows, salt, corn, flour, seed, shot, powder, and other necessities of life on the Missouri prairie. Stallings's store also yielded up the post office cash box and the county's tax receipts, totaling two thousand dollars. When the store and Stallings's home were both empty, the raiders turned to his bunkhouse and grocery on the east side of the square. Then to the other homes. There they found more of the same goods, along with beds, spinning wheels, lamps, clocks, canned vegetables, smoked meats, tools, and other treasures.

At last the groaning Mormon wagons pulled out, and the horsemen encircled their leader, David W. Patton, who was known as Captain Fearnot. His men came up with the title, and he was proud of it. Like fellow Mormon leaders Captain Bull and Captain Blackhawk, the assumed name inspired followers and helped confuse any civil authorities who might come around asking who led the Mormon raids. With the work in Gallatin finished, all eyes settled on Captain Fearnot. He paused, surveyed the pastoral winter scene, and said simply, "Burn it."

Although Gallatin was the county seat, it had been a town only officially since January. There was no courthouse, jail, church, or school. There were only ten homes and a blacksmith shop, along with Stallings's businesses, the tailor shop, and a tavern. In minutes it was all in flames, and the riders escorted their wagons north to Adam-ondi-Ahman. There the plunder was unloaded into "the Lord's Storehouse," a brick building overseen by the local bishop, to be used for the common good of the Mormon people. In their parlance, the property had not been stolen, but consecrated for the Lord's use.

How did it come to that? How did people who crossed the Mississippi to raise crops, tend stores, and make clothes descend into terror? Missourians were a stewpot of English and Irish, with a smattering of French, Canadian, and Scotch, all Catholics and Protestants, plus a handful of Jews, in a land awash with political activity, patriotism, and frontier spirit. As diverse as those people were, they saw themselves united when it came to distrusting, and eventually hating, the volatile Mormons. The sect was already unwelcome in New York, where it had been started by Joseph Smith in 1830. After a move to Ohio, Smith could see that their time there was also going to be brief. He needed a new plan and a new place to live, and just in time, divine revelations told him that his people needed to venture into the wilds of Missouri.

Unfortunately for them, frontier Missourians had even more reason than New Yorkers and Ohioans to hate Mormons. Very few Missourians were born west of the Mississippi. They came from Kentucky, Tennessee, and the Deep South. From Virginia, Ohio, and the Carolinas. They came prepared for deprivation, farm accidents, Indian confrontations, and hard weather. Every day was a fight for their lives and homes, and the general opinion was that the Mormons were just one more enemy to face.

Mormons tended to have a New England manner about them. They were stiff and overly devoted to their Sunday worship, and they insisted on very disciplined schools for their children. Missourians were mostly rough, self-sufficient folks, who thought a little schooling was more than enough, and they loved their corn liquor. They also thought Mormon religious ideas, based heavily on Smith's revelations, were strange. To make it worse, Mormons believed the Bible in most Missouri homes wasn't the whole holy story. Most Mormons settled on land owned by their church or squatted on public land. They paid no taxes, which never sits well with people who do pay taxes. Mormons also kept to themselves and protected their own. They had their own newspapers and created their own businesses, including blacksmith shops, feed stores, and general stores. There were so many of them, Missourians were afraid the Mormons would take over the government and impose their strange ways on everyone. And perhaps the greatest threat of all,

Mormons were opposed to slavery. Though there weren't many slaves in Missouri, Missouri was a slave state, and virtually everybody but the Mormons wanted to keep it that way.

In the Jackson County seat of Independence, the night of July 20, 1833, a non-Mormon meeting turned into an anti-Mormon mob. Both legal offices and taverns throughout the town had been incubating the discontent for hours before the meeting started. Attorneys, judges, sheriffs, and mayors smoked their cigars, poured through law books, and pounded desks. More common men drank and swore louder as the night went on. Then when the various factions finally came together in the meeting hall, it wasn't about enforcing the law. Sure, Mormons had broken some laws, but the main problem was that they just scared the Gentiles, as they called everyone who wasn't a Mormon. It was time to end the threat. Acting with a mob's courage and lack of restraint, one hundred men stormed out of the meeting hall, marched down the street, and destroyed the office of the Mormon newspaper, *The Evening and Morning Star*, loaded the printing press onto a wagon, and dumped it into the Missouri River. Then they tarred and feathered the local bishop, Edward Partridge. That seemed to go pretty well, so the men kept at it, night after night. They beat Mormon men and threatened their women. They made midnight visits to awaken families with the glare of torches, threatening to burn them out if they didn't leave. And the vigilante raids persisted until every single Mormon family had been run out of Jackson County by a mob of their gun-toting neighbors.

That was fine for the Gentiles of Jackson County. But nearly all of the Mormon exiles from Jackson simply moved up the road and settled in neighboring Clay and Ray counties. So for the rest of the state, 1833 was just the beginning of the trouble. The Mormons were livid about the expulsions from Jackson, and in their Old Testament frame of mind, they wanted vengeance.

Back in Kirtland, Ohio, Joseph Smith was mad too. But perhaps more important, he knew he had to maintain his hold on the leader-

Though there are no confirmed photographs of Joseph Smith, experts believe this image is Smith at about the age of thirty.

ship of the church, and that meant he had to meet the Gentile mobs with immediate and dramatic action. He called for a retaliatory march on Missouri and organized an army called "Zion's Camp." He personally strapped on his sword, armed, trained, and drilled a band of two hundred men, then led them all the way across Indiana and Illinois and beyond the Mississippi, bound for Independence, Missouri. Word of their advance preceded them, and western Missourians began to tighten the ranks of their own militia companies.

From 1807 to 1847, every able-bodied man in Missouri was required to serve in the state militia. There was, of course, a scarcity of laws, not to mention lawmen to enforce them, and the militia might be needed to preserve order. The armed units were also a bastion of the Constitution's second amendment. Besides, in those days, lots of people had fresh memories of invasions by English, French, and Indians. For that matter, in those days, folks weren't entirely sure the neighboring county or the U.S. government itself wouldn't invade. So legally, the militia couldn't march without orders from the governor. Yet the people of each county considered their militia to be their own private army. A few counties even proudly turned down the state's offer of guns and opted for volunteer militias, which outfitted themselves. That way, they weren't subject to the state's orders. Of course, they also had no legal authority to enforce the law.

In order for each county to raise a militia of fifty men, the state provided arms for forty-five men, and the officers were to provide their own weapons. The militias mustered out and drilled a few times a year with no particular purpose. But when the news arrived that Joseph Smith was coming with Zion's army, it sent all the units into action. They assembled the men, made sure they were well armed, and held drills, all preparing to fight the armed Mormon invasion. A storm was brewing, sure enough.

Meanwhile, Joseph Smith was having a terrible time keeping his little army on the move. They set out in May, pelted by spring storms and hampered by swollen streams and rivers. They were alternately hot and cold, often soaking wet, always hungry, and always exhausted. They didn't know the people they were going to fight, or even the Mormons they were going to defend. The suffering men's faith in Smith proved to be mighty thin motivation after their thousand-mile march, and their protests grew louder with each labored footstep. They repeatedly threatened to quit, but each time they did, Smith prevailed and pushed them forward.

Then, before they could reach Jackson County, an unseen enemy struck the Mormon army: cholera. Fourteen men died, stoking the dissent that already hampered the exhausted, underfed army. After all that sacrifice by his men, after all the times they had recommitted themselves to his cause, Smith gave up the effort, and the disgruntled men returned to Ohio. But they dared not speak up against Smith. After all, he said he'd received divine instructions to give up the mission, and no good Mormon could argue with that.

The anticlimactic Zion's Camp accomplished two things. First, it lit the fuse for pitched battle between the two factions. Second, it turned Smith to a more militant approach to all things Mormon. He would have no more of the grumbling that hampered Zion's Camp. He became increasingly heavy-handed in his demands for loyalty and unquestioning obedience. His rhetoric turned more threatening, containing increasing references to Old Testament violence, revenge, and the blood of enemies. And he restructured the church with a hierarchy under twelve apostles, awarding leadership positions to the most militant among them, especially those who had proven themselves loyal to him on the Zion's Camp march. Among them were Thomas Marsh, Orson Hyde, Sampson Avard, and Porter Rockwell, who would all prove to be major figures in the rise and eventual fall of the Mormons in Missouri.

On both sides, Mormon and Missourian, vigilante gangs rode, not to enforce the constitutional law of the land, but to enforce the mob's prejudice. Families were threatened. Crops were burned and livestock stolen. And so Missouri's first flames of vigilantism burned in whiskey-soaked saloons, in city meeting halls, and among hordes of night riders. But the spark was struck in the mind of Joseph Smith.

Propelled by Smith's promises of a utopia on the frontier, Mormons continued to migrate to Missouri. The more that Mormons poured into the state, the more that Missourians feared their plans for domination. By 1836, the climate surrounding Mormonism was so strained, it was generally agreed by both sides that the only way to have peace was to segregate the Mormons, giving them their own part of the state.

Since Ray County had been the scene of repeated violence against Mormons, by that time they'd all been chased to the north end of the county. So the legislature just let them stay there and called it Caldwell County. It was not so much as an accommodation to Mormonism, but to get them out of everyone else's hair. There, Mormons laid out their own county seat, Far West. To further isolate them, the state even marked off a six-mile-wide buffer zone in which nobody could settle.

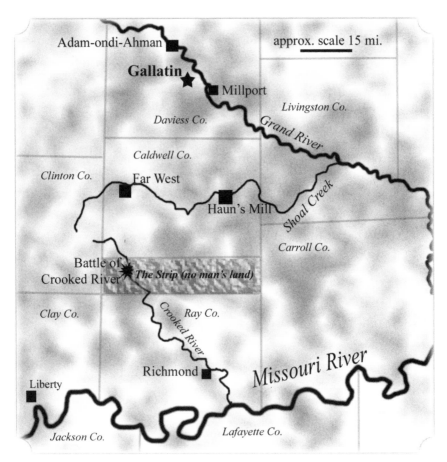

The area of the Mormon wars.

But in solving that problem, the legislature created a new one. They created the new Daviess County, north of Caldwell County, embracing the beautiful lands around Grand River, which flowed into the Missouri. So Mormons once again found themselves surrounded by Gentiles, and their roads to the area's two major waterways, the Grand and the mighty Missouri, far to the south, both ran through unfriendly territory.

By that time, Joseph Smith had run head-on into some serious legal troubleback in Ohio, including charges of bank fraud. He conveniently received a new divine revelation instructing him what to do next. It told him to join the throngs of the faithful in Missouri, beyond the reach of the Illinois courts, so off he went. Soon after his arrival in Missouri, he went to take a look at the new Daviess County. While exploring the countryside, he found three piles of rocks that brought on another revelation. He declared that the stones were actually the remnants of altars built by the biblical Adam after he and Eve were ex-pelled from the Garden of Eden. Smith's ongoing revelations told him that Adam would return at that very spot, the spot where those "altars" stood, so the Mormons needed to assemble there as soon as possible to enjoy the New Eden. There was one huge problem: The so-called altars weren't in the Mormons' home of Caldwell County, but in Daviess, the new county to their north.

Smith wasn't going to let a little thing like a county line stand in the way of heavenly direction. Under his supervision the Mormons started building a city called Adam-ondi-Ahman near the altars in Daviess County. The odd name of the town has variously been ascribed to Hebrew, Aramaic, and even French, but in fact it's not from any known language. It's most likely nothing but a combination of mis-spellings from various tongues. Smith said it meant something like "Adam's sacred ground," and that was good enough for his believers.

Hundreds of Mormons joined him in the New Eden, swelling their numbers to about 1,500 in Caldwell County and close to 1,000 in Daviess, where only about 500 non-Mormons lived. While the two non-Mormon towns of Gallatin and Millport had less than a dozen houses each, Adam-ondi-Ahman grew to about one hundred houses. It was an astonishing population boom on the frontier, and all those Mormons could be mobilized for any common cause. At their new town of Far West they dug the foundation for a temple, measuring eighty by one hundred feet and four feet deep, in half a day. That feat was militaristic in organization and scale, which made it downright frightening to non-Mormons.

The state gave these zealots their own county, the Gentiles complained, and they should be content to stay there in Caldwell. That's the way the non-Mormons understood the purpose of Caldwell County: to contain the Mormons. But the truth was, like all Americans, Mormons were free to settle wherever they wanted, including Daviess County. Legally though, Smith and his followers were on shaky ground. First, nearly all the Mormons were squatters, occupying huge tracts of land in common. Most of that land, even in Caldwell County, wouldn't even be opened to settlement for several more years. That didn't sit well with the other settlers who'd scrimped and saved to buy a few acres of their own. Where Mormons did own legal title to the land, many families often shared the property, so it was hard to tell who owned what and who was legally responsible for what. To make matters worse, Smith was using the same methods that got him in trouble in Ohio. Mormons freely created their own money, worthless promissory notes, and illegal deeds. When Gentiles filed criminal charges or sued to recover debts, the Mormons proved repeatedly in court that they answered only to their own courts in Caldwell County, where of course Gentiles could never prevail.

During that time there was an inverse Mormon movement. While Mormons in general became more militant, an increasing number of them objected to the violent turn their lives had taken in Missouri. They began to speak out, refuse to arm themselves, and fail to show up for military drills. Joseph Smith's loyal leaders were determined that

Mormon leader Sidney Rigdon inflamed his people when he delivered the "Salt sermon."

the unfaithful ones had to be brought back into line immediately, so in early summer, 1838, Mormon president Sidney Rigdon delivered what came to be called the "Salt sermon." Referring to the Bible's Matthew 5:13, he threatened dissenters, saying they were like salt that has lost its flavor, "good for nothing, but to be cast out, and to be trodden under foot of men." He went on, "When men embrace the gospel and afterwards lose their faith it is the duty of the Saints to trample them under their feet." And just in case that wasn't clear enough, he said anyone not responding to their leaders' call should be forced up on a horse with a pitchfork and made to ride at the front of the column into battle.

Then at their July 4 celebration, he said Mormons had to protect each other from their enemies, "And that mob that comes on us to disturb us, it shall be between us and them a war of extermination; for we will follow them until the last drop of their blood is spilled; or else they will have to exterminate us, for we will carry the seat of war to their own houses and their own families, and one party or the other shall be utterly destroyed."

From that time on, the Mormons went on the offensive. They organized a "Fur Company" to bring in livestock, an armed band of men who maintained a steady flow of captured cows, pigs, and horses into Far West and Adam-ondi-Ahman. Anything they took from the non-Mormons was divinely justified, they said, because it was consecrated for Mormon use. They began to embrace a new philosophy that the spilling of a Gentile's blood would save that Gentile from his sins. By killing him, they would actually be doing him an eternal favor. They repeated it and refined it until it became like scripture to them. And when one of the military unit leaders, armed with pistols, a rifle, and a sword, said those words with blood in his eyes, it was a rare Mormon who could refute them.

As if things weren't tense enough, Smith announced his intention to take over all of Daviess County and run the Missourians out. That further raised the level of militancy among his own people, but of course it had a similar effect on the non-Mormons. Gallatin, the county seat and home of Joseph McGee and friends, was smack in the middle between Adam-ondi-Ahman and Far West, with groups of armed Mormons traveling back and forth every day. The non-Mormons were going armed too. Oddly, by late 1837, the violence declined—yet it was an uneasy peace, with everyone more on edge than ever.

CHAPTER TWO

DIVINE VENGEANCE: THE MORMON WARS CONTINUE

Farmer James Stone, tired after a day of work in his fields, was just sitting down to dinner with his wife while their two infant children played on the floor. There was a rumble of hooves, a few seconds of paralyzing fear, then a sudden crash as the door was kicked open. Twelve armed Mormons filled the cabin, upset the table, and dragged James outside into the dust. While the children screamed and Mrs. Stone cried and pleaded, James was knocked to his knees. The leader held his saber aloft and calmly told James he would lose his head if he and his family didn't leave. The marauders mounted and galloped out of the yard, and the Stone family was on the move that night by ten, taking only a little food and the clothing they could quickly gather in their arms. When James quietly returned the next day for the rest of their belongings, he found that everything of value on the place had been taken and the house burned to the ground.

The Mormons justified such raids by saying the Gentiles had far more than they needed. Mormon families were taught to acquire just what their families required to live, and if there was any surplus, it was contributed to the common good. When a family ran short, they could turn to the warehouse and get what they needed. The Gentiles, on the other hand, had too much of everything, which the Mormon leaders declared a sin. Accordingly, Mormons saved the Gentiles from their sin by relieving them of their goods. But the Gentiles were just as determined, and raids were met by counter-raids. It was the day of vengeance and the night of fear. It was the reign of sword and torch.

The Mormon violence was all under the guiding hand of Joseph Smith, and all in the name of holy instructions revealed only to Smith. But beyond the mystical religious motivation, there was a more practical truth in the tragic timing of Joseph Smith's extreme evangelism: He had hungry people to feed. Smith was an uneducated, erratic opportunist who seemed to have no great, overarching plan. Or maybe his plan constantly changed to match the evolving terrain of politics, hungry followers, migrating Mormons, new Mormons joining the ranks, rebellious talk among the ranks of the faithful, and pressure from distrusting locals. He reacted to every new situation with a new heavenly revelation. During the time he lived in Far West he professed a major epiphany about once a month, with minor ones in between.

When Smith found the "altars," the three piles of rocks, and told his believers to gather for Adam's return, they did, in droves. Some of the earlier Mormon settlers had been quite wealthy, with most of them settling in the county seat of Far West. In contrast, July of 1838 saw the arrival of a group of wagons that would become known as "the poor train." They were people who had almost no possessions and even less money. Leaving from Kirtland, Ohio, 405 of them arrived, settling in rural Caldwell and Daviess counties, with 265 of them in Adam-ondi-Ahman. All those new people, arriving too late to plant, had no way to feed themselves. By fall, they were destitute, with no provisions for winter, and Smith had starving people looking to him for answers. So he turned to the Fur Company to steal more livestock, and to other Mormon gangs to steal produce and other staples. Smith appointed captains, who arranged the men in groups of ten, so the raids were better organized and more effective. As always, the stealing was justified because the goods were being consecrated for Mormon use.

Then came the first election day in Gallatin, August 6, 1838. William P. Penniston, a candidate for the state legislature, was running against Judge Josiah Morin, who had been courting the Mormon vote. Penniston was shaking hands and asking for votes when a contingent of Mormons rode into town. They'd been pouring into the county all spring and summer, but they weren't eligible to vote because they hadn't lived in the county long enough. Voters were registered by paying taxes, so that election day in Gallatin, the only registered voters were those who had paid taxes the previous fall. It was obvious that the Mormons had only come into town to disrupt the election.

Penniston climbed up on a barrel and loudly proclaimed that Mormons were liars and thieves and must be driven from the county. "If you suffer such men as these to vote," he shouted, "you will soon lose your suffrage." His harangue worked. When the divinely inspired Mormons tried to push their way into the polls, they were thrown out.

Then Penniston's cause was taken up by Dick Welding, the town drunk, who also happened to be the town bully. He shouted that Mormons had no more right to vote than Negroes. Of course that played well with the non-Mormons, who were almost universally slave owners. Mormon Samuel Brown tried to argue with him and was met with Welding's wildly swinging fists. Welding never landed a punch on Brown, but another Mormon grabbed him and pinned his arms, which provoked three more Missourians to jump Brown.

One of the brethren picked up a stick for a club, and of course a non-Mormon found one too. The brawling spread among small groups of men up and down the street. Rocks were thrown, men were bleeding, and then one creative Mormon warrior took a cup and saucer from the store, placed it in his kerchief, and smacked it on the porch to break it into chunks. He tied the corners, creating a most dangerous version of the medieval flail that was heavy, hard, and sharp. One Mormon ran

The Election Day brawl in Gallatin.

from the melee with a hunting knife between his shoulder blades and three men in pursuit, until Mormon John Butler stepped in with a club and flattened all three men with mighty blows. Another man caught up with Butler and whacked him in the back with a horse-whip handle, so Butler whirled and with an upper cut broke the man's jaw. When the fighting stopped there were several men on the ground too wounded to walk.

Both sides got what they wanted: Gentiles were terrorized and Mormons didn't vote. It had not been a matter of mob threats in the torchlight. It was man to man in the bold light of day. They had looked each other in the eye, spilled one another's blood, and gone home to prepare for all-out war.

And where was the law in all of this? Neither side could expect any help from law enforcement. Daviess County wouldn't even have a prosecuting attorney for another twenty years. There was no sheriff's office, no courthouse, and no jail, so Sheriff William Morgan was rarely seen in the county seat, Gallatin. He was usually working his farm like everyone else. In fact, after the trouble started, he was hard to find at all.

A county sheriff was virtually helpless when most of the problems in the county were caused by throngs of twenty to fifty armed men on horseback. Victims of threats, thefts, beatings, and kidnappings were afraid to bring charges. Or if they did, it was often hard to say who in the crowd had done exactly what. Furthermore, the victims generally didn't know the vigilantes, who lived miles away, so identification was impossible. Mormons riding across county lines to commit their crimes couldn't be brought back to trial in Gentile courts, so lawmen ended up with pockets full of warrants they couldn't serve. And since the law couldn't defend anyone from reprisals, the vigilantes from both camps ran at will.

There was no Daviess County militia, and some terrified citizens thought that might be their salvation. They pooled their money and sent John Comer with a wagon and two mounted guards to buy arms from the state warehouse in Richmond. Unfortunately, their wagon had to pass through the Mormons' Caldwell County, and on the way back the Mormon vigilantes seized all forty-five rifles, casks of powder, and two hundred pounds of lead, taking Comer and his guards as prisoners. Ray County sent its militia to free Comer and retake the guns, but the Mormons still had plenty. Three weeks later they drove everyone out of the town of Millburn, stripped it of food and supplies, and burned it.

When the wagons came into Far West overloaded with supplies, food, and household goods stolen from Gallatin, Reed Peck was among the men gathered in the Mormon headquarters of Adam-ondi-Ahman to unload the plunder. Most of the men were glad the supplies had been taken, but some, like Peck, had their doubts.

He really changed his outlook one night when he talked to a friend who'd been out with the raiders and learned that Mormons had been burning both Mormon and Gentile farms. Joseph Smith had a revelation that every house in Daviess County should be burned except those in their stronghold of Adam-ondi-Ahman. Accordingly, the faithful Mormons left their farmhouses and moved into town. Then the farms they left behind were torched by Mormon vigilantes under the command of Captain Seymour Brunson. And to keep everyone united in angry paranoia, they spread the word that it was the Gentiles who were burning the farms.

Captain Brunson and a force of twenty men rode through the night calling themselves the "Flying Horses of Daviess County." Typical of their attacks was the stop at one non-Mormon farm, where they were complete strangers. They made polite introductions and lied that they were intent on driving out the Mormons, which was wonderful news to the little farm family. After enjoying their hospitality and a warm dinner, Brunson and his men revealed their true identities, took everything they could carry, loaded the farmer's wagon and took that too, and burned the house to the ground.

The Flying Horses were one element of the Danites, the Mormons' own official vigilantes and enforcers. There are varying accounts of the origin of the name Danites, but it was based in the Old Testament, probably inspired by the book of Daniel, which says, "The Prophet Daniel has said the saints shall take the Kingdom and possess it forever" (Daniel 2:44). Within the Danites were even more violent, more secretive contingents that went by names like "the Destructives" and "Lady of Zion."

Sampson Avard was the Danites' organizer and leader. He called the meetings, choreographed their secret signs, and drafted the oath, which would endure as a common underpinning of vigilante action on the American frontier: a promise of mutual defense. If one in the group was attacked, all in the group vowed to rise to his defense. That sort of promise would prove its value in vigilante organizations for decades to come, because it was an easy code to defend, and hard to fault. After all, it makes sense that anyone under attack should be defended. But once a group of men had banded together for defense, it was a simple matter for brutal leaders to turn the men to offensive operations.

Mormons were frequently reminded that their leaders were divinely led, and therefore infallible. The rank and file were never to question whether their instructions were right or wrong. But peace-loving men like Reed Peck didn't like being told to ignore their homes in favor of whatever the military leaders ordered. He should have been putting in fall crops and making ready for winter. He needed to smoke meat and lay up firewood and hay. Instead he was drafted to help build a small, hidden, fall-back fortress, in case Adam-ondi-Ahman fell to Gentiles. It had a powder magazine and gun-ported brick walls, and was fully stocked with food, blankets, and other supplies. Peck and the others were sworn to secrecy about its location, and even the fact that it existed, under penalty of death.

Peck attended a Danite meeting, of which he would later write, "About 50 persons were initiated into the Society at the time I was introduced and at same time the oath was administered to all the novices at once of which I took advantage by remaining silent and accordingly avoided taking it." Peck was appointed adjutant, but whispered in confidence to his closest friends that he would never act in the post. Of course the Danite leader Avard knew there were dissenters like Peck, and he met them head on. At the next Danite meeting he declared that those who didn't follow willingly should be taken out in a field and their throats would be slit. Avard was right in step with the other Mormon demagogues, as by that time the Salt sermon, with its blood-spilling mentality, had become the standard for driving Mormons into service.

Tom Marsh and Orson Hyde, two of the Mormon elite, were as concerned as Peck. They were among those forced to ride with Captain Fearnot. They saw the terror and destruction, and that was enough for them. They brought their families to Ray County and reported to the non-Mormon county authorities.

That night, Marsh signed his name, handed the quill pen to his friend Hyde, and scanned the county leaders gathered at the office of Ray County justice of the peace Henry Jacobs. The affidavit Marsh and Hyde were signing told exactly what they'd seen of the Mormons from the inside. Signing that document was enough to place them squarely

Mormon refugee Orson Hyde.

in the gun sights of hundreds of Mormons, including some of their closest friends. But Marsh and Hyde did it so their testimony could be carried to the governor in an appeal for help. Several other men at the meeting penned their own letters, pleading for the governor to send the militia to put down the violence. Then two of the justices boarded a coach and left at a gallop for the state capitol in Jefferson City.

After riding through the night, the justices walked in to find the desk of new governor Lilburn Boggs already deluged with letters and affidavits about Mormon atrocities. Boggs had no choice but to respond with force, and yet he took the smallest step possible. He called out only the Ray County militia, directing them to act as a peace-keeping force under the command of Captain Samuel Bogart.

Everybody knew Bogart and his men were facing danger. Joseph Smith had been happy to let the state arm a militia for the Mormons' home of Caldwell County, just like all the other counties. But then Smith proclaimed the troops were "the Lord's" army, subject only to Smith's command, not the governor's.

Both sides were armed with the best muzzle-loading flintlock rifles of the time. They carried a mixture of good-quality guns that were available to the government, but it was not uncommon for a militiaman to turn his nose up at the gun the county bought for him and bring his own instead. Some relied on the Revolutionary-era Brown Bess, a hearty English musket in staggering .75 caliber that was limited to a range of about fifty yards. Some marksmen could hit a squirrel's head at three hundred yards with the lighter Kentucky long rifle in calibers as low as .36. Still others favored the new .69 caliber Springfield. And every man carried some combination of pistol, knife, and short sword.

Missouri's militiamen were the grandchildren of Revolutionary War veterans. Many of them had fought British and Indians in the War of 1812, and some had served in the Black Hawk War of 1832. Some units, like the St. Louis Grays, led by a tailor who designed their beautiful uniforms, were crack outfits with regular drills and matching muskets. One St. Louis newspaper, the *Daily Missouri Republican*, offered the city's militia for the distant Mormon struggle, saying, "His Excellency (the governor) has not called upon the Grays of this City. They are armed and equipped for service, and would be more efficient than any troops which he could muster, being better disciplined and prepared for an emergency than raw troops can be."

The newspaper was right. Out on the frontier, the troops were anything but efficient. People were busy from sunup to sundown just try-

The Brown Bess musket.

ing to feed their families. They had little time for meetings, instruction, and drills. When they did report for duty, they wore everything from Continental army uniforms to overalls and muck boots. Still, the staff of officers was in place, most of them receiving their appointments based on previous military service, and if the call to arms was made, men were sure to respond, ready to fight.

So even before Governor Boggs called for troops, Captain Bogart was out with a few men. Bogart was a general storekeeper, Methodist circuit preacher, and lifelong citizen-soldier. As a fifteen-year-old orphan he had enlisted in the army and fought at the Battle of New Orleans. Then when the Black Hawk War came along, he served as a major. The Mormons were a different kind of enemy, but not one from which he could turn away.

Bogart's men had just started working along the Ray County border, making sure no Mormons were squatting in the six-mile-wide no man's land and no Mormon raiding parties were moving through. They were camped in the field on October 18 when a severe snowstorm blew up. Unable to shelter and feed his men in such weather, the captain pulled his scarf down tight around his ears and sent them home. But just a few miles north, Mormons on a holy crusade wouldn't be put off by a little weather. The very next morning they galloped in to chase McGee, Worthington, and the other men out of Gallatin, then pillage and burn the little town.

News of that attack reached Bogart the same day as the governor's orders. He reassembled his men, this time the full force of fifty, all mounted and armed. On October 23, Bogart wrote to the governor:

> (Mormons) have been seen near & on the line between Ray &
> Caldwell, from consequence of which I have ordered out my
> company to prevent, if possible, any outrage on the County of
> Ray, & to range the line between Caldwell & Ray, & await your
> order & further assistance. I will camp at Fields, 12 miles north

of this tonight. I learn that the people of Ray are going to take
the law into their own hands & put an end to the Mormon war.

That time, Bogart's militia made a clean sweep of the six-mile-wide
strip, where they expelled a few Mormon families from their homes.
Three Mormons were intercepted and suspected of carrying messages,
so they were taken prisoner. The militia camped in the strip that
night on the Crooked River, just south of the Caldwell County line,
a neutral position where Bogart hoped to prevent any more Mormon
communication or vigilante action between Ray and Caldwell counties.

When Captain Fearnot heard that the militia had evicted Mormon
families and taken prisoners, he called for the drums to be sounded at
Far West, summoning the Mormon faithful to arms. About seventy of
them struck out in the dark of night and came upon Bogart's militia
camp, just across the shallow river below. They waited until dawn, then
advanced, rousing Bogart's sentry, who was nestled in the grass halfway
down the hill. Seeing the Mormon force approaching, he rose and fled
toward his camp in the trees below, shouting the alarm. He paid for his
loyalty with his life, as the first Mormon shot was fired.

The militia was on lower ground, but the Mormons made that a
superior position with their poor tactics. They were silhouetted against
the rising sun as they marched down the hill from the east. For the
militia soldiers, who were in the shelter of the trees, shooting over the
river bank, the Mormons made perfect targets.

The militia was also strengthened by the many veterans among its
ranks. But coming down the hill were men propelled by religious fervor, not to mention the threat by their leaders that they'd better be
brave in battle. The Mormons raised their cry, "God and Liberty!" and
charged, routing Bogart and his militia, who fled the scene, leaving
their prisoners behind. Captain Fearnot was severely wounded in the
charge and taken to a neighboring farm, where he died later in the day.
One other Mormon and three militiamen were killed that morning, but

the casualties were less important than the fact that the prisoners were freed. With the courageous Fearnot martyred, the Mormons considered it their victory.

The report reached the governor that night saying three of Bogart's men were killed, and calling the incident the Battle of Crooked River. This time Boggs's reaction was swift, sure, and more severe. He issued Executive Order No. 44, mobilizing two thousand militia under the command of Major General John B. Clark, saying, "Your orders are therefore to hasten your operations with all possible speed. The Mormons must be treated as enemies, and must be exterminated or driven from the state if necessary for the public peace." The order made no distinction between raiders, housewives, children, and peaceful Mormon farmers. It was clearly illegal, casting Governor Boggs as one more vigilante, commanding an army of government vigilantes.

Meanwhile, hundreds of farm-dwelling Mormons poured into Far West under Joseph Smith's orders and started building walls and blockhouses, intending to make the city their fortress. A few others, still clinging to the hope that peace was possible, and not wanting to enter a besieged fort, made their way to Haun's Mill. Jacob Haun was one of the early Mormons who'd been chased out of Jackson County in 1832. He'd settled on Shoal Creek, just two dozen miles from where the Crooked River fight took place and about the same distance from Far West. The Mormons gathering there hoped to present a non-threatening face to the militia, be spared from gunfire, and possibly negotiate their own settlement, regardless of what Joseph Smith and his army did. They rightly believed there was no reason why they couldn't live peacefully with everyone else in Missouri.

The Jackson County militia was in the field three days after Executive Order No. 44. However, they still had not received the order, so technically they were vigilantes, out to reap vengeance for the Crooked River battle. The force rose to an astonishing 240 men, who poured in from all the surrounding counties and included such prominent men as state senator Charles Ashby and Thomas O. Byron, clerk of Livingston County. They were led by Colonel William Jennings, Caldwell County sheriff.

Their scouts reported the gathering of Mormons at Haun's Mill, but of course they had no way of knowing the group was not gathering to make war. So at about 4:00 p.m., the militia surrounded Haun's Mill, which was nothing more than a farm with its outbuildings, and the Mormons looked up to see a hillside bristling with rifles. One Mormon started toward the troops, waving his hand in peace. Someone gave the order, "Fire!" and the poor peacemaker ran for cover, fortunate to lose only a finger in the fusillade. With that, the Mormon men all ran into the blacksmith shop. Most of the women and children fled down the creek, scattered into the woods, and in a matter of seconds heard the gunfire erupt again and continue in earnest on both sides.

Mormons fired from between the logs of the old blacksmith shop, where hardly any chinking remained. Casualties were few until "Charge!" was shouted on the hillside. The troops broke from their cover and ran to cluster around the little cabin. The militiamen boldly flung themselves against the log wall, right beside the ports where Mormon rifles protruded. The instant a weapon discharged, a militiaman poked his own rifle into the same hole and fired. Then the militiamen were firing, reloading, and firing again so fast, the Mormons had no chance to reload. All inside would have been slain had the few remaining not flung the door open and run for their lives.

Thomas McBride was among those who broke out, but at the age of seventy-eight, he didn't have the stamina to keep going. He turned, out of breath, and surrendered his musket to militiaman Jacob Rogers, who shot McBride. He fell wounded, and Rogers cut his body to pieces with a corn knife while he died. Militiamen pursued the escapees, firing until the call was made, "Quarter," meaning to have mercy on the survivors. But the command came very late, and few remained alive.

The militiamen returned to the blacksmith shop and found bodies wall-to-wall. Some Mormons were still alive, and the relentless militiamen shot nearly all of them dead. Ten-year-old Sardius Smith was found hiding under the blacksmith's bellows. As he pleaded for his life, the militia's William Reynolds put his musket against the boy's head and blew off the top of his skull, explaining to his friends, "Nits will make lice, and if he had lived he would have become a Mormon."

The few survivors were allowed to load their wounded into a wagon and leave. Still-seething militiamen were angry over the order to stop shooting, so they continued to mutilate Mormon bodies, threw them down a well, and thoroughly ransacked the Haun farm and mill. When it was over, three militiamen had minor wounds, and some thirty Mormons were killed, including two women who had refused to leave their husbands when the shooting started.

In the following days, the still-gathering militia entrenched itself outside Far West, ready for a siege, armed with their illegal orders from the governor. But the siege was short-lived, as Joseph Smith saw the futility of resisting. He surrendered, along with his brother Hiram Smith, Brigham Young, Avard the Danite, Salt-sermonizing Sidney Rigdon, and their flock. They were arrested and charged, but only a handful of them ended up being tried, sentenced, fined, or imprisoned. The greater result was that the Mormons were expelled from the state.

But vigilantes die hard, and that wasn't the end of the trouble.

When Smith and other Mormon leaders were charged with various crimes, they wisely requested and received a change of venue to Boonville. On the way there in the custody of Sheriff William Morgan and four deputies, they camped on Yellow Creek. That night, all the prisoners escaped, taking their guards' horses, and there was plenty of evidence to suggest that Sheriff Morgan and his deputies had been bribed to let them get away. Word of the escape got back to town ahead of the lawmen, who came walking wearily back into the village to meet an irate citizenry, still in a vigilante frame of mind. After all, those civilian soldiers had risked their lives to fight the Mormons, and then trusted the sheriff to get the Mormon leaders to trial, and now they were convinced that he let them escape. As Sheriff Morgan and his deputies approached the Gallatin town square, they saw the angry crowd start toward them. The deputies ran away into the woods, while the sheriff caught the full brunt of the townsmen's wrath. The long-haired Morgan was grabbed and dragged around the square by his hair. Still not satisfied, they rode him out of town on a steel rail, in a hazing so severe that the sheriff later died from his injuries.

The Mormons disappeared into Illinois, and among the Gentiles, the Mormon Wars became a distasteful memory. But the defeated Joseph Smith could not let it go and never stopped ranting against all things Missouri. Three years later the Mormons bought the tiny town of Nauvoo, in the northwest corner of Illinois. After settling there, Smith publicly announced a divine revelation that Missouri's ex-governor Boggs, the one who kicked them out of Missouri, would come to a violent death. By that time, Boggs was out of office, but that didn't matter to the vengeful Smith. It was the kind of premonition that some radical believer was bound to act on, which would really secure Smith's status as a prophet.

Before long, Porter Rockwell, one of Smith's bodyguards, slipped back into Missouri and introduced himself as Mr. Porter. When one of the Mormon leaders missed him in Nauvoo and asked Smith where Rockwell might be, Smith replied, "He has gone to Missouri to fulfill prophecies."

Rockwell was one of the original Danites, a huge man, rough, ready, belligerent, and willing to follow Smith into hell, if need be. But he was mostly unrecognized in Missouri, so he was able to enter the state unarmed and pass himself off as an out-of-work farmhand. It was easy enough for him to secure a job as a stable hand at a horse farm neighboring former governor Boggs's home in Independence. On May 6, 1842, about 9:00 p.m., Boggs was in his study reading the newspa-

Porter Rockwell, militant Mormon and confidant of Joseph Smith.

per and enjoying his retirement. Rockwell crept up to a window, just a few feet from the governor's side, his footsteps silent on the damp ground.

In his hand was a pistol, one of a pair stolen a few days before from a local baker. It was a muzzle-loading, single-shot flintlock, a trusty-enough firearm for the time, but only accurate at a short distance. To be sure he hit his mark, Rockwell had loaded it with six buckshot, pea-size lead balls that are lethal to deer at fifty yards if fired from a shotgun. As they exited the barrel and spread in an ever-widening circle, Rockwell thought, they were bound to disassemble the politician's head. But this wasn't a shotgun. This was a pistol, which held a much smaller powder charge and was designed to shoot a single ball, not shot. As a result, it was horribly inaccurate and woefully underpowered.

When Rockwell fired and the charge left the muzzle at the end of the weapon's short barrel, the gases dispersed instantly and the pressure behind the pellets dropped to almost nothing. They lost most of their power to penetrate. One pellet missed, one pierced Boggs's cheek and exited his mouth, and another went through his neck and he swallowed it. Two shot lodged against his skull with enough force to knock him unconscious, but not enough to pass through the bone. The governor slumped in his chair, and to Rockwell, it looked like he'd done what he came to do. He dropped the pistol and ran from the window, confident that his mission was accomplished. His hand rested on the other stolen weapon in his belt, reassuring him that he had one more shot, should anyone pursue him. But nobody did.

That was the common belief of what happened. But was Porter Rockwell truly the lone vigilante who attacked Boggs? Was he acting on Smith's orders? Circumstantial evidence continued to mount. Rockwell arrived back in Nauvoo on the very day the news of Governor Boggs's attack arrived. Smith presented him with a fine horse and carriage, and while Porter had been always been decidedly poor, he left his family to move into a tavern, and made it no secret that he had recently come into quite a sum of money. Of course the news of an assassination was premature, as Boggs not only survived his wounds but would live another twenty years.

Missouri tried to extradite both Smith and Rockwell from Illinois, but Smith went into hiding and Rockwell left the state. About a year later Rockwell was returning to Illinois through St. Louis, and amazingly, someone recognized him and he was arrested. A grand jury examined the charges, and, testifying in his own defense, he said he was a better shot than that; if he wanted to kill somebody, that person would be dead. It must have been a stout defense because the grand jury decided there was insufficient evidence, and he was acquitted of the charges. Of course it also helped his cause that the prosecution's key witness, an employee of the horse farm where Rockwell had worked, failed to show up for the trial. There's little doubt that he was strongly encouraged by Mormons not to testify against Rockwell. After all, he had a wife and children.

The prosecution was disappointed that there was no way to pursue the case any further. However, while awaiting the grand jury hearing, Rockwell had broken out of jail and been recaptured, so at least the prosecution had that. They settled for a conviction on the escape charge. Whether the judge was tired of the whole business, had been bribed, or had been threatened, he thought it was enough to sentence Rockwell to only five minutes in jail. The prosecution delayed his release for another five hours while they dug for more charges they could bring. But at last, they had to let him go.

Though Reed Peck, the dissenting Danite, furnished information to authorities both before and after the wars, he remained in the Mormon faith. Tom March, who signed the letter to the governor, was excommunicated but rejoined the church in 1857. March's companion Orson Hyde was disciplined by the church but repented and was reinstated as a leader. He continued to be vigorous in the faith, took nine wives, and fathered thirty-two children.

The Mormon Wars were over, and their effect on Missouri was profound. The popular opinion was that every illegal act against the Mormons was justified for two reasons. First, it got rid of the Mormons. Second, the militia's final actions, the brief siege of Far West and arrest of the Mormon leaders, were authorized by the state and didn't result in anybody getting killed. Those facts helped the law overlook all the previous, unauthorized raids.

Though the action was all in the western reaches of Missouri, it touched the whole state. The defeat of the armed Mormon horde was big news, widely reported and endlessly discussed. It wasn't the government that saved Missouri from the Mormons, but the men in the fields, rising up in their own interest. Common men, armed with the musket from over the mantel, carrying father's sword, and riding the family horse. Most people in the state never met a Mormon, but they feared and hated them, and the Mormon expulsion was seen as a victory for all Missourians.

After the first quarter of the nineteenth century, the people of the new state might have emerged from fighting the British, French, and Indians into a new era of peace and good citizenship. Instead, the Mormon conflict of the late 1830s taught them that civilian violence was a continuing part of frontier life. It left behind an entire generation schooled in vigilantism and empowered by government to take the law into their own hands. It would color the way Missouri's people dealt with slavery, the Civil War, and law enforcement for decades to come.

Chapter Three

The Slicker Wars Begin

If a person needed a place to hide out for a long time, he couldn't do better than the Missouri Ozarks. The hills provided lookouts with broad views over miles of terrain. Some hills had bald tops, and if people were summoned to meet, they could navigate toward the grassy summit from miles away. Of course the deep hollows were dark and cool and protected from winter winds. They held woods so dense, in some places two people could pass undetected within ten feet of each other. Fresh water flowed in countless streams and sparkling springs. But perhaps most attractive of all, there were the caves. The smaller ones offered shelter to lone travelers, while some were big enough to house scores of people, horses, wagons, goods, and machinery.

But there among the dark green hiding places, also came men who craved the light and insisted on bright, happy places to raise towns full of families. The West was dotted with patriarchs, men with a vision of themselves and their families leading the way, setting the standard for the great mass of more common people who looked to them for leadership and direction. Some believed they had a corner on greatness. And no wonder. The fledgling nation regularly birthed such men, then pushed them out into the wilderness. "Here," America said. "Prove yourself."

Necessary Evil

Hiram Kerr Turk was such a man. He came from a large and re-spected Virginia family that moved to Tennessee and left big footprints on both states. In 1839 he was making his own mark on the wilds of southwest Missouri. The town of Warsaw was no suburb of St. Louis. It wasn't even within a day's ride of the Missouri River, the Mississippi, or the railroad. It was a tiny burg in Benton County in the middle of the Ozark Mountains, surrounded by forests that were as deep and wild as any on the continent.

Colonel Turk, a veteran of the War of 1812, along with his sons, Nathan, Tom, and Jim, ran a little general store and dram shop, or tav-ern, in Warsaw. There they hosted the voting in the 1840 election, and a lot of people were in town when Andrew Jones came to the shop to vote and buy some cigars.

The Jones family, including Andrew and his sons Samuel, Isaac, and John, had been living about twenty miles south of Warsaw, along the Pomme de Terre River, since the early 1830s. They'd been sus-pected, but never convicted, of stealing horses and were generally considered about as ready to fight as the Turks. Both families had well-earned reputations for short tempers and plenty of nerve. On Election Day, when Andy Jones pulled out a paper dollar bill to pay for his cigars, Jim Turk objected that it was counterfeit and loudly refused to take it.

This was in an era when there was considerable debate about stan-dardizing American money. Some favored coins for their precious met-als. Some favored paper money for its convenience. And in an effort to stimulate local economies, the federal government authorized banks to print their own money. With every new law, every new technology, there's a dark mind calculating the best way to make hay out of it, and so it was with America's evolving currency. Scoundrels were bound to start printing illegal local money, and as early as 1832 there was a coun-terfeiting operation going on in the Missouri Ozarks. Everybody knew John Avy started it.

No one knows exactly when John Avy showed up in the Ozarks, but it didn't take him long to make a reputation, and soon men who had no apparent connection to him were turning to him for orders. There was a story of a farmer who awoke one cold morning to find one of his horses stolen. So he saddled the other one, bundled up, and started tracking the missing animal. As night fell, he found himself near a cabin, where he called out and asked for shelter for the night. The man in the cabin welcomed him, fed him, and made a pallet for him by the fire. In the morning, the farmer awoke to find that the horse he rode in on had been stolen. He had to walk all the way home, leaving his host shaking his head at the bad fortune. Of course the farmer had no way of knowing he'd taken shelter with one of Avy's men, and his two horses were once again sharing a stall at a neighboring farm.

Avy opened himself a bank in the bowels of the Ozarks, on Ha Ha Tonka Creek where it flowed into the Niangua River, an area recently vacated by the Osage Indians. Avy became the owner of a printing press and plates, and even a coin stamping machine, with which he began creating a fortune, all under the sheltering wings of his newly opened Bank of Niangua. He was so taken with this new way of making a living that he even copied Mexican currency and traded it southwest into Texas.

Andy Jones and his sons were longtime associates of John Avy, and it was widely believed that they had combined their talents in a variety of illegal ways. So on that November day when Jones paid Jim Turk for the cigars, he offered a bill printed by Avy for Avy's bank. Jim Turk refused it and accused Jones of passing counterfeit money. Jones grabbed the young Turk and hollered that nobody talked to him like that. Hiram Turk rose to the defense of his son and his store, grabbing Jones by the neck and hurling him out into the street.

There among the crowd, both the Jones and Turk families had friends, and the scuffle turned into an all-out brawl. It got really ugly when Jim's brother Tom Turk emerged from the store with an unsheathed knife. As he stepped into the street, the crowd parted in a widening circle, tense, waiting, watching the blade swing back and forth. Belligerent voices began to rise again. Threats were followed by counterthreats, until at last one man backed away, then another, and the violence passed into seething distrust.

Hiram Turk was elected justice of the peace that day. But that very afternoon, before he could take office, Andy Jones filed charges of assault against the Turk family. Once he'd told his story, the justice also added a charge of inciting a riot.

There was one other person in the store that day, Abraham C. Nowell, and he was no friend of the Turks. Not long before, the Turks filed suit against him in a dispute over a sliver of land Nowell sold them. In return, Nowell filed suit against them for failing to pay the full amount due on the land. He was the only customer besides Andy Jones who saw everything that happened in the store on Election Day, and he was the one man who was in a position to testify against the Turks.

The trial date came, and Nowell was riding into Warsaw with neighbor Julius Sutliff and some other men. Nowell was all set to tell what he'd seen and watch the court punish the Turks. As the riders slowed to cross a stream, Jim, Tom, and Hiram Turk, along with some friends, stepped out into the road. The riders stopped, and Sutliff asked, "What do you want, Turk?"

"I want that man right there," Jim Turk said, pointing at Nowell. "I'm going to pull him off his horse and whip him so he won't be thinking about going to court today or any other day."

Nowell countered that the two families just couldn't go on living in the area.

Jim interrupted to agree with him, pulling his pistol and walking forward to stand just to the left of Nowell's horse's head. He told Nowell it was time for him to move away.

Many men in the crowd were armed, but not Nowell. As the argument heated up and Turk waved his pistol more threateningly, Nowell knew he was truly in danger. His friend Sutliff's belt held a pistol within easy reach. One of the other men spoke to Jim, and that was enough to make him take his eyes off of Nowell. At that instant, Nowell grabbed Sutliff's gun, cocked it, and swung to his right, pointing the weapon under the neck of his mount, all in one lightning-quick motion. Jim jerked a pistol shot wildly over the horse's back, in the direction of where Nowell had been, just as Nowell hit the ground and fired, his shot entering Jim's belly, causing a massive wound on its way to his heart.

As Jim Turk fell dead on the trail, he accomplished his purpose of stopping Nowell from testifying, because Nowell jumped back on his horse and galloped away in the opposite direction from town. Jim's father, Hiram, left it for others to check his son, choosing to run to his horse, which was hidden in the brush. He lit out behind Nowell, but after an exhausting pursuit he had to give up. Andy Jones wisely left the county, knowing that the Turks would come after him if he stayed. Without a key witness, the Election Day charges against the Turks were dropped, but their freedom had been won at the loss of Jim's life. And the clumsy way those events unfolded would prove to be typical of the rest of the Turks' story.

About that time a Texas bounty hunter came looking for James Morton, a brother-in-law to Andy Jones, for a murder committed in Alabama. The bounty hunter stood to collect a $400 reward being offered by Alabama, and he generously offered to pay the local people for information. Still, he couldn't find a single person to help him locate Morton. Even the sheriff refused.

Then the bounty hunter asked the Turks. They were more than happy to help catch a relative of Andy's. They told the Texan to sit tight, and they'd fetch Morton for him. As promised, they watched Andy Jones's house until Morton appeared, then took him away. The Turks delivered the prisoner to the bounty hunter, who hauled him back to Alabama. There, it was determined that the murder was committed by a man with the same name from another state. The bounty hunter didn't get the reward, Morton was acquitted of the charges against him, and he returned to his wife.

Morton filed a complaint against Hiram Turk and his boys for kidnapping him. But those charges were dropped, which further infuriated Morton's brother-in-law, Andy Jones, who had quietly slipped back home by that time. He hated the Turks, he'd had enough of their high-handed ways, and he knew they'd kill him as soon as they found out he was back. So on July 17, 1841, he waited for the father, Hiram Turk, as he rode home after fetching his mail in town. Hiram smoked his pipe and enjoyed the evening air, the reins laying loose across the horse's neck. Jones didn't need to talk about it. He just rose up out of the brush and unloaded a shotgun into Hiram's face as he rode past. Hiram flopped backwards onto the trail, and the horse plodded on home.

Jones was charged with Hiram Turk's murder, but as was often the case in that era, if there were no witnesses, there was generally no conviction. So Jones was acquitted and remained a free man. Of course he also disappeared from the county for the second time. And that's the way it was. Punch and counterpunch. It was the Turks' turn to retaliate, and that's when the events of Benton County evolved from a family feud into a full-fledged vigilante war.

Tom Turk was even taller than his late father, standing six feet, eight inches. His black, wavy hair hung to his shoulder blades, a perfect counterpoint to his dark complexion, prominent hook nose, and angular features. He determined to organize his neighbors so they could protect one another and provide some law enforcement in their chaotic county. Tom called together the Turks' backers in the county and stood before the first meeting in a fringed hunting shirt, high black boots, and a red sash and belt, into which was tucked a Bowie knife and a pistol. He kept another knife in a sheath on the back of his neck.

After Tom's inspiring opening remarks, the neighbors all took a pledge of mutual protection. They swore they'd come when called and execute Tom's orders. Their method of enforcement would be slicking, or whipping with hickory switches. The term "slicking" was a common term on the frontier, and a fairly common method of punishment.

So Turk's band of vigilantes was called the Slickers. Their avowed purpose was to rid the county of livestock thieves and counterfeiters. But Tom Turk's first order of business was to locate Abraham Nowell and avenge his father. In the process, the Slickers made raids on local farms, intent on making someone tell where Nowell was. They would haul out the man of the house and tie him to a tree, often for hours, while they taunted him with the pain he was about to endure. Of course he had the option of telling the bunch what they wanted to know, but, in fact, nobody knew where Nowell was. Still, the poor victims were whipped until their flesh hung in strips and blood pooled around their feet. The level of terror in the area was without precedent.

One of the Turks' most trusted men in the Slickers was Ise Hobbs, known throughout the area as a superior physical specimen. He stood about six feet tall, perfectly proportioned, and was strong, agile, and the fastest man in the county in a foot race. On the frontier, men loved to make a contest of their chores, and Hobbs proved himself the best at everything, from cutting wheat to pitching horseshoes. At turkey shoots he could not be bested, always taking the prize with his Tennessee rifle, Old Abram. Furthermore, Hobbs was considered a man of backwoods integrity. Though he was as quick as anyone to take offense at a personal insult, as ready to fight, and as merciless against an enemy, he was particularly given to fighting over other people's honor, often taking up the banner of a woman or a smaller man. Such a figure in the ranks was a huge asset to the Turks, as men flocked to serve in the Slickers alongside Hobbs.

Meanwhile, the Slicker raids went on virtually unhampered. It was during this era that the Slickers became one of the rare success stories in Missouri vigilante history. There had been several murders in John Avy's neighborhood from the mid-1830s to 1841. Then the Slickers

Many a victim was helpless when the Slickers stormed onto property, armed with threats, intimidation, and sticks and ropes for beating. Some of their targets were punished, some were expelled from the community, and a few even lost their lives in the attacks.

made friends among Avy's ranks so they could spy on him. They also threatened Avy men into spying for them, whittling away at the criminal element. The clever Turks even brought attorneys into the Slickers and filed lawsuits against the crooks and their businesses.

One of the Turks' allies was county judge G. W. Moulder, who ruled that Avy's bank was not a bank at all, but a counterfeiting operation, and had to go. Of course, that didn't mean Avy was instantly out of business. It just meant he couldn't do business locally. The bank was Avy's cash cow, so he just continued to distribute his counterfeit loot farther away from home. Still, he couldn't let the judge's ruling pass without taking retribution. One evening just after dark, when the judge and some other men were returning home from Camden County, gunfire erupted from the brush along the road. It was only a few shots, and then it was over. The judge was slightly wounded, but a young man, Proctor Capps, was killed outright by a bullet to the chest.

The next day the sheriff went out to the spot and could see that the assault was made near the home of one of Avy's men. He arrested the man and put him in the Camden County jail. As jails of the time went, it was a pretty good one, with a steel door. So that night, when the Slickers came to get the man who killed young Capps, they came armed with sledgehammers to batter down the door. However, the Capps boy's father met them there and pleaded with them not to lynch the prisoner, but to let the law take its course. The Slickers bowed to the grieving father's plea, but the next day they were sorry for their bargain. During the night, the sheriff, who was an anti-Slicker, took the prisoner and disappeared. He wasn't about to take a further chance on losing his prisoner to a lynch mob.

By that time, John Avy could see the end in sight. Fighting against men was one thing, but fighting against judges, courts, and lawsuits was another. The Slickers were watching his house, so he couldn't even go home. He knew the Slickers were going to get him sooner or later, possibly with a bullet in the night, the same way he and his men had done to others so many times. So one afternoon as one of the Slickers was on his way home from doing his milling, Avy stepped out into the road. The terrified Slicker thought his time was over—but Avy held up his empty hands to show that he had no weapon, and said he wanted to make a deal. They agreed on a plan for the following evening. As the sun touched the horizon the next day, Avy, the man he stopped on the road, and one other Slicker who was a former Avy man, met on a bald above a secluded hollow. It was a perfect meeting place, where anyone could see if another person approached, and they could all be sure it was just the three of them.

"I'm turning my coat," Avy told them. "My time is at an end. I'll give you a list of the names you want, and I can tell you exactly the lives they've taken." All he wanted in return was a chance to pack up and leave without any more trouble. The deal was struck. Within twenty-four hours Avy's top two men were swinging from Ozark maple trees, and their leader had disappeared, never to be seen in the hills again. The Slickers found Avy's money-making operation right where he said it would be, in a big cave under an overhanging bluff, shrouded by trees. The raiders destroyed every sign of it. They rode every night for a week, until they'd worked their bloody way through every name on Avy's list. Some were killed by the mob, while others heard about the rampage and moved away before it was their turn.

Unfortunately, a lot of good families also moved away from the violence.

CHAPTER FOUR

SLICKER VENGEANCE

For a time the Slickers reigned. Not in the way Tom Turk intended, cleaning up the criminal element and protecting the settlers. Instead, every night there was a new act of violence or intimidation. One of the Slickers' favorite methods of intimidation was to simulate a grave in the targeted man's yard. A pile of dirt, a border of stones, and some hastily picked wildflowers did nicely. The horrifying sight was generally topped with a headstone, sometimes a rude cross, but more commonly a board bearing the man's name and his offense. It was more than enough to frighten men, women, and children into moving out of the county, and one by one, that's just what they did.

In fact, a few of the Slickers developed a lucrative real-estate business in the process. As a tortured man hung against a tree trunk, pleading for mercy, he would beg to sell immediately, and before the night was out, a Slicker had bought a farm at discount price. Meanwhile, nobody moved into the area, and there wasn't a new house built in the Slickers' territory for two years.

The worst of these attacks were led by various overzealous Slickers, and not the Turks, who were still interested in justice, not ill-gotten property. They never forgot about Abraham Nowell and were intent on avenging the murders of James and Hiram Turk. Then in 1842, Nowell made the mistake of thinking they'd forgotten about him, and he moved back into his old home. One morning he opened his front door and walked to the well with his wash pail, then back to the washstand beside the door. As he raised the bucket and poured it into the basin, Tom Turk's rifle cracked in the bushes and a bullet sailed past Nowell's ear. Nowell whirled in the direction of the shot, then Ise Hobbs's rifle thundered, and the bullet passed cleanly through Nowell's heart and out his back.

Andy Jones and his friends had been protesting to constables, lawyers, anyone who would listen, about the Slickers' reign of terror. Finally, in the wake of the murder of Nowell, the eighty-man Benton County militia was called out. Their leaders included Colonel D. C. Ballou and Captain John Holloway, veterans of the Black Hawk War, who showed up in full uniform, including sabers and plumed hats. They took to the field to locate Nowell's suspected killers, Turk and Hobbs, and to generally quell the Slicker activities. As the militia marched from farm to farm, frightened women and children became camp followers, moving with them and settling for the night wherever the militia camped. The women were more than happy to gather and prepare food for the men. Whichever home the militia stopped at for the night became their fort.

But the Slickers were not intimidated. Young Bob Turk and a friend jumped up on a fence rail and crowed like roosters, making fun of the strutting troops as they marched down the road. Later that night the militia was camped on the property of a local farmer named Dobbins, when Bob Turk fired a shot through the front door. Though it was a blind shot, meant to be a continuation of the taunting, it passed through the door and happened to strike Dobbins, killing him instantly. It was a mistake, but Dobbins was dead nonetheless.

He was one of a series of Slicker victims, most of whom died from various combinations of blood loss, shock, concussions, heart attacks, ruptured kidneys, and infection. In one such attack, a young man named Sammy Yates was pulled from his home and beaten severely. Tom Turk had targeted him, and his men did his bidding. But the next day Tom discovered that the Slickers had the wrong man. Young Yates was a cousin of the man they wanted.

Ise Hobbs was fed up with crimes like those being committed under the name of the Slickers. The violence had gone too far and had been inflicted on too many innocent people. At the same time, he was fed up with his old friend Tom Turk, with whom he had partnered to kill Nowell. The day of the shooting Hobbs was not surprised when Tom missed with his shot. After all, Tom was a knife man, and he was depending on Hobbs's skill with his legendary rifle, Old Abram. But when the militia started roaming the neighborhood, Tom's streak of cowardice began to surface, and he made sure the other Slickers knew that it was not his shot that killed Nowell, but Hobbs's. It wasn't that Hobbs didn't want to be recognized for his skill and courage, and Tom told the story as if he were praising Hobbs. But he told it too often to too many friends. Hobbs knew Tom was protecting himself, making sure it was common knowledge that Hobbs fired the fatal shot, just in case the militia caught up with them. Hobbs strongly suspected that Tom even missed his shot at Nowell on purpose, so Hobbs would have to kill him. Then, if anyone was hanged for the killing, it would be Hobbs.

There were other conflicts between the two men, like the time Hobbs took exception to Tom's remarks about a local girl. Over that issue they faced off in a field, both armed with scythe blades, but Tom walked away before any blow was struck.

At last, after weeks in the field, the militia's persistence paid off. Acting on a tip, they cornered Tom and Hobbs in the second story of a farmhouse. With the home surrounded, the family who lived there pleaded with Tom and Hobbs to give up, and they did. The militia took them to Bolivar to be tried for Nowell's murder. But before long the prosecutor determined that he didn't have a case. With no witnesses and no other evidence, and with the help of influential friends, both men were released without a trial.

However, one critically important thing happened while they were in jail. Tom Turk sealed his fate. He was so afraid of the gallows that he continued telling people that Hobbs had fired the fatal shot—and he told not just fellow Slickers, but militiamen and deputies. Hobbs became convinced that if they had come to trial, Tom would have testified against him. When they were released, the friendship was broken, and Hobbs's course was set.

Ever since Nowell's murder, both men had gone armed at all times. Yet Tom knew that was not enough to preserve his life, because someone would be waiting, someday. If it came to a shootout with Hobbs and he prevailed, someone would come to avenge Hobbs. He determined that the only way to stay alive was to move away and leave Benton County to Hobbs. But that wasn't enough for Hobbs. He wanted an end to Tom Turk. He knew Tom's habits, so it didn't take much surveillance to settle on his best opportunity for an assault. Scouting a trail from Tom's house he settled on a position behind a great root ball of a fallen tree. The next day, in preparation for leaving the county, Tom went to the blacksmith shop to have his horse shod, and returned home, rifle in hand, using the ramrod as a quirt, or whip. Hobbs watched from the shadows, saw Tom's big, black horse leave the shop, ran quickly to his hiding place, and waited. As Tom passed, Old Abram belched fire, and a ball passed into his side. Tom Turk fell dead in the trail.

As word spread, people gathered at the murder scene, talking and conjecturing about whether Hobbs did it or one of the anti-Slickers. A rain began to fall. About that time Tom's mother rode up to the little group. Without a word she dismounted, and refusing help from any of the strong men, the tiny woman raised her murdered son's body across her saddle and walked home leading the horse.

Mourners gathered in the parlor to view the corpse laid out on the dining table. Among them was Ise Hobbs, who raised a gentle hand to stroke the hair of his former confidant. "You've been a brave fellow, Tom," he said, "But they got you at last." It was the bold act of a defiant man, as everyone present was certain that Hobbs had killed Tom.

Of course the Turks weren't content to let it end there. Although a warrant was issued for Hobbs's arrest, nobody expected him to be convicted. Soon thereafter, Hobbs's brother Jefferson was riding in a wagon with their father when he was shot dead in an ambush. For Hobbs, seeing the grief and fear that wracked his father, it was worse than if he had been shot himself. Then, while the family was newly grieving over Jefferson's murder, Hobbs was arrested for killing Tom. Of course he had friends, and it only took a couple of hushed conversations, a threat, and a bribe for Hobbs to break out of the Warsaw jail. He told his family goodbye, tied a bag of apples and dried meat across his saddle, and fled from Benton County.

At that point the Slicker War moved out of southwestern Missouri. Two anti-Slickers who were known to be good trackers followed the fugitive Ise Hobbs when he left the county. They arrested him and had him locked up in Potosi. Again he escaped, and his pursuers chased him across Kentucky and all the way to Tennessee, where they arrested him a third time. That night they camped along the Buffalo River, just off the road near a ford. Huge chestnut trees sheltered them as the water gurgled past. It was really the first time the anti-Slickers had a chance to sit down and talk about it all. They were plenty tired of chasing Hobbs across three states, and they had a long trip home. He was going to be a lot of trouble, he was likely to escape again, and worst of all, the trackers were afraid they'd get him home and he'd be acquitted. So they prodded and taunted him until, even though handcuffed, Hobbs threw himself at them in a frustrated rage. Both guards fired on him, and he died far from home on that Tennessee riverbank.

Meanwhile, the Slickers had a tracker of their own, younger brother Nathan Turk. When Andy Jones, murderer of the Turk patriarch, Hiram, decided things were too hot in Benton County, he disappeared.

The Turks had been watching for an opportunity to put an end to Jones, and when they found out he was gone, they turned Nathan loose, like a bloodhound on a scent.

Jones and two of his closest associates, Louden Wray and Harvey White, along with Wray's son, left Missouri and headed south. Somewhere along the way they picked up a man named Reed. In a saloon in Bonham, Texas, they made the acquaintance of a local man named Mitchell, who threw in with them, and so began a spree of horse stealing. They would take one horse or a few, whatever they could get, and hide them away at Mitchell's scruffy little farm. When they'd accumulated enough, they'd make the ten-mile ride across the line into Indian Territory, where nobody asked any questions, and sell the stolen stock there.

In July 1844, they came upon a camp of friendly Native Americans. The Caddo reservation was nearby, and the little group of four men and a boy had been out catching wild horses. They camped for the night under a little cut bank that sheltered them from the relentless north Texas wind. To one side, the cut provided a sort of natural corral for the horses. Across the flat prairie Jones and friends saw the glow from the Indians' fire and came riding up.

The outlaws smiled and waved, making every pretense of a friendly visit and a desire to share the fire. There was nothing unusual about that. Besides, Native Americans were always under suspicion, always outmanned and outgunned, so they had to make friends wherever they could. The Caddo had no guns, and they had no choice but to accept the strangers' good-natured greeting. The white men dismounted and admired the Indians' horses. Then without warning, they turned, pulled their pistols, and opened fire on the unarmed Indians. Two of the Caddo were killed instantly, and two scrambled up the bank and ran to safety. The horrified boy screamed for mercy after seeing his brother and cousin shot dead, but Reed grabbed and held him while Mitchell pulled out his Bowie knife and in a single slash laid open the boy's belly. The take was twelve horses, four rifles, and the dead Indians' knives.

The two surviving Indians ran all the way back to the reservation and told their horrific story to the Fannin County sheriff. He already had warrants out for the Jones gang in horse stealing. He added murder warrants to the Missourians' trouble, and he intended to do something about it. Mitchell was one of the men named in the horse-stealing

Robert Coffee and Louis Bedoka, Caddo Indians wearing a mix of store-bought and traditional clothing. Although this photo was taken later, in about 1890, the men Nathan Turk was hunting had murdered and stolen from Caddo men who probably looked a lot like these two.

warrants, and he lived just seven miles from the site of the Indian murders, so the sheriff brought Mitchell in, and the Caddo survivors identified him as one of the murderers.

Mitchell wasn't going to hang alone, so he spilled the beans. He fingered the hangers-on of the group, Bob Jones, and two that he knew only as Jewland and Harris. He didn't know about Andy Jones, but he said Louden Wray and his son had taken most of the Caddo horses on a journey of over one hundred miles to Shreveport.

Loud was feeling good as he and the boy sold the Indian horses, along with Loud's own horse and saddle. Then he simply stole another one, a mare with a foal, for the trip home. When Loud and his son crossed the line back into Fannin County, deputies were waiting, and the Wrays were arrested. Like Mitchell, Loud wasn't going to let the others get away, and he told the sheriff that Andy Jones and Harvey White had headed south. They'd left the county, so there was nothing the sheriff could do but wait for them as he'd waited for the Wrays.

But someone else had been watching. Someone who wasn't limited by county lines. The tracking Slicker Nathan Turk was still on the trail, and he came to Texas armed with his family's talent for working up a crowd of vigilantes. With an impassioned plea on a Bonham, Texas, sidewalk, he related to the crowd of strangers how Andy Jones had made a coward's attack on his father, shooting him from ambush on a Missouri back road. Now Jones was leading a gang that stole horses and killed unarmed Indians in Texas. Where would it end? And in a matter of minutes, young Nathan found himself leading a posse of twenty armed vigilantes.

The trail was cold, but Jones and White had some of the Caddo horses and left a trail by selling them one by one as they traveled. Nathan Turk and his posse tracked them over 120 miles to the abandoned Fort Houston outside Palestine. Jones and White knew they were beyond the reach of the Fannin County sheriff but had no idea there was a relentless Slicker leading a pack of vigilantes after them. With no particular place to go, and believing they were safe, the two took refuge in a dilapidated building of the old outpost, where they drank until they passed out, then got up and did it again the next day.

In the dark of night, the gang of twenty armed men burst in on Jones and White as they slept. Young Nathan Turk was close enough to avenge his father with a single thrust of his knife, but he restrained himself. He was surrounded by Fannin County men who cared more for Texas justice than for retribution over something that happened back in Missouri. So Nathan had to be content with knowing the law would do the work for him.

All the men were arrested except Reed, who was never found. Andy Jones, White, Loud Wray, and Mitchell were convicted of horse stealing and murder, and they were hanged. Wray's son and three others of the gang, Bob Jones, Jewland, and Harris, were convicted only of theft. In a twist of cruel and unusual punishment, they were forced to leave the state after pulling the others up on hangman's ropes, where they slowly twisted and strangled to death. Standing in the front row was a somber Nathan Turk, satisfied that his father's murder was avenged.

Nathan decided he would only face more trouble from anti-Slickers back in Missouri, so while he pondered whether he could ever return, he drifted to Shreveport. There, he was killed in a barroom brawl. When news of his death finally reached Benton County, Missouri, the widow of Hiram Turk hugged her only living son, Robert, to her bosom and moved back to Tennessee. In later years she would say she never understood what her men were fighting about.

CHAPTER FIVE

THE BORDER WARS

Jesse James was a shirtless and barefoot fifteen-year-old boy sweating in the late May sun, hoeing the emerging rows of cabbage, turnips, potatoes, and onions in the family's garden. Suddenly, a dozen armed and blue-uniformed men came at a gallop out of the trees, into the yard, and right through the vegetables. They were Provisional Enrolled Missouri Militia, merciless anti-Southern fighters, and they weren't wandering around on an aimless patrol, but had ridden specifically to the James farm. They knew that Jesse's brother Frank was off fighting with William Quantrill's Confederate guerrillas, and they would do whatever it took to get somebody to tell them where Quantrill was camped.

The militiamen were on the right track. Frank had been riding with a little band of Quantrill's guerrillas led by Fernando Scott. Frank took them to his mother's farm for a welcome break from their raiding. They slipped into the woods not far from the house and set the horses to graze beside a little creek. The men napped, played cards, and generally enjoyed the shade, unaware of the brutality about to descend on the farm.

Some of the militiamen rode up around Jesse, and one struck him a blow with the butt of his pistol that sent the boy to his knees in

Jesse (left) and Frank James, in their teens before the Civil War.

the black loam. More riders reined up at the house, stormed in, then emerged, dragging Jesse's mother and stepfather, Dr. Reuben Samuel. The loud invaders were a terrifying sight, with pistols and swords in their hands and on their belts. They beat the Jameses, demanding to know where to find Quantrill. They pricked Jesse with bayonets and forced him to watch as they put a rope around his stepfather's neck and hanged him repeatedly from a tree in the front yard. They laughed and mocked the old doctor's gasps for air, then let him down just before he lost consciousness. As soon as he recovered, back up he'd go. At last, the cowardly stepfather was unable to resist more torture, and he gave up his wife's son, pointing to the woods where Frank and his friends were camped.

Just inside the trees, the soldiers spread out in a line and moved steadily deeper into the woods until they could see Frank and the others. A sergeant called for them to surrender, but the guerrillas answered with pistol shots, which were answered by a chorus of Union rifles. The Rebels kept firing while they mounted and made their escape, but two died there in the hail of militia bullets. The soldiers ran back for their mounts, which gave the guerrillas a chance to get a bit of a head start. But after riding a couple of miles the guerrillas made the mistake of thinking they were out of danger, stopped, and dismounted to gather themselves and secure their gear. Just then the militia came riding up again, firing wildly, and killing three more. Frank and the other survivors jumped into the saddle and, because they were better mounted, made good their escape in a dusty, galloping, cross-country chase.

Although old man Samuel survived, the cruel hangings at the hands of the soldiers caused him permanent brain damage. He and Jesse's mother, the outspoken, Yankee-hating Zerelda James Samuel, were both arrested, leaving Jesse alone on the farm with the hired hands. A few days later, after his mother signed a loyalty oath, was released from jail, and returned home, Jesse left.

That was in the middle of the Civil War, the summer of 1863, and Frank had already been serving the Southern cause for two years, first with the Confederate regulars, then with Quantrill. Jesse once visited Frank in the Quantrill camp, but as a boy too young to have whiskers, everyone agreed he needed to go back home and help on the farm. But then the Provisional Enrolled Militia raid on the farm cast the die, and Jesse rode back to join Frank. He proved he was old enough to ride with the charismatic Quantrill when he took the lives of at least

*Jesse James at age sixteen or seventeen, about the time he left
home to join Quantrill. Courtesy of Missouri History Museum.*

four men on the legendary raid that destroyed the town of Lawrence,
Kansas, in August.

By that time Jesse and others like him on both sides were living a
story that was more than a decade old. The brutality Jesse and his family suffered at the hands of the militia was common along the Missouri-
Kansas border, and each one who was attacked responded with more
ruthless attacks. The proving ground for those war-hardened guerrillas
began as early as 1852, amid worries of whether the territories of Kan-

sas and Nebraska would enter the Union as free or slave states. With the first shots of the Civil War still years in the future, and hundreds of miles away at Fort Sumter in South Carolina, lives were already on the line in western Missouri and eastern Kansas.

In other parts of the country the pending war was boiling on several political fires, but the issue that mattered for the James/Samuel family was slavery. They had money and a nice farm; they raised hemp, one of the few Missouri crops that really benefited from a workforce of slaves. As was the case with most of their neighbors, without their slaves their way of farming and living would change.

Slaves were the most valuable property most farmers owned, hard to come by, and hard to replace. Freeing them would cause far more damage than losing every horse, plow, rake, shovel, butter churn, and spinning wheel on the place. As for preserving the Union, pro-slavers and abolitionists were divided among themselves. On both sides, some thought the nation must be preserved at any cost, and some were sure the Union's time was past. Some were talking about secession, while some slave owners thought slavery could only be preserved by preserving the Union. They were sure that individual slave states leaving the Union, scattered among free states, would be weak and unable to sustain their slave trade.

Missouri had entered the Union as a slave state in 1821, and as a result was a mecca for Southerners, whether they owned slaves or not. They were attracted by the Democratic mindset and the agricultural opportunities, though there were virtually none of the sprawling plantations that had characterized slavery in the Deep South. For the average farm family, slavery was a matter of pride, tradition, and "don't tread on me" beliefs more than economics. The only Missouri crops that favored slave labor were hemp and cotton, and slave owners commonly had only one or two slaves, or perhaps a slave family, serving them. But Saline, Clay, Calloway, and Lafayette counties were in an area of Missouri known as Little Dixie, with more Southern traditions

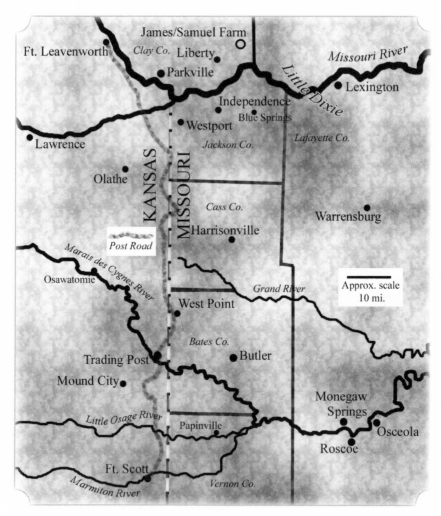

Map of the Missouri-Kansas border at the time of the Civil War.

and a higher concentration of slaves. In Little Dixie, especially in those counties that bordered Kansas, there was an overriding fear that Kansas would enter the Union as a free state, which would erode slavery across the whole of Missouri.

Disagreements led to tensions, then violence, and Kansas was as hotly contested by the vigilante rifle as it was by the governmental gavel.

Kansas Free-Staters raided into Missouri, and Missouri Bushwhackers raided into Kansas. Sometimes it was a handful of men, sometimes a hundred. On one trip they might issue a beating and a warning. On another they might burn a farmhouse and beat a man to death while his family watched. In those days they learned outlaw tactics, hardened their hearts, and were repeatedly galvanized by the attacks of their opponents.

In the late 1850s, Missouri slaves increasingly ran away to Kansas, and they had plenty of encouragement. Anti-slavers traveled from farm to farm, gathering slaves in the dark of night, telling them stories of the free life in New England and Canada. Of course many runaways were captured by their owners and returned. And a booming little business sprang up among slave hunters who brought them back for a bounty fee.

All that activity around slavery was prompted by the 1820 Missouri Compromise, and in the 1840s, a complex system of state bounties was established. Then in 1854, the Fugitive Slave Act made it just about impossible for slaves to escape, because it proclaimed that they were still slaves, even in free territory, and that it was a crime to help or hide them. Hundreds of Missouri slaves sued in court for their freedom between 1800 and 1860. Since they had no legal standing to bring suit, the Fugitive Slave Act established commissioners to adjudicate disputed cases. The commissioner was paid $5 if the slave was freed, but $10 if the slave was returned to his owner.

The law unintentionally created a boom in hunting runaway slaves. Of course some slave catchers didn't care whether the people they caught were legally bound or not. To them, any person of African descent found on free soil was fair game for capture, as somebody in the South would pay for him or her. Some opportunistic men even stole Missouri slaves, took them across the border into Kansas, then delivered them back to their Missouri owners, just to collect the bounty.

Eastern anti-slavery activists, like the New England Emigrant Aide Company, led by Eli Thayer, organized great companies of Free Soil families to move to Kansas. In late 1854 Thayer set out with several hundred people from Boston. Slavery advocates heard they were coming, and soon rumors abounded that the emigrants were heavily armed, and even more guns were being raised by eastern churches and shipped to Kansas Free-Staters. Of course, in the face of such a threat, Missouri pro-slavers raised their own arsenals.

Kansas went through a long period when elections included pro- or anti-slavery ordinances, and candidates for office promised to support or oppose slavery. To make sure Kansas didn't become a haven for Free Soil men and runaway slaves, some Missourians claimed an address in Kansas just so they could travel over there and vote. Entire wagons loaded with voters from Missouri showed up on election days. And of course both sides boldly stuffed ballot boxes.

On Election Day, March 30, 1855, thousands of Missourians poured over the border and cast their votes. They elected a new Kansas government and adopted a constitution that legalized slavery. In such a climate, out there on the American frontier, with law enforcement officers and courts carrying their own personal feelings about slavery, violence was bound to take a hand.

The fire had been smoldering for some time in Lawrence, Kansas, the same town destined to be sacked by Quantrill and his men, including Frank and Jesse James, in 1863. The place was a Free-Stater headquarters, where fights and arrests were common, along with corrupt officials and rigged local elections. The new Kansas government, determined that something be done about the abolitionists in Lawrence, called for a special territorial grand jury. The jury ordered the arrest of several Lawrence officials and the closing of the newspaper, among other things.

To enforce the orders, on May 21, 1856, a swarm of more than seven hundred Missouri vigilantes descended on the town with five cannon, all led by a federal marshal. The raiders demolished the newspaper office and its press, which was their main objective. But they didn't stop there. They burned the town indiscriminately, destroying homes and businesses without regard to what kind of products or services they offered, who owned them, or whether they had any connection to abolitionism. They even fired a few cannonballs into the stately brick Free State Hotel before setting it ablaze. All that was five years before the Civil War.

The Military Post Road, or Old Post Road, ran within about three miles of the border, from Fort Leavenworth in Kansas to Fort Scott in Indian Territory. Though most of it lay in Kansas, it dipped in and out of Missouri's Jackson, Cass, and Bates counties. It was a pipeline for Free-Staters and anti-slavery settlers, as well as pro-slavery people. Of course when feelings became heated and violence rose, it was a freeway for raiders from both sides.

In May 1856 John Brown descended the Post Road accompanied by his sons, taking off east into Missouri for his legendary first raid. They prowled along Pottawatomie Creek, looking for slaves, and the longer they rode without seeing a hard-laboring Negro, the more eager they became for some action. Brown and his boys weren't about to ride all that way without inflicting their personal brand of justice on someone. At last they came upon the James Doyle farm. The Doyles owned no slaves, but Brown knew Doyle and his sons to be slave hunters, men who caught runaway slaves and returned them to their owners for a bounty. Brown engaged the Doyles in friendly conversation, but Doyle, not knowing Brown, played his cards close to the chest. Brown tried, but he couldn't get Doyle to admit his pro-slavery activities. At last Brown became so frustrated that he gave up talking and flew at Doyle in a fury. He and his sons dragged Doyle and his sons out of the house into the front yard and hacked them to death with short swords, Bowie knives, and hatchets. Traveling on, they made an equally grisly attack on an elderly pro-slavery district attorney, Allen Wilkinson, and took his slaves with them. Then they found Dutch Bill Sherman at home. Using the same interrogation techniques that failed on Doyle,

Abolitionist John Brown.

the Browns got Dutch Bill to admit he'd led Bushwhacker raids, and then they cut off his hands before splitting his torso down the middle. By the time they quit, the murdering Browns had freed fourteen slaves. Of course when Brown stole slaves, he knew someone could find them and take them back to Missouri, so he went to great lengths to get them out of Kansas. On one of his slave-stealing raids, John Brown made off with eleven slaves, then spent almost three months delivering them to freedom in Canada.

In retaliation for Brown's raids, Charles Hamilton led a group of Bushwhackers north on the Post Road to kill five newly emigrated Free-Staters. Then Kansas Free-Stater James Montgomery raised a gang that chased Hamilton and his pro-slave men back to Missouri. Next, he organized a bigger band of two hundred men who rotated duty patrolling the southern section of the Post Road, as well as making slave-stealing raids into Missouri. Montgomery was the first to label his men Jayhawkers, although the name had been used before that time.

Pro-slavers used it as a slur, implying that slave stealers were birds who stole from another bird's nest, but it was taken as a boast by the Jayhawkers themselves.

Before the Civil War, virtually every community on the Missouri side had organized its own vigilance committee, so that when slaves were stolen, they could steal them back and kill the men who took them. As border violence continued, army troops began to patrol the Post Road to restore peace. But keeping things quiet was impossible on the long, winding trace. So every farmer went to his fields armed, and dozens of people died in the two years before the war was officially declared.

Some of the excursions across the border had a sense of military precision. In 1856, Mexican-American War veteran Major John W. Reid marched out of Westport, Missouri, with a force of pro-slavery men—and picked up more along the way until they numbered about three hundred. Their mission was to punish the anti-slavery hotbeds of Osawatomie, Topeka, and Lawrence. Miles before they neared Osawatomie, they were challenged by an early warning sentry, one of John Brown's loyal abolitionists. As the guard reached for his pistol, one of Reid's men calmly outdrew him and shot him dead. And the march continued.

Brown's scouts had already told him the raiders were coming, and he had gathered his own men from their homes and farms. With his force assembled, he realized that he was still outnumbered ten to one. To hole up in the town and try to defend it would lead to a siege, and that would be a disaster. If they pulled out and left the town to Reid and his men, it would be destroyed. Brown had to think of something else, a surprise that would offset the slavers' superior numbers.

He determined to engage the Missourians before they reached the town. He set an ambush, spreading his men along a line of woods near the road. It was August, midday, and as Brown's men enjoyed the sheltering trees, the sun beat mercilessly on the tired Missouri men who had marched all the way from Westport. No doubt their thoughts wandered to home and cool buttermilk.

As they came alongside the woods, Brown's men opened fire, and the surprised Missourians scattered, looking for cover where there was none. But they had an experienced leader, and that made all the difference. Reid braved the fire to rally his men, pulled his saber and rode down their line without regard to the abolitionist bullets buzzing around him. He commanded his men to turn their cannon on the men in the woods. A few volleys from their cannon and rifles established a new tone to the battle, and Reid led his men in a headlong charge. Brown's men fled in retreat, forced to cross the creek at their rear. As they were slowed down descending the bank, wading through the water, and climbing the opposite bank, Reid's furious men caught up and picked them off one by one.

All but a few of Brown's men were killed. A handful were taken prisoner, and at least one of them was executed the next day. The overwhelming pro-slave force went on to sack and burn Osawatomie after taking everything of value they could find, including guns, ammunition, clothing, wagons to haul the bounty in, and plenty of horses.

Small raids continued, like the one on May 19, 1858, when about thirty men led by Charles Hamilton crossed over into Kansas. Hamilton once lived in Trading Post, Kansas, where he was a pro-slavery man living among Free-Staters led by the Jayhawker James Montgomery. They ran Hamilton out of the state. After settling in Bates County, Missouri, making friends, and building a reputation as a pro-slavery, pro-Missouri man, he organized a meeting in Papinsville. He raised the crowd to a fever pitch and convinced them to join him on a raid to rid Kansas of the Free-Staters. Of course Hamilton also had a more personal agenda, as the targeted abolitionists were also the people who had chased him out of Kansas.

Hamilton led his men to Trading Post and rounded up a few antislavery men he knew personally. Though he herded them like cattle, forcing them to walk at gunpoint ahead of his little band of mounted vigilantes, and though they didn't know where he was taking them, they didn't really think he'd hurt them. After all, they knew Hamilton, and it hadn't been that long since he was their neighbor. Only one man resisted, blacksmith Eli Snyder. He refused to leave his forge and be a prisoner of Hamilton's band. Hamilton persisted, and the smith grabbed a shotgun from the corner of his shop, unleashing both barrels harmlessly in Hamilton's general direction, then running for the woods. By the time he'd gone a few steps the Missourians had their own guns at their shoulders and unleashed a volley that sent Snyder tumbling head over heels, severely wounded. They left him bleeding on the hillside behind his shop and continued on their mission.

As the group traveled, they rounded up more Free-State men, until the prisoners totaled eleven. Stopping alongside a washed-out ravine, Hamilton ordered the prisoners to walk down into the red-dirt ditch and stand along one side. He lined the force of thirty Missourians along the opposite bank and ordered them to open fire. There was a moment of silent hesitation, then one man protested that he would not fire on unarmed men. He mounted his horse and rode for home, as Hamilton turned back to his remaining men.

Urging his men to shoot, Hamilton said the Kansans were Free-Staters who would take everything from them. He then took his own rifle and fired the first shot. The others instantly followed his order, and the eleven helpless men fell. William Stilwell, Patrick Ross, William Colpetzer, Michael Robinson, and John Campbell were killed. Austin Hall, who was almost blind, was not hit, but cleverly fell to the dirt and pretended to be dead. Five others were badly wounded and left for dead.

The raid, which came to be known as the Marais des Cygnes massacre after the name of a nearby river, was lost in the swirling dust of the Civil War. After all, it was one of hundreds of similar acts of unfeeling violence over a period of over fifteen years. Investigators later determined that none of Hamilton's victims had any connection to James Montgomery, the man who was responsible for running Hamilton out of Kansas. As for the leader of the raid, Hamilton, he returned to his native Georgia and lived until 1880. Out of the thirty Missouri men who rode with Hamilton, only one man, William Griffith, was arrested. That was years later, in Bates County in the spring of 1863, when the state was under martial law. He was found guilty of murder and hanged. In a perfect example of the vengeful mindset of that time, one of the survivors of the massacre was given the honor of hanging him.

With such hate flourishing along the border, it's no wonder that when the war started, Missouri farms were attacked by Jayhawker leaders like Jim Lane and Charles Jennison, and their victims retaliated in guerrilla bands or joined the Confederate army in the hope of taking revenge. Upton Hayes was a peaceful freight hauler, driving his wagons from near Kansas City to far western towns. He also happened to be a slave owner, but he wanted nothing to do with the controversy. When the Jayhawkers captured one of his wagon trains, burned his house, took everything he owned, and freed his slaves, he suddenly turned very political and became a Missouri Bushwhacker. Cole Younger, the charismatic outlaw who rode with Jesse James, had a similar story. Younger's father was strongly loyal to the Union, but Jennison's men robbed and killed him. Younger and all his brothers who were old enough turned to the Rebel cause and rode with Quantrill's guerrillas.

When William Clarke Quantrill first came to the border, he assumed such aliases as William Clark and Charlie Hart. His true historical record is lost in veiled stories of spy activity and wanton killing on both sides of the issue, and on both sides of the border. Some say he was a man willing to participate in Kansas Free-Stater raids to free the Missouri slaves, just so he could gain an opportunity to turn his coat and help the Missourians slay the invaders from Kansas.

But the record is clear that one afternoon in November 1860, near Blue Springs in Jackson County, Missouri, six miles outside Indepen-

William Quantrill during the Civil War.

dence, a company of eight anti-slavery men, including Quantrill, rode toward the home of Morgan Walker, intent on taking his slaves. Walker was one of the original settlers there, and owned one thousand acres and twenty-six faithful slaves. The abolitionist raiders, coming out of Lawrence, Kansas, sent one man ahead. Arriving at dawn, a day before the rest of the group, the slave stealer slipped around the corner of Walker's barn, surprising the thirty-year-old black man who had come out before the sun to milk the cows. Though he was startled by the man in the shadows, the visitor's calm voice was reassuring. He said he had come to alert the slaves that they'd be liberated by that afternoon. Just be ready to run, he said, and they'd soon find themselves free, among men who could take them to safety.

But the slave was loyal to his master, Walker, and after a brief talk with the other slaves, they all determined to stay on the place. If the abolitionists captured and took them away, that was one thing, but they would not willingly leave the Walker farm. Of course they were motivated by equal parts loyalty and fear, because a runaway slave might be whipped or even hanged if he were captured.

Late that day, Quantrill left the rest of the raiding party camped in the woods about a mile west of Walker's home. Saying he was going to spy on the Walkers, he approached Walker's son Andrew as he worked in a field. He told Andrew the entire plan and urged him to go to his father and make ready a stout defense. Thanks to Quantrill's warning, dozens of neighbors gathered at the Walker home. When the raiders came just after dark, Morgan Walker was waiting with a few men in the house, while his son Andrew and others were in the harness room of the barn.

Quantrill and two other raiders walked up on the porch and knocked, while the others fanned out across the yard. When Morgan Walker opened the door, Quantrill politely, but pointedly, announced that they'd come to take his slaves, mules, and money. Walker calmly said his slaves were always free to leave, but he wouldn't let anyone force them to leave, and he was not giving up any of his other possessions. With that, Quantrill deftly stepped inside and slammed the door, leaving the bewildered raiders looking at each other. The door opened again, and gunfire erupted from the house and the harness room.

Walker was a deadly shot, and he immediately killed one man and wounded two from the doorway. While some raiders briefly exchanged shots with Walker, one circled around to the slave cabins to round up the slaves. But the slaves were as afraid of the raiders as they were secure with Walker, and they wouldn't come out of their cabins. By that time another raider had been killed. That left three, and two of those were wounded. The healthy one came across the yard, pulling a slave by the arm. He helped one injured raider onto a horse. Then he forced the slave up on a horse, jumped up behind him, and galloped away beside his injured companion, who slumped, barely hanging onto his saddle. The last raider in the yard was wounded in the heel, so he jumped up on their wagon and drove hard for the Kansas border as fast as he could go.

Walker's little army was flush with victory, and they talked excitedly about pursuing the Kansans. As they stood in the moonlit yard and looked around the group, they recognized their neighbors and realized that among them was the new man, William Quantrill. He'd never lived in that community, but some men knew they'd seen him before. Then everyone realized that Quantrill came in with the Kansans, but none of them knew it was his warning that saved the day. They started questioning him, and before long had his hands tied and a rope ready to hang him. Morgan Walker was among those ready to lynch him, and said that Quantrill was the one who spoke for the raiders at the house.

Morgan Walker, who defended his slaves from Kansas raiders.

Andrew Walker had been talking with the slaves, getting them settled, and when he returned and saw what was happening in the yard, he pointed his Hawken rifle over his head and fired one shot. Everyone stopped dead still. Striding through the crowd to stand beside Quantrill, Walker said, "I promised this man he would be saved, no matter what happened. With his warning we were ready for those scoundrels. If you want to hang this man, you'll have to do it after I'm dead."

Walker's endorsement was enough to convince the others of Quantrill's trustworthiness. They settled down and rested, agreeing that at first light they would set off in pursuit of the slave raiders. During the night, the one slave who was taken by the raiders waited until the men were asleep, then slipped out of the west side of their camp, circled around, and was waiting on Walker's porch when Walker and his friends awoke in the morning.

The returned slave led them straight to the camp of the two Jayhawkers, where one stood guard over his wounded partner, who lay on a blanket. When the Walker party was barely in rifle range, still over a hundred yards away, the healthy raider saw them, leveled his pistol, and dared the men to come in closer. But Walker refused the invitation, instead drawing down and placing a bullet through the man's forehead. Quantrill then walked calmly forward, ahead of the others, placed his Navy Colt in the wounded man's mouth, and pulled the trigger.

Some distrust of Quantrill lingered, even after he shot the raider. Suspicious men conjectured that Quantrill couldn't afford to leave the wounded man alive, because he would have told about more of Quantrill's anti-slavery activities in Kansas. But the suspicions faded quickly, simply because Quantrill rose up as an uncommonly violent defender of slavery. From that time on, Quantrill ruthlessly cast his lot against the Free-Staters. Men flocked to follow his unflinching leadership, and he taught them how to be relentlessly brutal.

CHAPTER SIX

THE BORDER DURING THE WAR

While the crescendo to the Civil War was a battle of words, law, and compromise in most of the nation, along the Missouri-Kansas border it was producing widows and orphans. Then, when the war started in earnest, the guerrillas, who'd already been killing, burning, and stealing, just went right on fighting. However, they quickly learned that their importance had soared overnight.

East of the Mississippi, from Maryland to the Carolinas and across the Deep South, staggering numbers of regular soldiers assembled, trained, marched, camped, and engaged in epic struggles. Infantry and artillery were supported by swarming, stinging cavalry. A regular cavalry company of one hundred skilled riders could harass an enemy brigade enough to turn a major engagement, or one spy could undermine a general's plans. In that setting, the eastern theater of the war, there wasn't a great deal that guerrillas could do to help or hinder.

At the same time, both North and South needed every bullet and body for battles like Shiloh, Gettysburg, Bull Run, Antietam, and Atlanta. Neither could afford to invest major armies and resources beyond the Mississippi. So there in the fearless and independent West, the guerrilla mindset gained full bloom.

Guerrilla units attracted the worst kind of men. Cruel men with no scruples. Men who didn't worry about killing the innocent who happened to be too close to the guilty. And yet the best of them were vigilantes serving noble ideals of enforcing laws, protecting the weak, and repelling invaders. Their leaders raised obedient forces who were loyal unto death under the barest of command structure, who fought with unflagging ferocity and merciless tactics. Guerrillas were willing to leave their homes and travel great distances, knowing they would strike a vicious blow when they arrived. No overarching strategy. No waiting for orders, supplies, weather, or the movements of another regiment. They moved at will and struck without mercy. When the raid was over, they'd scatter, go back to their homes and families, put on their overalls, and take off their boots. There was no way an outsider could know who was a raider and who wasn't.

While regular soldiers moved in great plodding masses, guerrillas struck like lightning. They had superior mounts because they stole the best horses they could find. They taught their horses to ground tie, grazing as long as the reins were dropped. It made for a faster getaway when horses weren't tied to anything. And such horses would stop on the spot if the rider was shot or thrown off.

They were wildly creative, attacking in unexpected ways and from unexpected directions. One of their favorite tactics was to gallop through an enemy camp firing at anything that moved. Just one pass, then they'd be gone before the resting men knew what hit them. While soldiers could be deadly accurate when firing at an enemy a hundred or two hundred yards away, the raiders were uniquely equipped for close combat. Quantrill's men trained to become superior horsemen, attacking with a revolver in each hand, another in their belt, the reins in their teeth, a carbine handy in its scabbard, a Bowie knife on their hip, and a dagger in their boot. Most of them carried four to six revolvers, so while regular soldiers reloaded their rifles, they could continue firing on and on.

In January 1861, Lincoln was elected president, Kansas entered the Union as a free state, and seven states seceded. Soon after, the people of Missouri decided to stay in the Union but also decided that if a war started, they wouldn't supply troops to either side. After the Rebel attack on Fort Sumter on March 22, President Lincoln called for two hundred troops from every state, and Missouri refused.

Things happened fast. Claiborne F. Jackson, a pro-slavery man, had just been elected governor. But he and his government soon had to flee to southwest Missouri, leaving the state with a Federally installed government that had not been elected. That government would hold office for the duration of the war, with the state under martial law. Right away, amateur military units started forming across the state.

On April 20 a band of two hundred secessionists, representing Jackson's legally elected state government, captured a small Federal arsenal at Liberty with one thousand rifles. Then they got ready to seize the much larger St. Louis arsenal, where sixty thousand arms were stored. Meanwhile, Congressman Frank Blair had organized the Home Guard militia unit from the German community. To avoid a conflict, the Home Guard smuggled those sixty thousand guns across the Mississippi into Alton, Illinois.

With one store of weapons in Jackson's hands and the other gone out of the state, it looked like there was nothing to fight about. But Governor Jackson was not going to simply disappear into the hills. He owed it to the people to be the governor they elected. In an effort to stand toe-to-toe with the Federals, Jackson called the Southern-sympathetic militia into camp, a bivouac they called Camp Jackson, a mere two miles west of downtown St. Louis. They set up their tents in a farm field, where many family members came to visit the troops and have picnics. Other people, including entire families, came simply to see the spectacle of the military gathering.

But that cheery scene looked to the Federals like the beginnings of a raid into Illinois to capture the guns. So the Home Guard was quickly mustered into regular Federal service and placed under Captain Nathaniel Lyon. On May 10 they surrounded Camp Jackson and demanded that the state forces surrender. Seeing that they were vastly outnumbered, the militia agreed to surrender the camp but refused to give up their guns. Both sides agreed that those were fair terms to settle the standoff for the time being. After all, they were all Missourians, neighbors, and friends. The thought of fighting one another was very strange, and even being armed and facing each other across the field was surreal. That could have been the end, but Lyon wanted to be sure the militia knew they were his prisoners, and he ordered them to march downtown under guard. Nobody was quite sure where that was leading, but the militia headed east, with Lyon's troops along their flanks. It was peaceful, but tension was high. Everything that was happening was new to everyone.

Then just when the march was going well, someone in the ranks of the regular troops fired his weapon. Of course the militia fired back in self-defense, and when the shooting stopped, more than thirty people were dead and over one hundred wounded, including women and children. That was the Camp Jackson affair, and that's how the Civil War started in Missouri. Ironically, just a month after the Confederate attack on Fort Sumter, this state that refused to fight became the place where armed infantry faced each other for the first time in the Civil War.

More militia units were organized on both sides, including the Reserve Corps, the State Guard, the Wide Awakes, the Minute Men, and of course the Missouri State Militia. Some of the units were legal, but most were not. Some were disbanded, and some absorbed into regular units of the Union or Confederacy. Some were given assignments, while others guarded places that didn't need guarding. Former governor Sterling Price, a slave owner who opposed secession, was livid with the Unionists over the Camp Jackson affair and took command of the state militia under Governor Jackson. The whole state became possessed by a military mindset.

The first shots between infantry units in the Civil War were fired just west of downtown St. Louis in the Camp Jackson affair.

Union soldiers roaming the state foolishly tried to keep order by resorting to the same kind of dirty work the guerrillas used. In Washington County, less than a hundred miles from St. Louis, a Union patrol decided to get rid of one of the area's major slave owners, Samuel Long. When they located him in the care of his son, they didn't care that he was a broken old man who could barely walk. They forced him to walk from the house at the point of a bayonet and refused his pleas to ride his horse. After only three quarters of a mile they tired of his slow pace and decided they'd gone far enough. They took him off to the side of the road, handed him his rifle, told him he was threatening soldiers of the U.S. Army, and shot him in the head. It's no wonder there were so many lost souls in Missouri, not sure who was fighting whom, or where they could fit in.

Left: Charles Jennison, Jayhawker captain of the 7th Regiment, Kansas Volunteer Cavalry. Right: Senator and Jayhawker leader James H. Lane.

When the Civil War started, Kansas raider Charles Jennison was commissioned a Union officer; he took the name Jennison's Jayhawkers for his regiment. Jim Lane was another leader who moved from lawless raiding into command of a Union regiment; he would later be elected one of the first U.S. senators from Kansas. Some of cavalry companies were Red Legs, adopting the red leggings worn by some pre-war Jayhawkers, which became a terrifying symbol along the border.

Victims of the Kansas Unionists included Confederate regulars, their families, their sympathizers, Union loyalists who were suspected of being Southern spies, and lots of people who just happened to be living in the wrong place at the wrong time. The raiders brought wagons or stole wagons, which were used to haul their plunder. They took dishes, furniture, tools, guns, and anything else that could be used by Union families and troops. They tore up hearths looking for treasure. They pulled quilts from beds. And what they didn't take, they destroyed. They burned crops and barns, smashed everything glass, and trampled vegetable gardens.

On one raid around Independence, Missouri, a marauding band of Jayhawkers hanged thirteen-year-old Harrison Young to make him tell where his father was serving in the Confederate army. When they let him down, Harrison told the men again that his father wasn't in the army, but was off working for a freight company, driving a wagon out west, which was true. But they didn't believe him and hanged him again. They let him down, and he didn't change his story, so they stretched his neck again. Harrison survived to tell the tale, and his nephew Harry Truman, born long after the war, would serve in World War I and become president of the United States. But in the 1860s, the Youngs and Trumans were one more family who learned to hate the Union troops.

The marauders demanded food, and all Harriet Young had to feed such a gang was biscuits, so she made biscuits. And more biscuits. And more. She made them until her wrists bled from rubbing on the edge of the wooden bowl as she mixed the dough. On another raid,

The Jayhawkers forced Harriet Young to make biscuits for them until her wrists bled, while they stole or destroyed everything of value on the farm. Her grandson Harry Truman would grow up to be president.

NECESSARY EVIL

Harry Truman's mother recalled that Lane's men shot the family's entire herd of four hundred hogs. They cut off the hams and threw them in wagons, then drove away, leaving the rest of the carcasses to rot. It was a devastating attack on people who used every part of the hog, from bacon to chops. Before they left, the Red Legs set both of the barns on fire. And it got worse. Truman's ancestors were soon victims of General Order Number 11.

There was so much of that kind of trouble along the Kansas border, in 1863 the army created a no-man's land. Order Number 11, issued August 25, made it illegal to live in the border counties. Every civilian had to leave unless they lived within a mile of a Union military post, and there were only a few of those. If they didn't move out, the whole family was arrested. If they had any grain in the field or the barn, they had to deliver it to the army. The army was then free to burn any that was left, to keep it from falling into Confederate hands.

The displaced people didn't have enough money to buy or rent another place, so some of them ended up living in virtual concentration camps, clustered around army posts, eating scant government rations. There was unsettled land available in the sparsely populated counties in the middle of the state, and some families became squatters there. Some moved in with relatives in other parts of the state, and some gave up on Missouri entirely, never to return to the land they once loved.

Order Number 11 reduced the border violence, but as might be expected, sparked new unrest and violence in Green, Washington, Wright, and other counties, all the way from Taney to Lafayette. They were home to five new Missouri Militia cavalry regiments whose purpose was mainly a series of patrols, scouting operations, and detachments. Riding in groups of five to a hundred men, usually under the command of non-commissioned officers, often with no specific military objective, they were free to wage war on their own terms, and took their objectives where they found them. As Lewis Adams of the 5th said in later years, "We killed men, women, and children" (oral history, Roy

Wibble, Hillsboro). In the eyes of the Southern sympathizers they were a bunch of Bushwhacking, women killing, baby killing, horse stealing, home burning, thieving marauders. Of course the same opinions were expressed for the Missouri State Militia, Home Guard, and Provisional Enrolled Missouri Militia. But Unionists saw them all as efficient and brave soldiers who helped defend Missouri's citizens from the roving hordes of Confederates—the true Bushwhackers, women killers, baby killers, horse stealers, home burners, and thieving marauders.

The Missouri State Militia (MSM) was formed in 1862, comprising ten thousand men, fourteen cavalry regiments, and one infantry. Many were slave owners. They were all Missourians. They knew local people, sympathies, roads, hiding places, hollows, and caves. They knew who was kin to whom, and who was lying to protect whom. About that same time the Union army declared that it was generally desirable punishment to burn the homes and fields of anyone who helped the Confederate regulars or the Bushwhackers. Their idea of helping the enemy might be as simple as letting them graze their horses. At that point, hell was turned loose in the state.

The original Enrolled Missouri Militia (EMM) was the product of the Union army's Order No. 19, also issued in 1862. In essence, the order required every breathing man to join the EMM, or if he was a Southern sympathizer, take an oath of loyalty and pay a commutation tax. Many men had the Southern sympathy but not $10 for the tax, so they ended up serving against their beliefs. It was a pitiful service, some uniformed, some not, some with government arms, and some with their own shotguns and muzzle-loading rifles. They guarded bridges, crossroads, and wagon trains, often on duty for a couple of months, then sent home. But the Provisional Enrolled Missouri Militia was a hand-picked group of EMM members who had real military experience or who were especially good fighters. And most of those units rode through the state making their own war, much like the MSM.

Then there was Alf Bolin, a backwoods opportunist with no con-science. He had no real political views and owned no slaves, but he associated himself with the South simply to justify his raids on de-fenseless folks, some of whom were associated with the Union. He was credited with several murders, and the truth of exactly which lives he took was lost in the smoke of war. But there's no doubt he was a violent man who didn't hesitate to fire his pistol into the heart of an unarmed man. He became such a terror in Taney County and along the Arkansas border, the Union army in that part of Missouri devised a plan to get rid of him. An incredibly courageous young Iowa soldier, Corporal Zack Thomas, volunteered to carry it out.

Bolin was known to stop for food at the home of a Mrs. Foster, whose husband was a Confederate officer imprisoned at Springfield. A young Union sergeant went unseen to the Foster home and worked out an exchange with the woman. The army would release her husband if she'd help them eliminate Bolin. She had no allegiance to Bolin and was very afraid she'd never see her husband again, so of course she agreed to help. In February 1863, young Corporal Thomas walked through the cold for two days, dressed in a Confederate uniform but unarmed, pretending to be sick and trying to get back home. Arriving at the Fos-ter home, he identified himself as the man sent to get Bolin, and Mrs. Foster took him in. She was surprised that he came with no gun, but that had to be part of his performance, for people he met on the road. She had no gun, and he had to find a weapon. Mrs. Foster went to the shed and brought in a coulter, a sharp steel blade that's attached to a plow ahead of the plowshare to break the hard soil. It was perfect, so Thomas retired to the attic to await Bolin.

After four more days, the outlaw Bolin finally arrived and made himself at home by the fire, waiting for Mrs. Foster to set the table. He knew the house well and noticed the coulter on the hearth, where it didn't belong. When he asked what it was doing there, Mrs. Foster explained that it needed to be sharpened. After all, winter was about over, and she had to get out and break the ground for spring planting soon. Bolin bought the story.

About that time Thomas moved around in the attic, intending for Bolin to hear him and wonder who it was. Mrs. Foster explained that it was a sick soldier in gray making his way home. Bolin insisted that Thomas come down where he could see him, and though he was suspicious, Thomas was young and unshaven, and looked pretty sick and tired. So Bolin accepted the story and relaxed.

Thomas would have only one chance. If he didn't get Bolin the first time, he knew the outlaw's pistols would be out and blazing away, ending his young life. So he waited for his moment. He found it an hour later, after they had all shared a hot meal of bacon, greens, and skillet bread. A satisfied Bolin bent to the fireplace to light his pipe from the coals. Thomas was ready and reached for the coulter. With a mighty whack, he split Bolin's head. It took a few stabs with Bolin's own belt knife to finish the job, but it was done.

Bolin was a bad man, but there were worse. Killing him was as much a public relations stunt as anything, aimed at convincing Missourians that the army was there to help them. When Bolin was killed, a company of soldiers was sent for the body, and they stopped at every farmhouse along the way, knocked on the door, and reported that Union soldiers had killed Bolin. They hauled him all the way from the Foster farm to Forsythe for public display and burial. On the way, they cut off his head and put it on a pole in Ozark. The brainwashing was so successful, people played music and danced in the streets up and down the county. It was an act of pure Union army vigilantism, and there was no doubt that the hills were a little safer when it was done.

Not that the civilians felt much better. Missourians, especially in that corner of the state, still lived in terror. Forsythe, the Taney County seat, changed hands several times during the war. In 1863 the Union troops, the same ones who arranged the assassination of Bolin, decided it was too much trouble to defend the town. They pulled out in 1863. As they left, they set fire to the courthouse to keep it out of Rebel hands. In those days it was mighty hard to tell who was friend and who was enemy.

Another man who struck terror among Unionists was Private John Highley. He first enlisted in the Missouri State Guard, then mustered into the regular Confederate army. But army life was too slow for Highley, and he deserted to wage his own war. Highley finally became such a scourge that the Federals sent the Missouri State Militia to hunt him down. Rather than try to chase him with a whole regiment, Major John Herderm sent a few brave and bloodthirsty members of Company E under Sergeant Henry B. Milks. They chased Highley relentlessly, all the way into Illinois, and caught up with him April 6, 1864. On April 8, the Missouri commander General Ewing received this message:

> To General Ewing:
>
> Captain Milks, 3rd Cavalry, Missouri State Militia Stationed at Farmington, Missouri, has just returned from Prairie Du Rocher, Illinois, where he was sent with some members of the Captain's E Company, after some bandits. He reports a complete success, having had a fight with a notorious gang of robbers, killed three and wounding several among them the notorious Bushwhacker and guerrilla chief, John Highley, who had long been the terror of this part of the State.
>
> John N. Herderm Third MSM

In 1864 Bushwhacker activity picked up because everybody knew that Sterling Price, who was by then a Confederate general, was getting ready for an invasion of the state. Almost two hundred Southern guerrillas under "Bloody Bill" Anderson camped on Young's Creek, about three miles outside Centralia. On September 7, the same day Price fought the Battle of Fort Donelson near Pilot Knob, Anderson rode into town with a force of about eighty, including Jesse and Frank James, to see what they could find out about Federal troop movements. The village of a dozen houses, two hotels, and two stores was generally sympathetic to the South, but that didn't stop Anderson's men from beating the few Union men and stealing food and whiskey. By the time a stagecoach rolled in, they were ready to tangle with whoever was inside. The passengers included Sheriff James Waugh and Unionist congressman William Rollins. The raiders robbed the passengers and surely would have killed Rollins if they knew who he was. But he gave them a false name, then hid under a stairway in a hotel until it was over.

Sheriff Rollins's life was no doubt saved when the guerrillas were distracted by the whistle and roar of a train pulling into the station. The engineer saw what was going on and tried to keep rolling, but the brakeman was applying the brakes, and the train came to a halt. The guerrillas swarmed the train, hauled all 150 passengers out into the street, and found themselves looking at 23 unarmed Union soldiers. They were members of the 1st Iowa Cavalry on their way home on furlough. Anderson, wearing a Confederate cavalry officer's hat and a Union officer's coat, told them to line up. When two stopped to whisper, Bloody Bill pulled a pistol and shot them dead. Then he commanded the soldiers to strip their clothes, and when they were down to their long underwear, Anderson asked if there was a sergeant among them. Thomas Morton Goodman stepped forward, expecting to be shot, but Anderson pulled him out of line to be traded for one of his own men who had recently been captured. Then Anderson explained, "You Federals," he shouted, "have just killed six of my soldiers, scalped them, and left them on the prairie" (Jay Monaghan, *Civil War on the Western Border, 1854–1865,* Boston: Little, Brown and Co., 1955). Rebel pistols were cocked, and with a nod to his right-hand man, Archie Clements, the prisoners were cut down, accompanied by the screams of the witnesses. The guerrillas set fire to the depot, then set the train on fire, opened the throttle, and sent it blazing down the track.

Major A. V. E. Johnston commanded 155 men of the 39th Missouri Mounted Infantry who were camped on the opposite side of Centralia

Major A. V. E. Johnston, who pursued Bloody Bill Anderson after Centralia, led his men into a guerrilla bloodbath.

from Anderson's camp. Seeing the smoke from the depot, Johnston and his men rode into town to see what was going on. They found the massacred Iowa troops dead beside the tracks, and the guerrillas gone back to their camp. The furious major looked at the Iowa boys with tears in his eyes and determined to chase Anderson immediately. He didn't realize that Anderson was happy to be chased. Scouts had already told Anderson the Yankees were in town, so he sent a detachment back as decoys to lure the Federals right down to where the entire Rebel force was camped. Johnston took the bait.

Heading south out of Centralia, Johnston trailed the little band of guerrillas for over two miles, and then clearly saw them, walking their horses lazily up the rise ahead. When Johnston charged them at a gallop, the decoys took off too. In moments, the Union men topped the rise and saw Anderson and about eighty men in the little valley below, sitting on their horses, nestled in a little arc of woods. Johnston followed procedure, dismounting his men to form a skirmish line. That was the way mounted infantry fought. Their horses were mere transportation, and the men were not trained in cavalry tactics. But by dismounting, they gave up any advantage over Anderson's men, some of the best horsemen and marksmen in the entire war.

The forces were barely a hundred yards apart. "Will you surrender?" Johnston innocently called across the field. The Rebels' answer was to let their reins fall, fill their hands with pistols, and charge. Johnston gave the order to fire on the approaching riders, but his men were armed with muzzle-loading Enfields, so each man got one shot, and that was it. Then Anderson's men were on them; they galloped directly through the infantry line, unloading their pistols into blue shirts. As soon as they passed, the rest of the two hundred Bushwhackers poured out of the trees, half from the left, and half from the right. A few of the Yankees were able to mount horses and run, but they were chased, some as far as the outskirts of Centralia, and killed. It's believed that three men escaped, but the major and the rest of his command died. Only three of the guerrillas were lost. When Bloody Bill Anderson was killed later in the war, he was carrying six pistols and had twelve human scalps swinging from his belt.

At the time of the Confederate surrender in spring 1865, Quantrill was a Confederate colonel of the Partisan Rangers. With a group of loyal men he tried to make his way past Union lines to Kentucky, but he was surrounded. In the fighting that followed, Quantrill was shot multiple times and died a couple of days later in a hospital. One of the enduring images for the men in the fighting was that of a loyal man standing over the wounded commander to protect him, fighting until his own pistols were spent, then with Quantrill's pistols until he was dead. Such scenes were seared into the minds of the guerrillas, etching memories that could not be outrun or outlived.

The impact of the war on the rest of the 1800s in Missouri cannot be overstated. The lines had been forever blurred between self-appointed saviors and legal authorities. Survivors of the war on both sides, male and female, were tattooed with visual images, written reports, and family histories of atrocities, and from those stories the people formed a unique view of law enforcement. While some guerrillas were happy to retire and even leave their beloved Missouri, others were equally happy to continue their role as self-appointed enforcers of the right and defenders of home and family.

Chapter Seven

Equipped by War

Southern guerrillas hanged Jesse James. Not the well-known outlaw Jesse Woodson James, but the obscure backwoodsman Jesse Ballard James. The war had barely begun, following the Battle of Wilson's Creek in 1861, when a band of Confederate irregulars came down through Douglas, Ozark, Howell, and Oregon counties on a relentless revenge raid. Of course they were experienced men who had been raiding through that part of the state for years during the long-standing trouble over slavery. Their mission was to hang or run out of southern Missouri any Northern sympathizers, and they learned that James had been milling grain for Union troops. He milled grain for the Rebels and guerrillas too, but that didn't matter to the raiders. His bigger crime was that his son Hiram had signed up in the Union army. Hiram was wounded at Wilson's Creek and was recuperating at home when the guerrillas came.

Unfortunately for James's neighbor Riley Brown, he was helping James at the mill that day. The raiders hanged both James and Brown near Bennett Springs, a mile southeast of Dora. In a rarity, they posed for a photograph with their victims. After the son Hiram recovered from his wounds, he enlisted again and continued fighting for the Union.

President Lincoln had ordered that Rolla, the terminus of the railroad, was to be held at all cost. So while Union troops worked on building fortifications there, the county was also home to Southern sympathizers, guerrillas, and veterans of both sides. Before the war, J. A. Davidson brought his wife and four children west from Virginia to settle outside Rolla. He was a simple farmer who wanted no part of the war. However, like every other man, he was required by law to join the Enrolled Missouri Militia (EMM). He served in the 82nd Regiment for about six months, September 1863 to April 1864, digging trenches and guarding the railroad at Rolla against attacks that never came. But whether he carried a rifle or a shovel, his duties mattered little to the Bushwhackers when they came around making inquiries about who was in the militia. Late one summer night, marauders reined their horses into the yard of the Davidson cabin and called for the man of the house. He knew what the call meant, but all he'd done was what the law made him and all his neighbors do, join the EMM. So Davidson walked out into the yard, sure he could explain to the men there that he didn't want any trouble. But he never got a chance. The men pulled their pistols and dropped him in a hail of gunfire.

Martial law meant that every county had a provost marshal, a one-man judge and jury who handled every military case, including those in which civilians were involved. In Iron County, a Bushwhacker named Sam Trollinger was arrested in the fall of 1861 and brought before the provost marshal. He signed the loyalty oath and was released, then was arrested again in November 1862 after local farmers complained that he had stolen their horses. They were his neighbors, so of course they knew him when he rode into each of their yards leading a gang of a dozen armed men. He greeted them when he entered their homes and tipped his hat when he left. But while he was in the houses visiting, his men were rounding up the farmers' best horses to be taken to the Confederate regulars. When he was arrested, rather than admitting that he was the leader of a guerrilla band, he mournfully pled that he was coerced into the raids. He said some men came to his house and told him they'd take his horses if he didn't go with them to steal horses from his neighbors. In fact, that's the technique Trollinger used to get men to ride with him. After all, he told the provost marshal, he took the loyalty oath last year, so they shouldn't punish him for what those bad men forced him to do!

Trollinger was so full of hot air, he could make up a story to weasel his way into or out of any situation. The provost marshal's log records that Trollinger testified:

> I had a gun when I was first arrested which was taken from me by the authorities. I have not had a gun of my own since. I borrowed a gun of Jim Barton's last spring and again in the fall to kill hogs and gobblers. I borrowed it off and on whenever I wanted it.

> Nearly all my neighbors are secesh. I am called a strong Southern rights man I am a Constitutional Union man. I don't know that I am a secession sympathizer.

> I have not done anything for or against the USA government. Before being arrested the first time Ben Talbot and his gang came along. He asked me to join his band. I refused to do it. He then said he would take my horse if I did not go along with him. John Stricklin (my son-in-law) and myself then went along with them. We staid four days and returned home. There was about 20 or 25 of us The band stole five horses while I was with them. He Talbot afterwards returned one of them to Jarvis Some of my union neighbors blamed me for being instrumental in having their horses stolen.

But there was a lot more than that to Trollinger. He and his men repeatedly raided a British immigrant named Elihu Shepherd, who had a booming pottery-making business. Josiah Morgan, foreman of the operation, was particularly belligerent toward Trollinger, so one night Trollinger and his men took Morgan from his home and murdered him. That story came to light when one of the men who was there with Trollinger, William H. Webb, went to the army for protection. He gave a full statement, telling how Trollinger and some others came to his home and invited him to go with them to buy whiskey. But instead, they picked up the factory foreman Morgan, so Webb said he was leaving and having nothing to do with that business. Trollinger pulled his revolver and asked Webb, "Are you sure that's what you want to do, Billy Webb?" Webb was forced to ride along and watch them murder Morgan. There was nothing connecting Shepherd or Morgan directly to the Union, but several of the plant's workers served in the army or were otherwise connected. So Shepherd's pottery business was all but shut down by the terrorism, and finally the guerrillas burned his factories.

On a dark winter night toward the end of the war, Private Morris M. Adams was riding in a patrol by Company M, 3rd Missouri State Militia Cavalry, tracking Trollinger and his right-hand man, James Edward Barton. Adams was an expert, relentless tracker, who'd earned a reputation for getting rid of key guerrillas. When Trollinger and Barton stopped to drink from a spring on Neal's Creek near the Black River, Adams and the others rode up on them, shot them dead, and cut off their heads. Others who rode with Adams were afraid of retaliation and would never talk about what they did during the war, but Adams had no such fear and freely told his story.

During the war, Nevada, the seat of Vernon County, was almost a ghost town. About half of the population of 450 had moved out, the government was suspended, and the courthouse was locked up. A Cedar County militia detachment stopped to rest at the hotel but never made it to their rooms. Bill Marchbanks and his band of Southern guerrillas had been following them, and they rode into the dismounted troops, firing wildly, scattering them and killing two. When the report reached St. Clair County, a regiment of their militia rode out to take re-

106

Captain Bill Marchbanks commanded the
Vernon County Bushwhackers who attacked
Federal militia at Nevada, in a photo taken
many years after the war.

venge on the guerrillas, but it took them two days to get organized and
get to Nevada. Of course by that time the guerrillas were long gone.
The militiamen didn't ride all that way for nothing, so they turned their
wrath on the town, setting fire to every home and business. When they
returned home, they found that their own homes had been burned by
yet another band of Southern guerrillas.

Such raids by guerrillas of both sides found targets of opportunity everywhere they went. Sometimes it was a partisan's store or barn,
sometimes an individual. In fact, many a family trying to avoid the war
and tend their farm simply found it impossible. Sometimes the farmers
helped the passing troops, out of decency and good manners. Some-

times they were threatened with their lives if they didn't help. But in every case, a band of armed men storming into a farmyard got whatever they wanted. Then an opposing force would often hear about it and punish the family for helping the enemy.

Family stories were changed forever because Missouri had wallowed in an era of such unprecedented savagery and paranoia. Peace-loving civilians were in just as much danger as returning veterans and wives whose husbands were away at war. As families laid down to sleep at night, they never knew when they might be awakened by the sound of dozens of horses, pistol shots, shouted commands, or maybe even the crackle of a fire consuming their home. The terror was neverending, year after year.

Families were divided, as were Masonic lodges and town councils. It was a lucky pastor who could hold a few people in the seats, the secessionists on one side of the aisle and loyalists on the other. Communities that once gathered for socials, rolling up the rugs, playing music, and dancing never saw one another. Men gossiped on street corners and women in stores. Nobody knew who was pretending to favor one side while providing information to the other. Nobody knew whose loyalty had shifted. Nobody knew whom to trust. The vengeful, brutal, and criminal nature of the violence that occurred before, during, and after the war in Missouri cannot be overstated.

After the war, most Union Bushwhackers were free to go home in peace, as were the militiamen who'd committed murders, burned homes, and broken other laws. At the same time, it was hard for Confederate veterans to keep their heads up. They wouldn't be pardoned until 1872. If they had any Confederate money, it was worthless. If they had a home they could return to, gardens and fields were barren, and the livestock was gone. Any former Rebel had to get in line behind the Union veterans when it came to jobs. They were barred from claiming land under the 1862 Homestead Act. Southern veterans had to take an oath of allegiance to the Union, and yet weren't allowed to hold office.

They couldn't vote, but the newly freed slaves could. With all that going against them, plus the tide of public opinion, the humiliation of defeat, the loss of relatives and other comrades in arms, along with all the Yankees moving into Missouri, a lot of Confederate veterans just picked up and moved out. Boone County had 2,600 voters in 1860. But in 1866 that was down to 900, and by 1868, just 350.

By that time, Missouri was home to three generations of citizens schooled in violence, galvanized in the belief that governments couldn't be trusted and open to the idea that it was their right and obligation to take the law into their own hands. People who'd spent years watching their belongings being stolen, their relatives butchered, and their homes burned, couldn't help but be hardened.

The whole southwestern part of the state, from the western border to the Ozarks, was a wild and inviting place for scoundrels of all stripes. There were no stores in the newly reopened border counties, and it was almost impossible to find a doctor, preacher, or schoolteacher. Then slowly, tough, decent people became brave enough to move back in. In fact, after the war there were three parallel immigrations to Missouri. There was the smattering of Southerners, especially from Virginia, Tennessee, and the Carolinas. They joined longtime Missourians returning to the places from which they'd been uprooted. There was also a wave of Yankees and easterners. To that group, Missouri was the frontier, a wide-open Eden, waiting to be civilized. Some of them brought an antagonistic "we won" attitude. Most brought a decidedly eastern, European, cosmopolitan, and even puritanical approach to what should be done with the state. To them, it was like clay, and someone had to mold it.

One upright citizen who dared to re-enter the vacant lands was a hero of the Union cause, Brigadier General Joseph Bailey, renowned not for his combat leadership, but for building a dam that turned a river battle in the Union's favor. He settled in sparsely populated Vernon County. Since veterans, especially former officers, were generally

*Brigadier General Joseph Bailey during the
Civil War.*

respected by partisans of both sides after the conflict, Bailey found himself elected sheriff. On the other hand, the county seat, Nevada, was the scene of those raids and counter-raids in which the city was repeatedly burned by one side, then the other, so plenty of ill feelings lingered.

Like many veterans, Bailey believed his own legend. Furthermore, he was one of that generation of Missourians who longed for a return to peace. He viewed himself as a civilized public servant, not a rough-riding crusader, so he went about his job armed only with his substantial ego, and not a firearm. However, such men as Bailey did well to remember that they were Yankees holding positions of authority within the stronghold of lingering Southern loyalties.

So in the spring of 1866, working in his normal manner, he served a pig-stealing warrant on the Pixley brothers, Lewis and Perry, by simply riding his gray horse out to their house, knocking on the front door, and telling them they needed to come to jail. They complained that they didn't steal any pigs, and that Old Man Williams, the man who accused them, was no good. Bailey had to say he didn't know whether they did it or not. He patiently explained that they'd have a chance to clear their name. After that, the boys came along just fine, but as they walked out they grabbed their gun belts hanging by the door. They had Remington revolvers in holsters from which the flap had been cut away, making for a faster draw. Those were souvenirs of the boys' days as Southern guerrillas. "Oh, you'll need to leave those thumbers here," Bailey said, pointing to the single-action guns.

The Pixley boys insisted on going armed, saying they were afraid of Old Man Williams. They'd heard he'd been telling people he'd go gunning for them. "We gotta be able to defend ourselves out there on the road, Sheriff," Lewis said. "What about when we bond out and we're coming home without you protecting us? We'll need them then, for sure." Perry, the quiet one, nodded.

Bailey agreed they could turn the pistols over when they got to the jail, and that's how they left. It was quite friendly, and Bailey even helped them drive up their horses from the pasture.

After they'd ridden a ways and were approaching a creek, the road began to narrow. The Pixleys slowed their horses just a little, allowing the sheriff to ease on ahead. When he was just beyond arm's length away, Lewis was ready, pulled his revolver, and the last sound Bailey heard was the cli-click of the hammer. The pistol roared and a single .44 bullet pierced the sheriff's cap and entered his skull. Bailey immediately went limp and fell face down from his horse at the edge of the water.

There was no discussion. Both Pixleys knew what the killing meant, and they had to work fast. They pulled him through the creek, then along the bank about 150 feet, over a little hill, and into a ravine. There was some standing water, about eight inches deep, back in the gully, and they concealed him there, leaving him face down in the pool. On the way back to their horses, they picked up Bailey's cap and stuffed it into the hollow of a tree.

They took Bailey's horse, went to the home of some friends, Eslinger and Williams, and begged them to help figure out a plan to get away, offering Bailey's gray horse as payment. Putting their heads together, they thought of another friend, Tom Ingraham, who had a canoe. They were sure he'd help. Lewis and Perry would go ahead and cross the Marmaton River in Ingraham's canoe, then hide out in the woods and wait for Ingraham to bring their family across a couple of days later.

But before their plan could be carried out, a posse closed in, led by district attorney John T. Birdseye. The Pixley boys were possibly the West's worst getaway artists. The posse found the obvious marks where the boys dragged Bailey's body. Following the trail, they saw the cap, then the body, and just kept following the Pixleys' tracks. When they got to the house Eslinger and Williams shared, there was Sheriff Bailey's gray horse grazing nearby. Birdseye told Eslinger and Williams they were the prime suspects in the sheriff's murder, considering the tracks and the horse. It didn't take much persuading to get the pair to put the blame on the Pixleys and lead the posse to Ingraham's house. By that time, the brothers were already across the river, and the Pixley family was waiting for their ride to meet Lewis and Perry. Eslinger and Williams were released, and Ingraham was arrested, cursing and threatening his captors all the way to the Nevada jail.

In later years it would be said that Ingraham was a Quantrill man. However, he was never mustered into Southern service and is not listed in any of the rolls of Quantrill's raiders. He may have ridden with them for a while, but his only significant link to Quantrill is that he married the widow of Pony Hill, one of the most notorious of all the Bushwhackers. Besides that, Ingraham was still steamed up because those Union soldiers burned Nevada when they left. Ingraham was not a vigilante but merely a misguided loudmouth who hated the Union.

That night the posse evolved into a vigilance committee. It just seemed to organize itself. Unlike most mobs, it didn't need a leader. It was something spontaneous that everyone agreed to, almost like a natural course of events. Their sheriff had been killed, and they weren't about to stand for that kind of violence from secessionist scum. The Pixleys were out of reach, but Ingraham was close at hand.

The mob armed themselves and moved in on the jail. There they found Ingraham guarded by deputies who were in no mood to argue with quick and easy justice. There was no shouting and no burning torches or threats. The deputies just opened the jail, turned Ingraham over, and he was hanged by the neck until dead. Deputy Sheriff John Shaw was even happy to let the mob string him up in his barn. But then he became worried that his wife wouldn't like it if she saw him there when she went out to feed the chickens, so they took down the dead Ingraham, carried him a quarter mile down the road, and hanged him again in a sturdy blackjack oak.

After a while, when the family didn't show up, the Pixley boys had to face the fact that they weren't coming, and the pair couldn't wait any longer. They took off for the tall timber. Though rewards totaling $3,000 were posted, no one ever collected, because the Pixleys were never heard from again. They were cowardly murderers who shot a lawman from the back, then ran out on their family.

It must also be said that like many men, the Pixleys gave up on doing anything right. They were penniless men who couldn't struggle on the legal side of the ledger any longer. Like many of their neighbors and countless people across the state, the Pixleys were isolated on their little farm with no money, desperate to keep their family fed. In their case, the beginning of the end was one stolen hog.

Even those who had no part in the war felt its lingering effects in the years to follow. In Missouri City in October 1866, Joseph and Abraham Titus, aged twenty-two and twenty, stopped for a drink at a local tavern. The boys' grandfather had been a slave owner, and some of their relatives were suspected of riding with Quantrill and other guerrillas. Confederate loyalty was part of their heritage, and everybody knew it. As they sipped their beer, Liberty town marshal G. S. Elgin spoke loudly, so everyone in the place could hear him, about the smell of Titus secessionist trash. He detested former Rebels and took delight in insulting them, taunting them about losing the war. The Titus boys tried to ignore the drunken Elgin, but he continued to press the matter. Knowing he could easily make an excuse to arrest them, they left their beers and quietly walked out into the autumn night, mounted their horses, and turned them toward home. But they never got out of pistol range. Elgin stepped to the doorway of the tavern and fired, hitting both of them in the back, killing them instantly. The horses took off up the road carrying empty saddles, cruel messages to the family of what happened to the two bright young men.

Elgin knew his victims had older brothers and plenty of friends in Clay County, so he decided it was a real good time to visit his father-in-law, William Tatman, near Platte City. As soon as Joseph and Abraham were in the ground, the other Titus sons, John, Thomas, and Noah, along with their brother-in-law John Blevins, became vigilantes. They went before a friendly justice of the peace, presented their case, were sworn in as deputy county sheriffs, and were given a warrant for Elgin's arrest. They were so careful to keep it legal, when they got to Platte City, they even had a justice there endorse the warrant.

The next morning Elgin's father-in-law found the Titus brothers and Blevins hiding in his barn. He ran back to the house and warned Elgin, who bolted out a back door and through an orchard, firing over his shoulder at the deputies on his tail. They returned the fire and Elgin fell, wounded in several places. The men then approached the fallen marshal and each put a bullet into his heart.

Of course Elgin had his supporters too, and murder warrants were issued for the Titus boys. The justification of the warrant was, of course, that when Elgin was wounded he was no longer a threat, though they executed him. All four men were arrested and lodged in the Liberty jail. Then after about four months they broke out of jail, a stout one from which they could not have escaped without help. In the summer of 1870 they were captured again but never stood trial because they had a legal warrant, and Elgin was clearly resisting arrest when they shot him. It all depended on how the story was told. Elgin was dead proof that it just didn't pay to go against the grain in a hotbed of former Southern guerrilla families.

Some former guerrillas continued raiding as if the war had never ended. Douglas County was home to "Captain" Lock Alsup, who led a band of thirty men, raiding farms, taking what they needed, and controlling the county sheriff and tax collector. They were former Southern Bushwhackers, and anybody who had served the Union was under constant threat from Alsup's gang. Legend has it that farmer and Union veteran John Hatfield came to Douglas County on a stolen horse, one jump ahead of an Arkansas posse. However he got there, the Alsups befriended him, but that didn't last long, because he took up with the widow Davis, who had recently jilted Shelton Alsup. When Hatfield married the woman and started enjoying life on her farm, there were several confrontations between the two families, including shots fired, with Shelton being wounded. Finally, the Alsups determined they would have the Davis farm. When the widow turned down their offer to buy it, the Alsups came ready to take it like they took everything else they wanted, at the point of a gun.

Hatfield had already written to the governor at least four times, begging for help, saying the Alsups had threatened him, but there was no response. One morning a gang of over fifty Alsup vigilantes surrounded the farmhouse with a warrant signed by Judge Lock Alsup for Hatfield on stealing the horse in Arkansas. Hatfield knew he'd never live to see a trial at the hands of the Alsups, so he refused to come out, and a gunfight erupted that lasted until noon. Seeing no good outcome, Hatfield hollered out and offered to surrender to Brown Wyatt, a constable that everybody knew was an honest man. The Alsups agreed, and that ended the siege.

The honest constable showed up at the house later with a deputy sheriff, and the surrender went peacefully. But before they rode out, Wyatt tied Hatfield's hands to his saddle horn and tied his feet together under the horse's belly. After riding just two miles, a gang of Alsups rode out of the bushes, blocking the road, and ordered the lawmen to step aside. They opened fire on Hatfield, and he was hit about three dozen times, including twenty-eight wounds that would have been fatal. The Alsups, the deputy, and the constable watched the horse wander away with its bouncing, lifeless cargo.

Later, Shelton called on the widow Davis, who was now the widow Hatfield, gave her a wagon and team, and forced her to sign a deed and leave the farm so the Alsups could have it. With tactics like that, the Alsup reign of terror continued until near the end of the century.

Some Confederate veterans, including Jesse and Frank James, had a price on their head. When the James boys tried to surrender, they had to run from a hail of gunfire. That's why they immediately began their career of robbery and murder, targeting institutions that had a Yankee flavor to them. Banks. Then railroads. They frequently rode with fellow former guerrillas of the Younger family, who joined them in the nation's first train robbery. They hit the St. Louis, Iron Mountain and Southern Railway at Gads Hill, Missouri. Of course since nobody had ever robbed a train before, it caught the sheriff completely off guard. His posse didn't get organized until the next day, and it was far too late to catch the fleet gang. But a small vigilante force came a lot closer.

In making their escape through Texas County the James-Younger gang's horses began to tire, and they needed fresh mounts to keep moving. But taking time to stop and trade horses was just too risky. The less attention they attracted, the better. So when they found a farm with a good stock of horses grazing unattended, they helped themselves to a swap, plus one extra horse in case one of the new ones didn't prove to be durable. They put a note in the hollow of a tree near the pasture gate, along with enough money to make a sweet deal, thinking that would keep the farmer quiet.

But the bribe didn't work. In less than twenty-four hours the owner of the horses noticed the unapproved exchange and was outraged. It didn't matter whether the bandits left equally good mounts and a little cash. It was a case of horse stealing. The long, slow process of locating a lawman, filing charges, and hoping he and his deputies would give chase was just not an option, so the farmer gathered a couple of neighbors. They armed themselves, saddled up, and rode after the horse thieves. But fortunately for the farmers, after two exhausting days, they gave up and returned home without catching sight of their quarry. If they'd known they were chasing the James and Younger brothers, no doubt they'd have never chosen to style themselves as vigilantes at all.

That night the Jameses and Youngers were confident of their escape and stopped at the Moses Bean Inn at Drynob. It was on the Osage Fork of the Gasconade River, near Bean Ford, which was of course named for old Moses. There the boys could not only get a good night's rest, but also get their horses' feet tended at the blacksmith shop. Moses had given refuge to plenty of Confederate irregulars during the war, so he knew better than to ask too many questions. Whatever those boys were up to, they were good Missouri stock, he figured. And that's the way the Jameses and Youngers made their way home, trading on Southern courtesy.

Higher-bred folks who took to white-collar crimes couldn't count on such hospitality. There were plenty of carpetbaggers and other scallywags who worked themselves into positions of money and influence within a short time after the war. A group of three such men took advantage of a set of worthless railroad bonds that dated back to 1857, before the war. The bonds had never been funded and were totally worthless. Then, in a secret meeting, the county attorney, J. R. Cline, and county judge J. C. Stevenson reissued the bonds to themselves and a friend, T. E. Dutro, knowing the only way to pay them off would be a tax on the citizenry of the county.

It was a clever—but clearly illegal—trick, and the law clamped down hard. They were arrested and charged with bond fraud. Of course, they bailed themselves out, confident that they were safe walking the streets of civilized society, but as *The New York Times* reported, "this confidence was fatal."

Their next mistake was trying to get away on the same train together on April 24, 1872. Destitute farmers and laborers who were trying to rebuild their lives in the postwar economy were in no mood to pay railroad taxes. And though it was seven years past the end of the war, they were still ready to return to their guerrilla tactics. They piled debris on the track, forcing the train to pull onto a spur and stop. Four men boarded the engine with pistols leveled at the engineer and fireman.

Forty more men surrounded the train and called out for the suit-and-tie-wearing crooks, Cline, Stevenson, and Dutro. Cline, the attorney, confident that he could talk his way out of anything, stepped out and held up his hands. In part, he became the victim of innovations in the pistol at the tail end of the war. By the early 1870s most men had bought new revolvers or converted their old ones to the new self-contained cartridges, replacing the old cap-and-ball designs. Bullets made reloading faster and the pistols more accurate, and of course the bullets were cheap and expendable. Before Cline could open his mouth, he was gunned down, as many in the crowd emptied their revolvers into his lifeless body. Then they stood around him reloading and commenting on the miracle of rapid-fire revolvers.

Stevenson barricaded himself into the baggage car, but the mob broke in, firing as they came. His body was thrown off beside Cline's. Then the vigilantes had to search the passenger car to find Dutro cowering under the seats. He was shot and wounded on the spot, but in deference to the other frightened passengers, he was dragged out, still alive, to die beside his co-conspirators. Rather than put him out of his misery, vigilante guards stood over him, listening to his screams for aid, and forbidding anyone to come near until midnight, when he finally died, still moaning.

The legal wrangling over the bonds continued for years, and three judges went to prison because they refused to enforce a higher court's order to start making the citizens pay them off. It's said that the last appeal from a bond owner wasn't dropped until the 1940s. But thanks to the line in the dirt drawn by a few dozen vigilantes, the people of Cass County never paid a penny of railroad taxes.

That was the brand of men who came out of the war, unafraid of trouble and ready to fight it. They were men who had seen the worst kind of depredations, who had suffered horrible deprivations, and who had looked squarely into the barrel of many a villain's gun. Veterans of both sides, the Grand Army of the Republic and United Confederate Veterans, met in reunions for years to come. They marched in parades, shared their pride in Missouri, and were reminded that they shaped our nation's history, together.

Chapter Eight

The Archetype: James Butler Hickok

The Civil War was on-the-job training. In uniform along with farm boys and factory laborers were career military officers steeped in outdated strategies. Furthermore, nobody had given much thought to the command and supply of an army scattered across a nation with few railroads, few towns, and divided loyalties.

Thousands of men joined for various reasons, and few had any idea what they were getting themselves into. Furthermore, the war started in the late winter of 1861–1862. Winter, when everything is harder. The men were cold and moved more slowly getting out of their tents. July mud would have dried to crumbles in a few hours, but January mud would grab and hold wagon wheels for days on end. Repairs on rail lines and telegraph wires were delayed. Galloping riders hid their faces from the wind and struggled to keep up a decent pace. In the next four years a few of the greatest, bloodiest battles of the war, like the Battle of Nashville, were fought between storms of snow and freezing rain. But starting about Christmas, the prevailing mentality was to hunker down and wait for warmer weather.

Even in January, wagon drivers might be needed on short notice, so the army had to keep them on the payroll. But since they did little more than wait out the winter weather, such civilian employees, including wagon master James Butler Hickok, were reduced to a subsistence pay of two dollars a day. They were only able to get by because they were on or near army posts, where the sutler sold everything at friendly soldier's prices. Still, a meal, a drink, and a little tobacco was about as far as the money went.

Hickok was in charge of one hundred teams of oxen, six oxen, or three yoke, to a team. Each wagon carried about three thousand pounds of cargo, or slightly less if the roads were especially bad or the terrain particularly hilly. A dozen wagons was considered the general train for a regiment, so Hickok's responsibility was considerable, overseeing enough livestock and wagons to mobilize eight regiments, with plenty of oxen for replacements.

Horses and mules were faster than oxen, of course. But every riding horse the army could get its hands on went for cavalry. Wagons were pulled by draft horses. As strong and dependable as they were, the heavier the wagons and worse the terrain, the more the job called for oxen. And of course the farther west one traveled, the poorer and fewer the roads. Out where Hickok was serving, there were plenty of places where the wagons were cutting their own way, following game trails and Indian trails, so all things considered, the oxen assured a complete trip, and usually the fastest trip.

General Samuel L. Curtis was an Iowa congressman who resigned his seat to serve the Union cause. After distinguishing himself early in the conflict and rising to brigadier general, he was sent to Missouri, where he was given command of the Union's Army of the Southwest. He established his headquarters, Camp Curtis, at Otterville, fortified with a mile of entrenchments where the railroad bridge crossed the Lamine River. That was the terminus of the northern railroad lines in 1861. Even though Missouri was under martial law, bands of Rebels large and small, official and guerrilla, would roam the state for the duration of the war. But from his location near the Missouri River, Curtis could exercise some control over the western part of the state.

At Camp Curtis, James Butler Hickok, known as Bill, oversaw his wagon and teams. Hickok had sunk pretty low, nursing a bunch of cattle. After all, he'd signed up to be a civilian scout, not a wagoner. And as an abolitionist, he believed in what he was doing. While he was a boy, his parents' Illinois farm had been a stop for runaway slaves on the Underground Railroad. He was an excellent shot and liked roaming the woods to bring home game for the family. He left home at eighteen to be a Kansas farmer, was elected constable for a small town at nineteen, drove a stagecoach, worked as a wagon driver for a freight company, and got into a shootout in which he killed his first man. As the war

General Samuel L. Curtis, commander of the Union's Army of the Southwest.

approached, he even did some spying for Jim Lane's fierce abolitionist guerrillas, the Red Legs. Exactly what role he filled is unclear. But the unofficial association seems to have set a pattern he continued through the war. He never enlisted in the regular army.

All things considered, it wasn't a bad way to spend the winter, sharing a civilian barracks with the other wagoners, getting wagons in prime condition, repairing and saddle-soaping harnesses, and seeing to the health of the milling oxen. He had certainly been to more exciting places, but he figured a man can't eat a steady diet of adventure.

Then just when he was getting used to army routine, on February 10, 1862, a wool-coated sergeant rousted him before reveille. Hickok bundled up and followed him to a meeting with the quartermaster that would do more than interrupt his sleep. It would thrust him into truly dangerous situations. It would set him on a course to find out who he really was. The quartermaster looked up from his paperwork and dryly told Hickok he was promoted to chief wagon master, given a raise to the startling salary of $100 a month, and put in charge of a train of twelve wagons that was to leave the fort as soon as possible.

Hickok was chosen for promotion from all the wagon masters because the trip he was about to take was a dangerous one, and he'd already seen combat. His officers also knew he was a scout before becoming a wagoner. Hickok was a true Union man who was loyal to the army, while many of the teamsters were simply men who needed a job. And finally, teamsters and wagon masters were hired, promoted, and fired by the quartermaster. Bill had the sense and charisma to make a friend of his employer. The quartermaster knew him to be a man of proper wit and sobriety, far above the cut of the other men in the barracks. Bill Hickok had a cool head when one was needed.

Hickok packed his gear and tucked two Colt revolvers into his belt, as was his custom. He selected his teamsters for the mission from the ranks of the sober, and thanks to their cold-weather diligence, the wagons and oxen were ready. The men all understood the risk of attacks by

James Butler Hickok in his thirties.

bands of Rebel guerrillas who prowled up and down the Missouri River like coyotes looking for prey. Just three months before, a huge train of fifty wagons had been captured by Rebels, with the wagon masters taken prisoner. They were all freed by a counter-raid, but still, in those days, the marauders could come from anywhere.

Even without the human threat, the cargo was risky enough, including cans of lamp oil riding in the same wagons with tins, casks, and half barrels of gunpowder. As the wagons bounced and twisted over the rocky, rutted prairie, the containers were twisted and banged until they leaked, leaving wagon beds rife with oil and the trail sprinkled with powder. Fire and explosion were constant threats. Any spark could be the igniter, and steel wheel rims made plenty of sparks against flint and other rocks. And when negotiating down hills, the drivers made every effort not to use their brakes, because those could heat up in a hurry. Hills were the devil, because neither a runaway wagon nor exploded wagon was an attractive prospect.

General Curtis commanded an army that was spread from Fort Leavenworth in Kansas to Springfield, where the post was badly in need of food, shoes, blankets, and ammunition. When winter shut things down, huge stocks of supplies were on the way west to Fort Leavenworth, but had to be left at Camp Curtis. Then the railroad tracks were completed to Sedalia, and the Camp Curtis supplies were moved there. So the plan was for Hickok's train to set out empty and pick up half their cargo in Fort Leavenworth, some sixty miles west. Then they'd return for the rest of the load at Sedalia before proceeding south to their ultimate destination, Springfield.

The trip to Fort Leavenworth was blistering cold and lashed by the unrelenting prairie wind, but otherwise uneventful. Each man was an island on his wagon. All things considered, they were glad to be out of camp. With the wagons empty, Hickok pressed them hard, even after dark, because the roads were getting better as they got closer they got to Westport, the town that would later became Kansas City. And just beyond Westport was the fort. They made the run safely and pulled into the fort in the early hours of morning. Drivers and animals rested while soldiers loaded the wagons, spreading out the goods to make a half-load in each. It was mainly powder, shot, and fuses, which had been under heavy guard in the fort. In Sedalia the train would pick up food, medicine, and other such supplies.

Leaving the following dawn with a soldier escort, the train headed south on the Military Post Road, crossing the Kansas River at Grinter's ferry and turning east along the Santa Fe Trail. They made it through Westport and then were out into open country, rolling and grassy, stretching invitingly before them, marked with tree-lined hollows and dry creek beds. Then, the train entered one of those hollows and it suddenly filled with Confederate guerrillas, dressed in a motley mix of overalls, homemade coats, and other civilian attire, all sporting hunting rifles and shotguns.

The Bushwhackers had chosen the perfect place for the ambush. It was a smart plan, but Hickok should have been smarter by sending his scout out sooner. He must have been surprised that the Rebels would pull such a stunt that close to town. The guerrillas not only took the wagons and goods, but also made prisoners of the whole bunch of men. Turning the train northeast, the Rebels headed toward a rendezvous on the Missouri River, where they would deliver the prize to Confederate regulars.

Somehow, in the mass of horses, wagons, and men, Hickok was able to escape. He knew he couldn't go back and retake the train by himself, so he had to collect his emotions and use his brain. There were army camps to the west, east, and south, but they were all miles away. By the time he got help, the wagons, the supplies, and the poor prisoners would all be in the hands of the Confederate regulars. But it was only a mile or so to Independence, and he could run that far. Not that the local sheriff would get involved in a military matter like this. No, Hickok was going to have to handle this himself, and maybe in town he could get a handful of men to back him up.

The details of Hickok's actions are lost in the western Missouri winds, but with a handful of men from Independence, he went back and found the wagon train on the banks of the river, waiting to rendezvous with the Confederate regulars. Before the night was over, Hickok had the wagons, oxen, and men all safely back in hand. He had no time to mess with guerrilla prisoners, so he sent them on their way with a warning not to mess with any Union trains again. There must have been plenty of slaps on the back for Hickok.

Passing through Independence to get back on the road to Sedalia, Hickok halted the train. He told the men to eat, drink, and get some rest. They'd be leaving soon after dawn. If ever he had been full of himself, it must have been that night. He had not only fulfilled his mission

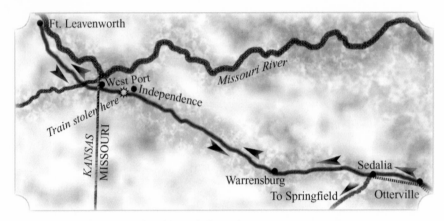

Map showing the route taken by Hickok's stolen wagon train in 1861.

for the army, but he had done it with a personal act of leadership and bravado, outside of army command. Furthermore, he had snatched victory from the jaws of an embarrassing failure.

Before retiring for the night, Hickok stepped into an almost-empty saloon, where he found a friendly bartender worrying about an unhappy mob of drunks outside. It seems the barkeep had thrown a loudmouth out of the place and roughed him up in the process. The drunk's friends gathered outside and were getting ready to go back in and take revenge on the frightened bartender.

People of the town knew there was trouble brewing, and they gathered across the street to watch the little crowd of a half dozen ruffians gathering. Stepping outside, Hickok swiped at his mustache, leaned against a porch post, and surveyed the street. The quiet corners. The blackened alleys. The pools of light. The muttering gang that milled a hundred feet away in front of the feed store.

When the angry men started toward the saloon, Hickok took one step, placing himself in their line of march and in front of the big lantern beside the door, making himself an ominous, featureless silhouette. After all, he was only a kid of twenty-four, and hiding his youth would be to his advantage. The Colt handles on his hips were plainly visible. When the men were no more than ten feet away, with a lightning move Hickok skinned the big revolvers with backhanded draws and let go with a shot from each: blam! blam! into the starry sky.

Nothing stirred, save the gray smoke that swirled gently about Hickok. He took one step toward a beanpole who seemed to be the leader. Whatever was said between them was all it took to send the gang on their way and keep the bartender safe. Twice that night, first against the guerrillas, and then against the mob, by his cool-headed, hot-handed action, Hickok was the law where there was no law. He was a man alone, who saw the right, and took it upon himself to do right, regardless of his personal peril.

The next morning Hickok rode up and down the line, inspected his train, and decided they were ready to pull out. At the time, there was no way they could know, but the supplies they were delivering would be used at the Battle of Pea Ridge, Arkansas, which would secure Union control of Missouri for the rest of the war. Hickok led the wagons down Main Street, and there on the edge of the square another group of townspeople was gathered. Hickok paused the train, wondering if it was another secessionist bunch and he was going to have to go into action again.

Then smiles and good wishes came from them, and Hickok nodded. A woman called from a room above the Golden Swan: "I saw it all. You were Wild, Bill."

"That's him," one of the men agreed. "Wild Bill."

Bill Hickok was smooth as a cat, moving from one adventure to another, leaving few tracks. In March 1862, in Arkansas, he spied on the Confederates for Curtis, then stayed on to serve as a civilian sharpshooter at the Battle of Pea Ridge. In 1863 he was spying on Southern sympathizers around the Union stronghold of Rolla and passing his information to his brother Lorenzo, who was by that time a Union teamster, as Bill had been. For a while he was a detective for the provost marshal, specializing in chasing down deserters. At some point during the war he began using the alias William Haycock so he could move freely among Union lines, Confederate lines, and the civilian world. And on the approach to the Battle of Westport, Bill spied in the camp of General Price, then informed his old Union commander, General Curtis, on the strength and movements of the Rebel forces.

Though he was suited to spying and detective work, he was at his best when he stood toe to toe with evil. Hickok killed Dave Tutt in Springfield, Missouri, in the first fast-draw pistol duel in Western history. That event in 1865 solidified the identity of Wild Bill Hickok in the public mind. Hickok was a U.S. marshal in Kansas in the late 1860s, worked as a sheriff's deputy in Hays, and was elected sheriff of Ellis County. He killed several troublemakers in shootouts during those years. He became marshal of Abilene, and several more bad men went to cheap graves because of Hickok's twin Colt revolvers.

At last his eyesight failed, and he turned to gambling and away from gunplay. He told friends his shooting days were over, but still he was able to disarm men who threatened him, simply by his fearless resolve. Nobody could face him down, and it took a coward named Jack McCall to end his life with a shot from behind while Hickok was playing poker in a saloon.

He was the archetypal steel-nerved lawman. With a badge or without, he stood for peace, liberty, and civility, and he simply did what needed to be done for the values he held dear.

CHAPTER NINE

THE VIGILANTE AS VICTIM: SAM HILDEBRAND

It was a typically hot June day in 1862, the golden rye in the field shimmering against the deep green shadows of the encircling woods. Shirtless black men in overalls quietly mowed the rye, their scythes rocking in a slow dance, as other men came behind them, busily stacking the dry, grain-bearing cuttings into shocks.

Back in the brush on the south side of the field, Sam Hildebrand kept both eyes open as he aimed. Sighting almost a hundred yards down the long barrel of his Springfield rifle, which he had named "Kill-Devil," he had a clear view of Firman McIlvaine. He was out there in a blousy white shirt, under a broad straw hat, sweating, an abolitionist doing the same work as his hired hands. But all Hildebrand could think about was how McIlvaine had murdered his brother. Hildebrand had waited three days, sleeping under an overhanging rock, crawling through brush and up and down hills, circling that field, just for this shot.

The farmer finished whetting his scythe and lowered it to the ground, then leaned on the handle, scanning the field, satisfied with the good work being done. They'd be finished with this field well before dark. He started to swing the scythe again, just when Hildebrand breathed in, then slowly exhaled, gently squeezing the trigger. With a sudden jolt, the rifle cut loose. One shot. Dead center. And McIlvaine collapsed into the Missouri dust, a .58 caliber hole through his chest.

What kind of man would lie in wait for such an ambush? A man who was loyal to the Union when the Civil War began. One who was happy to see his older brother go off to join the army, and who would have done the same if he wasn't needed to keep the farm for his mother and little brother. But the bloody culture of warfare that pervaded Missouri turned Hildebrand into a cunning, deadly Rebel, a hunted killer with a growing reward on his head.

It all started with horses being stolen in St. Francois County, and with Hildebrand's distant cousin Allen Roan, who was known to be a Southern sympathizer. In the gathering storm of Civil War, more and more livestock disappeared. Any time that happened, it was assumed that beef and pigs were stolen to feed troops of one side or the other, and that horses were stolen for cavalry mounts and to pull army wagons. It was on one such raid in August 1861 that Allen Roan and his friend Tom Cooper ran some horses from the field of a farmer named Ringer, an avowed Union loyalist. They didn't scout the field very carefully before their raid, or they'd have seen that Ringer was outside his house, with a clear view of the grounds. He saw the boys taking his horses, mounted a horse that was already saddled and tied at the porch, and chased Roan and Cooper, firing his pistol. He couldn't hit anything at a gallop, but they stopped, turned, and returned his fire, hitting him twice in the chest.

There were no witnesses, but Roan and Cooper were suspected because they were loudmouthed about their Southern sympathies. Folks looked around the country at the young men who hadn't gone off to war and might be capable of horse-stealing raids. A lot of people wondered if Sam Hildebrand and his younger brother Frank were in it with their cousin Roan. On the contrary, Sam and Frank leaned toward the Union, and their older brother William was already in Federal service.

More important, Sam and Frank knew Roan was involved in stealing stock for the Rebels and had tried repeatedly to convince him that he was playing with fire and needed to stay out of the whole mess.

One evening about a month later, twenty-five-year-old Sam was turning under cornstalks on the little farm he shared with his wife, Margaret, and their five children. It was just a mile from his widowed mother, who was still on the farm established by Hildebrand's grandparents, where his father had died in 1850. Hildebrand was just over six feet tall and very thin. He appeared almost feminine, with his close-set blue eyes, delicate lips, high-pitched voice, fair complexion, and

Sam Hildebrand, early in the war, in a captured Federal uniform with twin Colt revolvers.

rosy cheeks. Though he wore a beard, it was sparse. For all that, he was an imposing man because he stood very erect and exuded courage and purpose.

Allen Roan approached across the field, leading a sorrel horse he wanted to trade for one of Hildebrand's. It was a stout animal, which both men agreed would be good for the field, and Roan said he didn't need a plow horse, so he'd like to trade for another riding horse. Hildebrand had a riding horse to spare, so they shook hands and made the swap. The next day, Hildebrand went to hitch the new horse and try him with the plow but found him hardly broken to the harness at all. Hildebrand swore under his breath at his cousin, who must have known the horse wouldn't pull. Hildebrand sure didn't need to spend his time training another horse, so he took it to a neighbor, Mr. Rogers, and traded it for two pigs.

At the dawn of war, county militia units were raised, and one of them was the Big River Mills Vigilance Committee. They were led by the unrelenting Firman McIlvaine, who persisted at investigating Roan, Cooper, and the Hildebrands. In his travels, snooping around the county, asking about recent livestock transactions, he found a horse that was stolen from one of the vigilance committee members, John Dunwoody. It was the sorrel horse Rogers got from Hildebrand, which Hildebrand got from Roan.

That was all McIlvaine needed to know. Although St. Francois County had a sheriff, the danger and confusion of war were too much for him, and the law had been given over to the vigilance committee. They had sworn death to anyone implicated in stealing horses for the Southern cause. Soon word got around to Hildebrand that the committee was coming for him and young Frank. They knew it was hopeless to reason with the crusading McIlvaine, so Sam left his house, and Frank left their mother's house, and the brothers set up a small camp in the woods below a bluff. They waited and watched, but the committee still didn't appear near either house.

In the little camp they were shielded from the worst of the wind, but it was October, and every night seemed colder than the last. One night after three weeks of roughing it, Sam slipped back to the house for more blankets. It was about 11:00 p.m., and everything was still, so he walked quietly to the door and whispered for his wife. Margaret opened the door, pulled him inside, and held him tightly. They talked, and she fixed a hot supper for him as he told her where he and Frank were camped. Don't worry, he told her, nobody would find them there. But they didn't know the house was being watched all day and night, every day and night. When Sam had crossed his field in the darkness, a runner went for the committee, and by the time Sam put the first bite of cornbread in his mouth, he heard the thump of a fence rail hitting the ground.

He peered through a crack in the door, and the moonlight revealed a line of armed vigilantes creeping toward the house and settling themselves along the fence. Sam didn't hesitate, but grabbed his pistol, and stuffing the cornbread into his shirt, ran for a gap in their line as rifles cracked all around him. He ducked behind a little molasses mill, which pinged with the impact of nine shots. Then, as the marauders reloaded, he rose and sprinted another two hundred yards, where he disappeared into the trees.

The vigilantes went home for the night, and in the days that followed, Margaret found ways to skirt the roads and make her way around to Sam and Frank's camp with food and blankets. But they knew they couldn't maintain that way of life, especially with winter coming on, so Sam and Margaret bundled up the children and moved to a little cabin in the southern part of the county called Flat Woods.

Frank could have gone with them, but he stayed in the woods, intent on getting back to help their mother and the farm. He was sure he'd find a way to clear the family name. After thinking it over a couple more days, he left the camp and, looking over his shoulder with every step, made his way to an old family friend, Justice of the Peace Franklin

Murphy. Murphy suggested that Frank prove his loyalty by enlisting in a Union-friendly militia. Frank agreed that would remove all suspicion from himself, and maybe even clear Sam's name too. So Frank went to nearby Potosi, where T. D. Castleman commanded four regiments of the Missouri Home Guard, a Unionist militia, and announced to the clerk that he was there to sign up. But when Frank and his enlistment papers reached Castleman's office, he found Frank's name on the army's list of wanted men. Frank was arrested, and although he should have been taken before the army's provost marshal, he was instead turned over to none other than the merciless Firman McIlvaine and his vigilance committee.

McIlvaine and his mob rode hard for Potosi, fetched their prisoner, and took him to the man who sent Frank to Potosi in the first place, Justice Frank Murphy, expecting him to hold a little trial and convict Frank of stealing horses for the Rebels. Of course, Murphy told them, he could do nothing except note the charges against Frank and allow him to post bond pending a trial. That wasn't enough for McIlvaine, so the gang simply hauled Frank to another justice, R. M. Cole, who told them roughly the same thing. Disgusted, they rode away from Cole's office to a remote place where McIlvaine ramrodded his own version of a trial. Frank was not allowed to speak but was found guilty, stood under a tree, still protesting his innocence and begging for his life, and was hanged. The mob then threw his body into a sinkhole. That was November 20, and the mob kept its secret. Nobody in Frank's family had any idea what happened to him until a month later, when two boys out hunting discovered the body.

That alone might have been enough to turn Sam into a Rebel and a man-hunter, but there was more to come. By the spring of 1862 the committee had been legalized as a state militia unit, commanded by James Craig and Joe McCahan, charged with disarming Southern sympathizers and seizing all manner of arms and other contraband that could help the Rebel cause. Under the militia banner, the numbers swelled with men who had been refusing to serve in the committee because of its vigilante methods. But the militia made it perfectly legal for them to hunt men, including Sam Hildebrand.

McIlvaine and his compatriots finally traced Hildebrand to his cabin in Flat Woods, then returned with eighty armed and mounted men of the militia to either arrest or assassinate him. Hildebrand was hauling wood that morning. He just finished unloading the wagon and was walking into the house when he heard, then saw, the militia, mounted and in full charge. Again, when most men would run away from the firing, Hildebrand ran directly toward them and through their lines, hopped a fence, and was off toward the woods. The soldiers fired as best they could while spinning their excited mounts, and though hundreds of bullets missed the mark, one struck Hildebrand, breaking his kneecap. He continued to run in horrible pain, knowing the men on horseback would need only a few seconds to throw down a rail fence and begin the chase again. That gave him just the lead he needed to reach a gulley, where he completely covered himself with leaves. Though the soldiers milled all around him, they never spotted his hiding place, concluding that he had made a clean escape into the woods.

Poor Margaret saw it all from the house. Then she was horrified to see the militiamen—frustrated because they couldn't find Sam—turn their fury on the house. Putting Margaret and the two children out, they burned the house to the ground, along with everything else the family owned. There was nothing for Margaret to do but leave that night to stay with nearby family. The next day she found Sam and, with the help of a trusted neighbor, got him into the hands of some Confederate raiders, who got him to Greene County, Arkansas, where they were safe from Yankee patrols.

Captain Nathan Bolin, who commanded the guerrillas, loosely reported to Brigadier General M. Jeff Thompson of the Missouri State Guard. Thompson had been defeated by Union forces at Fredericktown and retired across the Arkansas line, leaving southeast Missouri in Yan-

Brigadier General M. Jeff Thompson, who may have met with Hildebrand.

kee hands but continuing to raid freely and frequently over the border into Missouri. He was called "the Swamp Fox of the Confederacy," and his men were known as "Swamp Rats," for their pesky attacks on the Yanks in the swampy land between St. Louis and Ste. Genevieve. By that time in his career, Thompson was a veteran of several commands at various posts, and he had even been a Yankee prisoner for a while. He was happy to have Bolin and his guerrillas in the Southern cause, but his hands were full with his regular troops. So although Bolin and his men claimed to be under Thompson's command, they were strictly on their own in planning their patrols and raids. It's doubtful that Hildebrand ever met with Thompson, but he claimed that the general appointed him a major, an appointment that was never recorded.

Nonetheless, the camaraderie of fighting men, Bolin's ruthless style, and swamp raiding all fit Hildebrand perfectly. He cared not a lick for

*Mingo Swamps, the inhospitable land through which
Hildebrand and his comrades raided, hid, and escaped.*

the politics of war, nor for marching in orderly lines. But as he said, "I was fully satisfied that the 'Bushwacking department' was the place for me, with the continent for a battlefield and the everlasting woods for my headquarters" (Kirby Ross, ed., *Autobiography of Samuel S. Hildebrand,* University of Arkansas Press, Fayetteville, 2005).

Through that winter Hildebrand nursed his shot-up knee. The following June he made his first trip back to Flat Woods, and he went alone. It had little to do with military operations, and everything to do with personal vigilante vengeance.

The first thing he did was track down George Cornicious, a farmer who'd told McIlvaine's raiding party where to find Hildebrand at his Flat Woods house, which led to the bullet in his knee. Hildebrand spent two days patiently waiting for the perfect opportunity. Shooting the informer was easy, but Hildebrand wanted to remember it, so he marked the event by cutting a notch with his pocket knife into the stock of his rifle, Kill-Devil. A fitting remembrance, he figured, and he tried to do it after every killing, although he probably forgot to cut a few in the heat of battle.

He then spent two more days trailing McIlvaine, again waiting for a good shot from cover. He found that on the edge of the rye field, as the Rebel-hunting farmer leaned against his scythe.

Those killings set in motion a series of horrid retributions. If they couldn't get Hildebrand, his enemies thought, they'd get the ones closest to him. In July 1861, another force of militia, the 1st United States Reserve Corps, marched from St. Louis under Captain Bernard Essroger. The 1st was a huge regiment of questionable legality, initially composed mostly of St. Louis Germans, mostly Republicans, but with local companies raised in various counties. Although the first members were sworn into Federal service, many of the later ones were not. Some were in uniform, and some were not. They elected their captains, who made their own decisions about their mission. When the orders came down to disarm and seize the property of suspected Southern sympathizers, there was chaos, and it's not surprising that Sam called them vigilantes.

On July 6, a mob comprising men from McIlvaine's old committee and a militia unit of Frenchmen under the command of a man known to Sam only as Captain Flanche, marched to the old Hildebrand homestead, where Sam's mother lived alone with Sam's youngest brother, Henry. They told the terrified old lady she had to leave immediately. So she clutched her Bible to her breast and waited for some family members to move her and her bed to the home of her brother, Harvey McKee, in Jefferson County.

The mob then proceeded to the St. Joseph lead mines near Big River Mills. Sam's brother Washington was down in the mine with a man named Landusky. Captain Flanche commanded the two men to come out of the mine and stand against a nearby tree. There they were cut to pieces by a fusillade from the troops, and their bodies were left where they fell. Both were nominal Union men, but neither had played any role in the war. It was just Wash's bad fortune to be Sam's brother, and Landusky's to be in the mine with him.

Soon after, Essroger and his men paid a visit to John Roan, the father of the accused horse thief Allen Roan, who'd traded the sorrel to Sam. John was in his fifties, and took no side in the war, but had furnished another son, Allen's older brother, to the Union. However, maybe even a greater sin than being Allen's father was being distantly related to Sam. Essroger ordered the white-haired gentleman out of his rocking chair and out into the yard. As he walked with his hands raised to heaven and a prayer on his lips, they opened his back with a hail of gunfire.

On July 23, about two weeks after Sam's mother had been ordered out of the Hildebrand homestead, leaving it empty, men of the 1st U.S. Reserve Corps returned to burn it. Sam would later say Essroger was there, as well as a Captain Adolph. They piled fence rails and other wood scraps inside as kindling and lit the house ablaze, then the barn. Meanwhile, two boys who had been working in the fields stood transfixed, watching their beautiful home go up in flames. It was Sam's

The log cabin built by friends for Hildebrand's mother after militia raiders burned her home.

brother Henry and an orphan boy who'd been hired to help Henry work the farm. Essroger told thirteen-year-old Henry to get on the plow horse, leave the county, and never return. Of course Henry obeyed the order, but as he approached a distance of just over a hundred yards away, the troops opened fire, peppering the boy with .50 caliber slugs. The merciless troops laughed as the orphan boy ran for his life; he was never heard from again.

All those mob activities took place during the war, but were unrelated to the war. Though they were rationalized, they were not justified. Though some were done by men in uniform, they were illegal. The militia claimed they were lawfully punishing people who gave support to the nation's Confederate enemies, but the truth is that the raids were pure violence for the sake of violence, by Unionists against fellow Unionists.

While those attacks were going on in the middle of July, Sam headed north from Arkansas on his second foray into St. Francois County, having no idea of what had been done to his mother, or Wash, or what was about to be done to Mr. Roan and little Henry. He was accompanied by his associate Devilish Tom (Thomas Haile) and another man, and they disguised themselves in captured Union uniforms, as guerrillas often did. The blue outfits enabled them to travel freely through enemy country, even in daylight. They could gather information and spy on the Federals, and even use the deception to get close enough to pull their pistols on unsuspecting victims.

When they were almost to Flat Woods, Sam and his companions encountered a man walking along the road and asked him if he'd seen any Rebels in the neighborhood. The man took one look at the Union uniforms and proudly replied that he had been spying among the Confederates all day. He'd gathered a lot of good information and was on his way to Greenville to report to the Federal troops there. The three Rebels in disguise offered to go with him, and Hildebrand hoisted the fellow up on his horse. Then after they'd gone a little way, Hildebrand shoved the little fellow off the horse, told him he was Sam Hildebrand, and shot him dead. Another notch in Kill-Devil.

As Hildebrand traveled through that country he'd been housed and fed several times by a man named Stokes, but Hildebrand suspected the man was plotting to turn him in to the army. So he decided to set a trap to find out for sure. He stopped by Stokes's house and visited, and as usual Stokes invited Hildebrand to stay the night. But Hildebrand politely refused his hospitality and told Stokes exactly where he was going to camp. A little later that same night, Devilish Tom and the other man then called on Stokes, wearing their Union uniforms, and Stokes greeted them warmly. "I know where Sam Hildebrand is camped. He's alone, and we can take him." The two imposters egged him on, and Stokes could hardly wait to fetch his rifle and lead them to Hildebrand.

Thomas Haile—Devilish Tom—was Hildebrand's frequent companion on his raids across southeast Missouri.

Of course before they traveled very far, Hildebrand met them on the road, told Stokes he was a dirty snake, and Stokes became the next notch on Kill-Devil.

That was typical of the way Hildebrand and his men operated throughout the war, sometimes wearing Union uniforms, spying on the spies, and other times riding into the midst of Union camps in mad cavalry charges. Once Hildebrand was in town wearing plain clothes and chatting with two women on the street in an effort to get information about troop movements, when a company of Federal cavalry came riding along. Seeing a chance to get the desired information firsthand, Hildebrand boldly turned his horse in beside them and struck up a conversation with the commanding officer. Hildebrand enticed the officer to disclose their objective, then said, "I'd sure favor to join up with you and get those Rebels." The officer replied that he appreciated Hildebrand's eagerness but didn't want any men who hadn't been trained. Hildebrand then pretended that his horse was coming up lame, gradually fell back, and disappeared down a side street. As always, Hildebrand and his men disappeared into the Missouri timber, then reassembled at a predetermined rendezvous, and there they made a plan to attack that Union officer and his cavalry.

It was guerrilla warfare at its best, directed at a mix of regular troops and Union-loyal civilians. It was mostly unauthorized, and without the oversight of anyone in uniform. By far, most of the eighty-four notches in Kill-Devil's stock by the end of the war were made in the service of the Confederate cause. But a few of Hildebrand's killings were nothing but personal vendettas against those who had so brutalized his innocent family. He was forced to become a vigilante and right the wrongs the law refused to address.

CHAPTER TEN

NO SURRENDER FOR SAM

When the war came to an end, Hildebrand vowed to go on fighting. But his patient wife, Margaret, saw a chance to have peace in their lives for the first time in a long time. She told him, "If you burn the rat, we'll lose the barn," a twist on the old wisdom that one doesn't burn one's barn to get rid of one rat. If he didn't seize the chance for peace then, there would be no end to the fighting until their whole family was destroyed. Sam's loyalty to her and his children overrode his fighting spirit, so he joined a Confederate unit at its surrender and signed the loyalty oath.

Sam and Margaret rented a little farm, got in a crop of corn, and lived in abject poverty for a while. But Sam remained a vigilant champion of justice. People knew they could turn to him for help, and they did. So it was that a friend came to tell him of his sister, whose husband had left her to take up living with a black woman in Arkansas. A couple of days later Hildebrand and his friend abducted the wandering husband and his mistress, tied them together face to face, and drowned them in a farm pond.

After Hildebrand was charged, then released, in that double murder, he lived with the fear that haunted all vigilantes, that someone would come to avenge the husband—or maybe another of his long-passed killings. Sam and Margaret decided they could only have peace by moving again, so they rented a little farm in Washington County. But there too they felt threatened by men who refused to bury the hatchet. During the war, many rewards had been offered for Hildebrand's capture, and after the war some continued, while new ones were offered. It was unclear which rewards were still active at any given time, and some men just heard rumors that there was money to be made killing Hildebrand, and that was enough for them. They didn't need any details. It was certain that some of the rewards were to be paid "dead or alive," and in the years following the war there was at least $300 still hanging over his head.

Hearing that a vigilante force had been organized to arrest or kill him, Hildebrand found work away from home to remove the danger from his family. Yet it was inevitable that he'd be found, and it finally happened in June 1869, after the war had been over for four years. A lone bounty hunter, the son of a county judge, stationed himself outside the Hildebrand home. During the day he watched from the woods. After dark he slipped in beside the fence. Night after night he waited, watching Margaret and the children, knowing Sam would show up sooner or later.

At last his patience was rewarded. It was well past dark, and the young man was dozing under a blanket beside a shed, when a noise startled him awake. There was his quarry creeping home to spend a rare night with his beloved family. The hunter had waited that long, so he was willing to sit even longer to get a daylight shot. When Hildebrand emerged in the morning light to fetch water, a shot rang out. But the young assailant's nerves got the best of him, and the shot he intended for the heart hit Hildebrand in the thigh. Hildebrand was able to get back into the house and grab Kill-Devil, and by the time he came out to face his would-be assassin, the terrified ambusher had panicked and fled. He was not about to go face to face with Sam Hildebrand.

The only known portrait of Buck Highley, who helped Hildebrand escape but then gave in to the posse's threats of jail.

Sam gave Margaret a parting hug and told her he'd be all right. Then he limped over to a neighboring farm and hid in the corncrib until the farmer appeared in the yard. Sam leveled a pistol at the man and demanded to be taken to home of his cousin, the wife of William Madison "Buck" Highley, about five miles away. Buck was the brother of John Highley, the Confederate soldier turned guerrilla who was hunted down and killed by Federal troops in Illinois. So once again Hildebrand turned to his faithful family, and the Highleys were more than happy to help. They dressed his wound, and then Buck hid him in the bed of the wagon and took him to the home of Hildebrand's uncle John Williams, where they believed he'd be safe until he healed.

But Washington County was crawling with men who held war-forged grudges, who hoped to be part of Sam Hildebrand's demise, and who hoped to snag a little piece of the reward. One of them was the neighbor who'd found himself staring down the barrel of Hildebrand's Remington pistol in his corncrib. He was only too happy to point the posse, headed by Washington County sheriff John Breckenridge, to the Highley farm. Of course Hildebrand knew that was a possibility, but he assumed Buck would keep his mouth shut and be nothing but a dead end for the posse.

When the posse arrived at the Highley place, Buck pleaded ignorance. He hadn't seen anybody. That farmer must be mistaken. But after repeated questioning, Sheriff Breckenridge told Highley and his wife they were both under arrest for aiding a fugitive. They were going to prison for years, he told them. Highley would have suffered anything to help Hildebrand. And yet, he couldn't let his wife go through arrest and a trial, much less a prison term. Just tell me where you took him, Breckenridge said, and we'll let you go. So at last Highley revealed that he took their fugitive cousin to the Williams farm.

The next morning Uncle John Williams walked from the log house to the barn to feed and soon returned at the prod of several gun barrels in his back. "Sam Hildebrand! Come out with your hands up, Sam Hildebrand, or we'll fill that house with hot lead," Sheriff Breckenridge called. When Hildebrand moved to open the door, the vigilantes did just as they promised, unleashing a hail of gunfire at the door and windows, with complete disregard for Hildebrand's aunt and a young niece who cowered with him inside. During that assault one man ran toward the house from another direction, intending to fire through a chink in the home's logs, but Hildebrand saw him and fired first, placing a slashing wound across the man's chest.

The group holding Hildebrand's uncle then forced him onto the porch so he was leaning a bit with his right hand against the door frame. "Open up, Sam," the frightened old man called, "or they'll shoot me for sure!"

When Hildebrand had joined the Confederate Bushwhackers he had his only known photograph taken in a dark wool coat, wearing a

The 1861 Remington revolver, favored by Hildebrand and other guerrillas for its sturdy frame. Note the heavy top strap, above the cylinder, which distinguishes it from the Colt of the same era.

kepi and a two-inch-wide belt, into which were tucked a pair of Army Colt revolvers. However, as the war went on, Hildebrand decided, like many men, that the Remington New Model Army .44 was a superior weapon because of its heavy top strap, a structural feature that was lacking in the Colt. If it came to hand-to-hand fighting, the thirteen-inch-long pistol was an excellent club. If a man's pistol was dropped, thrown, hit by a slashing saber, or stepped on by galloping cavalry horses, some thought the Remington was more likely to survive than the Colt. So it was that Hildebrand was in the Williams house with his ever-present pair of Remington revolvers, as well as a sheath knife and several pocket knives.

Hildebrand called out to reassure his uncle. Then suddenly he opened the door, not in surrender, but with pistols in both hands, instantly firing with his right hand under his uncle's arm, into the sheriff's groin, and crossing with his left to place a ball in the shoulder of the man on the other side. The group left the trembling uncle on the porch and sprinted for cover, with Hildebrand still firing, striking one man in the cheek.

While the sheriff was taken to the doctor and runners were sent for more men, the remaining posse settled into good hiding places and continued to pour sporadic fire into the house all day. Both Hildebrand's aunt and the little girl had been slightly wounded by the posse's firing, so a truce was called while they went out to safety. Though his aunt begged the posse to let her take water back in to Hildebrand, the enforcers refused.

When Deputy Sheriff Jim McLain arrived with fifteen more men, they too had to take cover, because Hildebrand was firing at everything that moved. McLain knew what to do. He immediately gave the order to burn the house. He wadded up several balls of candlewick and soaked them in coal oil. Then he climbed to the roof of the Williamses' old cabin, which still stood right beside the main house. From there he was able to reach over and lodge the fireballs against the stick chimney of the cabin where Sam was holding forth, and set them to burning.

Then, thinking he could use the old cabin as a cover to get close to his prey, McLain slipped inside. It was only a couple of steps from the back door of that cabin to the back door of the newer one. But that was a trap Hildebrand had arranged beforehand, and he saw McLain's every move through a chink beside the door. As McLain stepped cautiously into the open doorway, Hildebrand placed a bullet squarely in his heart.

The fire around the chimney failed to produce any result, because as soon as shingles would ignite, Hildebrand would knock them off. While Hildebrand was thus occupied at the rear of the building, one crusader decided that was the time to make his move at the front. Unfortunately for him, Hildebrand was thinking the same thing. As the man approached the house, Kill-Devil again spoke death, and the man sprawled across the porch. His friends, not knowing whether he was alive or dead, ran to pull him to safety. Darkness was falling, and as the posse focused on getting the man off the porch, Hildebrand chose that as his time to escape. He pried up a floorboard and slipped out under the floor, crawling across the yard and right between two of the mob. They had no idea he was there until he rose and ran away into the tall grass beyond the fence. Though they fired until their guns were empty, he disappeared. The wound in his thigh, now two days old, was so painful that he was unable to run any farther, so dropped to the ground and kept crawling away from the posse. The revolvers were still tucked into his belt, but he was unable to carry Kill-Devil while on all fours. He had no choice but to abandon his trusted rifle in the dirt of the Williamses' cornfield. Then he kept crawling two more miles to safety at the home of a friend.

Hildebrand passed through friendly hands and ended up in the care of Dr. Abram W. Keith, who provided a hiding place in the basement of his spacious Big River Mills home. He brought a trusted friend into his confidence, and over the next few weeks the two men met with Hildebrand to write down the tale he told them of the incredible life he had lived since the start of the war. Thanks to them, he was able to tell the whole story, which resulted in a book that was published as his autobiography.

In July, Hildebrand wrote a letter that was published in newspapers as distant as *The New York Times*, begging to be left alone. But it was too little, too late. The militia was swarming across southern Missouri looking for him. The *Times* reported, "In order to obtain information about the haunts and habits of Hilderbrand [sic] it was sometimes deemed necessary to frighten and torture certain persons who were believed to have the information desired." It went on in detail, "Several men were hung up by the neck until they told what they knew." The militia was really a vigilante mob, but by early August they had given up the search.

Since the merciless militia campaign didn't work, the governor of Missouri ordered that standing posses be raised in Washington County and each county south to the Arkansas line. He couldn't very well say that so much effort was being expended to bring in one man, so the posses were publicly announced as a general cleanup of lawlessness. But in fact, all the work was aimed at the killing of Sam Hildebrand.

Hildebrand was finally forced to surrender, not to men or a government, but to a fate he never sought, a life in exile. It was simply not safe for Hildebrand and his family to live anywhere near his beloved St. Francois County anymore, so he and Margaret moved to Texas. Unfortunately, the peace they found there was short-lived, as she died a year later.

For Sam, without his Margaret, Texas felt even farther from home. In one last effort to move closer to his beloved kin, Hildebrand took his children to Pinckneyville, Illinois, about twenty-five miles from Ste. Genevieve, and rented a farm under an assumed name in the spring of 1872. From there, he thought, he might take the children to visit their

Sam's son Henry Hildebrand. The children moved many times with their parents, and were at last reared by relatives, married, and had children of their own. Photo courtesy of Jan Hite.

Missouri relatives now and then, and in time, maybe he could even move back home with them.

Hildebrand was never a heavy drinker, but he missed the company of other men, and he enjoyed an occasional beer. One night he went into town for a beer at a tavern, where he was surprised by the bartender, a Missouri man who said, "Hey, I know you. You're Sam Hildebrand." Hildebrand told the man his new name, but the bartender knew he was right. "Sure as I'm standing here, you're Sam Hildebrand," he insisted.

"You're a liar," Hildebrand replied, and repeated his new chosen name. The bartender was not about to let Hildebrand call him a liar, and Hildebrand said the bartender was just as much as calling him a liar. In no time at all, the two red-faced men were nose to nose and about to explode. There was a push, then a fist to the chest. In another time and place the bartender might have been asking for a quick trip to the cemetery. But Hildebrand couldn't afford trouble. He had to back down. He turned and left the bar, his heart pounding so loudly he was sure every man in the place could hear it.

Outside, he pondered the dangerous situation into which he had just stepped. The bartender wouldn't keep quiet. After all, the name of Sam Hildebrand was popular barroom conversation, even when he wasn't nearby. And it in no time at all, word of the sighting would spread back to Missouri. Pretty soon Pinckneyville would be crawling with men hoping to collect the reward on Hildebrand. It wasn't only his life at stake. He'd risked that before. But he stood to lose his newfound peace and this new beginning with his children at his knee. With Margaret gone, he was all the children had, and he refused to leave them orphaned. Yes, the old trouble still hounded him, and he had to shut the bartender's mouth to save himself and his family.

As soon as Hildebrand left the tavern, the infuriated bartender sent a friend to fetch the town marshal. The marshal sauntered over, hoping by that time the man who argued with the bartender would have cooled down and gone elsewhere to drink. But as he strolled around the corner of the tavern, he peered down an alley and saw something that didn't look right. On closer inspection, it was Hildebrand, looking through the tavern window with his rifle in hand. He was lining up a shot, the marshal thought. Of course the lawman had no idea who Hildebrand was, and whether he would have actually fired through the window is open to speculation. But the marshal decided to err on the side of safety, acting quickly to grab a board at his feet and whack Hildebrand a mighty blow to the head. The marshal and two deputies took him before a justice of the peace, where the bartender identified him as the man who started the trouble. He was fined five dollars for disturbing the peace and sentenced to jail on a charge of attempted murder.

The three lawmen then left the office of the justice, escorting the prisoner to the jail, and they neither knew nor cared that he was Sam Hildebrand. But Hildebrand knew he couldn't go to jail, because his true identity would be discovered. Whether it was revealed in the prosecuting attorney's investigation, or by word of mouth, or by people dropping by the jail to take a look at him, sooner or later they'd know for sure whom they had in their cell. Then they'd send him back to a Missouri hangman's noose. The deputies had relieved him of his two Remington revolvers, a Bowie knife, and two pocketknives. But they missed another knife in the pocket of his vest.

The deputies' pistols were holstered under their coats. After all, there were three of them and only one of Hildebrand. As usual, Hildebrand's plan was to run toward the greatest danger and depend on other men's lack of skill. By disabling the man closest to him, Deputy John Ragland, he hoped to gain enough of an edge to escape before the others could decide to act. He deftly and quietly peeled the pocketknife, then whirled to bury it to the bone in Ragland's knee, pulling it up and laying the meat open for the length of his thigh. But Ragland's reflexes were better than Hildebrand expected, and far quicker than those of the other two men. Even with the shock and pain of the knife wound, he found the presence of mind to slip his Smith & Wesson double action pistol from its shoulder holster and squeeze the trigger as it came out. When the muzzle exploded, it was squarely against Hildebrand's temple, and he collapsed dead into the street.

Though he was buried as an unknown person, a couple of lawmen from St. Francois County read the story of the killing in the newspaper and thought it might be Hildebrand. They traveled to Pinckneyville, Hildebrand was exhumed, and they identified him. He was then returned to his beloved Missouri and buried on John Williams's farm, in a spot that eventually became the Hampton Cemetery. His daughter Rebecca sewed a new shirt in which he was buried. Then Hildebrand's children grew up in the homes of their Missouri kinfolk, loved and nurtured, and had families of their own, proud to be associated with the name Hildebrand.

Anyone who hears the story of Jesse James and has any doubt that he was forced into a life of crime after the war, need only listen to the story of Sam Hildebrand. He too was a man who sought peace but would not be allowed to rest. He was a vigilante pursued by vigilantes. A man who saw himself as a righteous defender of the people, and whose enemies saw him as a threat they had to eliminate.

While war crimes in the name of the winning side went largely unpunished, Hildebrand was one of many men who could never go home or live in peace again after the war. Major John N. Edwards, adjutant and chronicler for Confederate general Jo Shelby, wrote in his book *Noted Guerrillas*:

> It required, indeed, all the excesses of the civil war of 1861–5 to produce the genuine American Guerrilla —more enterprising by far, more deadly, more capable of immense physical endurance, more fitted by nature for deeds of reckless hardihood, and given over to less of penitence or pleading when face to face with the final end, than any French or Spanish, Italian or

Mexican Guerrilla notorious in song or story. He simply lived the life that was in him, and took the worst or best as it came and as fate decreed it. Circumstances made him unsparing, and not any predisposition in race or rearing. Fought first with fire, he fought back with the torch; and branded as an outlaw first in despite of all reason, he made of the infamous badge a birth-right and boasted of it as a blood-red inheritance while flaunting it in the face of a civilization which denounced the criminals while condoning the crimes that made them such.

CHAPTER ELEVEN

OUTSIDE THE LINES

The public and the media generally based judgment of the law on how the case turned out. The question was, did the bad guys get what they deserved? Frustrated lawmen had so few legal crime-fighting tools that doing it the legal way sometimes just wasn't enough.

The standard for extralegal law enforcement was set during the war. Both sides arrested men and sent them to prison, set up ambushes, and sometimes simply dragged men from their homes and beat, shot, tortured, or hanged them. With the state under martial law, the Union army installed a network of provost marshals throughout the state who processed warrants, arrests, and prosecutions of countless people in every county. Bounty hunters ran down slaves, deserting soldiers, people who helped the enemy, and criminals. It's no wonder the legal boundaries were blurred.

Sometimes it was unclear who was serving what purpose. William P. Adair and several other local men were arrested by Union troops in 1863. Their crime: guerrilla activities, including stealing horses. Their victims: families who helped the Southern guerrillas or had men in the Southern service.

William Adair was one of the founders of Ironton, a justice of the peace and a Union man from the beginning of the war. He enlisted in the Union army, and when his first unit was dissolved, he became his own guerrilla. As he stood before the provost marshal, it was a surreal scene. He was guilty, of course, of stealing horses, but he stole them for the Union army from Southern sympathizers. The marshal explained that the army could do that, but Adair couldn't, but it seemed like splitting hairs to Adair. The marshal asked him if he'd like to enlist in the army again instead of being prosecuted for stealing horses, and Adair was more than happy to do so. When he was released, he simply enlisted as a captain and served in Company F, 47th Regiment Missouri Infantry, spending the duration of the war in uniform.

One of the best late-nineteenth-century crime-fighting tools was the posse, a quickly organized mob of farmers, clerks, railroad hands, and blacksmiths. They weren't trained in law enforcement, and the civil rights of the men they chased weren't an issue. Many of the men who were most ready to ride were the veterans. They'd fought for law and order, and if law and order needed restoring, they would be first in line. There was often no time to swear a posse to an oath, because getting after the bad guys quickly was essential. A posse differed from any other vigilante mob only in that it had a lawman in the lead, and there was a slightly better chance the captured parties might live to stand trial.

Back in 1833, in Greene County, Joseph Ferguson got into a fistfight with fellow farmer Jacob Sigler, and he was so mad, he went home and got his rifle. When he came back Sigler was armed too. They were so riled up and so afraid the other was going to shoot first, that they both fired and both fell wounded. The difference was that Ferguson got up, walked over, and finished off Sigler.

Later the sheriff went to Ferguson's cabin, where he was laid up with his wounds, and told him he was under arrest. Then the sheriff went back to town, got the county judge, and brought him to Ferguson for a trial. But Ferguson wasn't quite as hurt as he acted. While the sheriff and judge waited, he went to the outhouse and never came back. The infuriated sheriff mounted a good-size posse and took off after him.

They stopped at the nearby home of a couple of Ferguson's friends, who said yep, they knew where he went, but nope, they weren't going to help the law find him. The sheriff had his posse tie them to trees and beat them with switches. Still, neither one would talk, and Ferguson made good his escape to Texas and a new life. Nobody said a critical word about the beatings. The sheriff was just doing what he had to do, and it was too bad it didn't work.

Over in the little Bates County town of Butler, the druggist James Richardson said meek dry goods merchant James Hill owed him five dollars. Richardson was a secessionist drunk who left town when the war started in 1861. Before leaving, he turned the disputed note over to farmer Jasper Browning for collection and, just for good measure, threatened to kill Hill when he came back.

Richardson came back in a few months, and the five dollars was the first thing on his mind. Browning hadn't bothered to collect it, so Richardson took him along to get the money and kill Hill for no good reason. Hill knew Richardson was back, and he was watching out his front window. When he saw the pair approaching his house, he ran out the back door to the smokehouse with his shotgun. In seconds he was cornered there, and Browning watched as Richardson kicked open the smokehouse door and Hill fired, wounding his assailant in the arm. Hill ran toward the house but only got a few steps before Richardson dropped him with a pistol shot, then walked over and put two more bullets into his brain.

Sheriff Alexander Spencer did things the right way, investigating, then obtaining a writ from the judge, before organizing a little posse. Everyone seemed to think it was quite appropriate that the posse included the murdered merchant's irate brother John Hill. They tracked Richardson to the home of doctor Frederick Teany, where he'd gone to get his wounded arm treated. Sheriff Spencer and a deputy quietly slipped in and found Richardson asleep. He woke up to the sound of Spencer's revolver being cocked, then felt the muzzle against his head.

A deputy took the pistols from Richardson's belt as the curious posse pressed through the door. John Hill emerged from the group, took one of Richardson's own pistols from the deputy's hand, and fired into his black heart, killing him instantly.

Farmer Browning hadn't shot at Hill during the corncrib affair, but he was with Richardson on the night of Hill's murder, and that was enough. The posse rode out and surrounded his house, and when he ran for the woods, John Hill had the honor of firing and killing him. Everybody, including the sheriff and the county judge, agreed that it was a heck of a shot and justice had been well served.

Private investigation for hire is as old as law, filling a needed role in law enforcement, going places and doing things that duly authorized lawmen couldn't or wouldn't. Private detectives didn't have badges— or even licenses—in early nineteenth-century Missouri. They were maverick individuals who worked alone, until the advent of the Pinkerton Detective Agency. The Chicago-based agency started in 1850 but didn't amount to much until the Civil War, when Allan Pinkerton was hired by President Abraham Lincoln for a variety of security services.

Pinkerton was a rabid abolitionist, and his home in Dublin, Illinois, was a stop on the Underground Railroad. He even worked with John Brown at least once in getting a group of runaway slaves all the way to Canada. His detective agency solved several railroad crimes; that's when he first met Abraham Lincoln, who was attorney for one of the lines. Later, in 1861, he was investigating a planned train robbery and happened to come across evidence of a plot to assassinate the president. He alerted Lincoln, who changed his travel plans to avoid the attack, and then hired Pinkerton to assemble a force of men to protect the president and take on some other jobs like spying and intercepting shipments of Southern supplies.

After the war Pinkerton didn't know exactly what to do with his agency, but as time went on, he figured out how big the market for his services could be. His experience with the federal government and

Allen Pinkerton pictured with President Lincoln at an army camp during the Civil War.

Union army gave him credibility wherever he went. Banks and rail-roads were eager to put him on their payroll. The American Bankers Association hired the company to investigate bank robbery, burglary, and forgery cases. Pinkerton agents were also assigned to transport money and other valuables.

Although he adopted a picture of an eye for his logo and touted the agency's investigative skills, Pinkerton agents had more dangerous work that they went armed for. A Pinkerton man wore a business suit, usually with a vest. Such an outfit concealed a shoulder holster and usually another holstered pistol on his belt. Most of them also liked pocket pistols, smaller guns in lower calibers that could slip unnoticed into a coat or pants pocket. And every man carried a knife or two.

As they went around the country armed to the teeth, Pinkerton men were paid very well. The combination of money and guns gave them great confidence. And because their employers, mainly the banks and railroads, were so flush, the agents could get just about anything else they needed, including free rail travel, a special railcar, or an entire train just for them. Hotel rooms. The best horses. There was also ample money to pry secrets from informants.

Pinkerton's agency was hailed for its successes, but its failures were often spectacular. When they blundered, more money was usually thrown at the problem, which sometimes helped, but not always. Of course the Pinkertons were criticized by disappointed clients and by the public. And yet, the banks and railroads had little choice but to continue funding them. The crimes were continuing anyway, so at least the Pinkertons offered some chance of nailing the criminals.

The main reason for their success is that they were a bought-and-paid-for vigilante force, unencumbered by the laws and customs that controlled sheriffs, police, marshals, and constables. They hired people to commit crimes. They crossed city, county, and state lines at will, and when they got there they had no more legal standing than any other vigilante. In one of their most famous cases, they crossed the border into Canada to catch one of the Reno brothers. Pinkerton's men became a private anti-crime army that did whatever necessary to accomplish their task. In the lawless world in which they operated, their methods were seldom questioned. In other words, they got away with just about whatever they wanted to do. That meant they went about their business with unbridled violence. They shot first if necessary and, in many cases, a dead crook was just as good as an arrested one. Sometimes better, because the dead ones didn't escape from jail and didn't get acquitted by a court. As with all vigilantes, a trail of blood bore testament to their good decisions and bad. But whatever the agency's results, Pinkerton had the market to himself. When businesses needed help, they called him.

Some big companies had their own security men. Most of them had no training but were hired because they'd proven themselves in military service or police work, or just by being brutes. They were men who could handle hobos hopping trains and drunks in the passenger cars, but when it came to real detective work they were no help at all. So as time went by and bigger cases came up, including frauds, extortions, and especially robberies, the big companies turned to Pinkerton. In time, his customers included stage lines, freighters, and short-line railroads.

Adams Express Company, the nation's biggest and most successful freighter, was one of those companies with its own agents, but they couldn't even come close to stopping the Reno gang. The Reno brothers, John, Simeon, Frank, and William, lived with their family on a farm outside Rockford, Illinois, until the boys' continued scrapes with the law prompted a move. They found a place just across the Mississippi, near St. Louis, and were living there when all four joined the Union regulars. While the army offered a chance to redeem their character, they continued down the lower road. None finished out their enlistment, but instead deserted, some of them signing up again to collect the enlistment bonus. They were all back home by 1863 and still looking for trouble.

In 1866 they headquartered themselves at Seymour, Indiana, and made an art of robbing trains. They would commandeer the train, kick off the engineer and fireman, and run it up the line where they could plunder it at their leisure before escaping. The major victim of their robberies was Adams Express.

Pinkerton was already working for Adams on a case-by-case basis; he was credited with recovering some $70,000 from outlaws who preyed on Adams in 1866. So in 1867, Adams hired the Pinkerton agency specifically to capture the Reno gang. It was an opportunity for a sensational public relations story that would give Pinkerton the attention of every major rail line in the country.

John Reno, leader of the family criminal enterprise, was in his late twenties, a little shorter than average at five feet, five inches, clean shaven, with auburn hair. He looked like anything but a leader of men, but he was a calculator; he had a knack for smart planning and a cool head when there was trouble. With Pinkerton on their trail, things were getting too hot around Seymour, and John decided to extend their territory.

Gallatin, Missouri, the seat of Daviess County, was not far from Kansas City, all the way across the state from the Renos' home in Indiana. Gallatin wasn't on a major river, road, or railroad. It was a long, difficult trip, and no one knows why John Reno went there. Maybe he just headed west until he found a target. Maybe someone on the train told him Gallatin was a prosperous place where the clerk and treasurer

Left: John Reno. Right: Frank Reno, the man Pinkerton wished he could catch.

*Frank Sparks, trusted companion of John
Reno, who refused to incriminate his friends.*

both kept their money in the new clerk's office in the courthouse. One thing's for sure, if it was hard for John to get there, it would be just as hard for any lawman to chase him home. He took only his most trusted gang member, Frank Sparks, and told younger brother Frank Reno that if they didn't return, Frank Reno was to take over leadership of the gang.

The Daviess County sheriff was John Ballinger. His father, Gabriel Louis Ballinger, was a fearless man who led an expedition all the way to the Mexican border to trade for mules when he was only twenty-five, commanded a cavalry militia against hostile Indians when he was thirty, and settled in Daviess County to farm and preach. John was cut from the same cloth. He served the Union as commander of Company G of the 1st Missouri State Mounted Cavalry of Volunteers for two years. He was a Republican, elected to the first Gallatin City Council in 1858. He became postmaster, then was elected sheriff while he and his wife, Mary Buckols Ballinger, were raising the first of their two daughters, Ethil. (Hattie came along later.) He was even Sunday school superintendent.

John Reno and Frank Sparks took the train west, arriving at the Daviess-Caldwell county line on Saturday, November 16, 1867. They settled in at a tavern and picked up the rest of the men they needed, including Daniel and Silas Smith, Burdet Clifton, and Clay Abel. One of them was a close friend of Deliverance Nichols, deputy county clerk, who loved to talk about how much money sat in the Daviess County coffers. The little gang sat around a bottle of whiskey and discussed how easy it would be to walk in and take the county's money. John and Frank had enough men to rob a train, when really all they needed was the two of them. That was John's first mistake, including more people than he needed. It was more people who could get caught.

His second mistake was waiting. If they'd proceeded with the robbery that Saturday night, they would have had a full day's head start before the theft was discovered on Monday morning. But the west Missouri corn liquor was good, so he and the others lay out in the woods until Sunday night.

Stationing two men as lookouts and taking the others with them, John and Frank had no trouble getting into the courthouse and finding both the treasurer's and the clerk's safes. The treasurer's was a formidable—but small—bank-style safe the men blew open with a little gunpowder. The other was a wooden locking box with hinges they easily pried off with a crow bar. There were later reports that county officials were negligent, and one or both of the safes wasn't locked. The safes were locked, of course, or the bandits wouldn't have needed to destroy them to open them. When the job was done, John and Frank paid off the gang members and told them to scatter, then left town with over $23,000 in cash and a bundle of warrants, which were IOUs from people who couldn't pay their taxes and were worthless to the robbers.

Sheriff Ballinger slept through the robbery like everyone else. Even the explosion in the middle of the night was muffled by the brick courthouse walls. So the next day Ballinger was furious and hot on the trail of the robbers. Silas Smith was the first arrested when he tried to spend some counterfeit gold coins that everyone in town knew had been in the county safe since the Civil War. Of course he didn't want to be the only one of the gang to fall, and as Ballinger questioned Smith, he hinted that he wasn't sure he could keep a mob from lynching him. After all, it was a crime against everyone in the county, Ballinger remarked. But if Smith named the others, people would appreciate that. So Smith spilled the beans about his brother Daniel and Burdet Clifton. Finally he named John and Frank. Ballinger dropped his cigar. The infamous John Reno robbing the county treasury, right there in little old Gallatin.

Daniel and Burdet were jailed immediately, and Ballinger set off tracking John and Frank. The pair left town on foot, waded the Chillicothe River, and stopped to divide the rest of the loot, each taking half the money. Realizing the warrants were worthless to them, they buried them inside a corn shock and walked on a little way before tossing away the crow bar. They found a place to sleep with a farm family who were no doubt paid well for their hospitality, not to mention for keeping their mouths shut. The next morning the bandits hopped a train—sitting far apart—and arrived back in Seymour.

Ballinger knew John Reno and Frank Sparks had gone back to Indiana, far out of his jurisdiction. But the iron-willed county sheriff wasn't going to let a little thing like a state line, much less a county line, keep him from getting his men. He swore in Joab Woodruff and Alex M. Irving as deputies, and the three of them boarded the train for Seymour. Woodruff had served as a captain in the state militia and after the war was in charge of enrolling the returning Confederate soldiers and making sure they signed the loyalty oath. He was afraid of no man. Irving was a veteran of the Illinois infantry, a blacksmith and wagon maker. He was strong as an ox, and a good man in case things came to a tussle. The little three-man posse went to Indiana with no legal authority. Arriving without badges or fanfare, they started quietly asking questions. Soon they had won the confidence and help of three local men, Robert Winscott, a saloon operator; Phil Oates, a professional gambler; and Walter Meara, a freight hauler at the railroad station. The three told Ballinger everything he needed to know about John Reno.

On December 3 at 3:00 a.m. John walked through a hotel lobby and headed for the bar. Ballinger and Irving silently closed in behind him. Across the room John noted a man in the big easy chair wearing the sort of rough jeans and brush hat that were common out west, but were rarely seen in eastern cities like Seymour. He had an idea that the westerner could be trouble. When the man in the hat, Joab Woodruff, pulled a pistol from under his coat, John turned to leave, but he was staring at two more Colts in the hands of Ballinger and Irving. They handcuffed Reno, marched him to the train station, and had him and Sparks back in the Daviess County jail by the next day.

There's no question that the arrest was justified and necessary. But it was also illegal, an act of vigilantism. It was over before anyone could do anything about it, and for that matter nobody in a position of authority wanted to do anything about it. Except Allan Pinkerton. It embarrassed him, because his company was under contract to Adams Express to catch John Reno and his brothers. So he concocted a story, a public relations masterpiece, that became the official and popular version of what happened. Pinkerton's story didn't even mention Ballinger. Actually, the same informants, Winscott, Meara, and Oates, had worked as informants for Pinkerton from time to time. So in the Pinkerton version, Reno was tricked into going to the train station, where he was arrested by the pistol-toting trio of local men, who were working undercover for Pinkerton. It made them feel like heroes, and it made Pinkerton look good, as if he had a small army of men working for him in all walks of life. But in reality all Winscott, Oates, and Meara did was provide information to Ballinger and his deputies.

Back in Gallatin, Silas Smith and Clifton had been released for turn-ing state's evidence, which really amounted to identifying John Reno. That's all they'd say about the robbery, but that was the main thing Ball-inger wanted. Daniel Smith had not confessed but was in jail, where he was joined by Reno and Frank Sparks. Ballinger never found Abel, but that was a very small matter with the notorious Reno locked up. Men gathered in the streets and talked of a lynching. They were afraid there wasn't enough evidence to convict the men, and they sure didn't want to let them get off unpunished. Even more important, they wanted the county's money returned. Maybe lynching one or two of them would persuade whoever was left to turn over the money.

Ballinger was worried but confident. He wasn't going to let any-body get lynched out of his jail. At the same time, the mobs of men in the street worried the prisoners, so Ballinger used that to his advantage. No threatening move was made toward the jail, and nobody came to deliver a threat to Ballinger. But he put out a call for volunteers to guard the jail, hiring ten edgy young men, including Henry McDougal, Jehiel T. Day, Crow Dunn, Will Hargis, Clay Peniston, and Thomson Brosius. Armed with Winchesters and pistols, they kept a twenty-four-hour-a-day watch, in plain sight, so everybody knew they were there. John Reno in particular watched the armed guards and was sure the crowd wanted him, which was partly his ego at work. Thus Ballinger felt like John was close to confessing and taking a prison sentence in preference to a mob hanging. But the other men were a different matter. John would not testify against Daniel Smith and Sparks. Period. And Ballinger couldn't get those two to pin the robbery on each other. Silas Smith had fingered only Reno but had nothing to say about the others.

At last, John became so afraid of being lynched, he confessed ev-erything to Ballinger on December 10. He even promised to give the money back, if only the sheriff would save him from the mob. Ballinger cuffed him, put him on a horse, and followed him to the corn shock to retrieve the warrants, which were worth over $4,000 to the county.

They rode back to town, where Ballinger sat down and penned a letter to Governor Thomas Fletcher. In fact, there had already been lots of letters. Indiana's governor was pressuring Fletcher to extradite John to Indiana. Pinkerton desperately wanted him brought back and was begging the Indiana governor to stay after Fletcher: If John were punished in Indiana, it would be clear to everyone that the Pinkerton agency brought him to justice. And there were plenty of crimes the people of Indiana wanted to pin on John and his gang. He'd already been identified by witnesses of an Adams Express robbery. On the other hand, those witness statements were a long way from a conviction. Meanwhile, Ballinger wrote, "We have the confessions of Smith and Clifton against him and he [Reno] frankly comes out and admits the whole affair" (letter, Missouri State Archives). We must prosecute him in Missouri, he insisted, where we know we can convict him, based on the confession. He begged the governor not to send him back to Indiana, where he might get off.

Late one night just before Christmas, when McDougal and two of the other young guards were on duty, Sheriff Ballinger, Major Joseph H. McGee, and Bob Grantham came in carrying rifles. Joseph McGee was the young tailor who was burned out by the Mormons back in the 1840s. He continued his tailoring business and taught school in Gallatin, and by the time John and Frank were in jail, McGee had served many years as county clerk. But beyond his clerking skills, McGee had an unquenchable adventurous streak. He took a couple of years to try his hand at the California gold rush in 1850, and during the war he rose to the rank of major in the Union army's Company A, 1st Cavalry. In later years he would become common pleas judge and even served as U.S. marshal. In 1867 he had a personal interest in getting John Reno convicted because McGee was the clerk whose safe had been burgled. His deputy clerk, Deliverance Nichols, had disappeared, so McGee especially wanted to get John to admit whether Nichols had helped with the robbery. Fellow guard Robert H. Grantham was a veteran of the 1ˢᵗ Missouri State Militia Cavalry, a fearless man and no stranger to action. He even had a special interest in the Renos because he grew up in Indiana.

Without a word, the sheriff opened the cell, handcuffed Sparks, and led him out into the darkness with McGee and Grantham. Back at the jail, the young guards exchanged puzzled looks. Several minutes went by. Then, from a wooded gulch at the edge of town they heard several rifle shots. McDougal was astonished as the other two shook their heads and agreed, "Poor Sparks."

Ballinger, McGee, and Grantham returned to the jail, took out Silas Smith in the same silent way, and walked away, telling young McDougal to come with them. Smith was not taken to the secluded ditch, but to the courthouse lawn, in the middle of town, under a spreading oak. There McGee asked Smith if he had anything to say before he died. If he was going to confess, that was the time. Smith simply begged to pray, fell down on his knees and went on for some time, forgiving everyone, including the men about to hang him, and proclaiming his innocence in the process. A noose was slipped over his head, the rope thrown over a big limb, and the clerk McGee commanded, "String him up." The gentle McDougal thought to himself, "This is hell, but here I am among the vigilantes of the far West, and I'm one of them." He had no choice but to grab the deadly line along with the other men and heave to, lifting Smith into the air, choking and kicking like a fish.

After a few seconds they let him flop to the grass, and the men got right in his face. "Don't die with a lie on your lips," McGee charged him. "Confess now! Did you and Sparks rob the county treasury?" Again Smith said he was innocent, and up he went into the boughs. And a third time, and still he wouldn't confess.

All that time, Sparks was still in the secluded gulch under the care of the young guards. There he had knelt, closed his eyes, and endured McGee's gunshots, bullets zinging past his ears, but he had been just as tight-lipped as Silas Smith. His faked shooting, and Smith's hanging, were all a show to get one of them to confess or accuse the other. In the end, both Frank Sparks and Burdet Clifton were released because there was no evidence to prosecute them. Even John Reno would never say a word against them.

Sparks went home to Seymour, Indiana, where Frank Reno took over as leader of the gang. In 1868, after only one more year of spectacular train robberies and murders, various members of the gang, including Sparks, were captured by the Pinkertons in Indiana and Illinois. Ironically, the stories of the rest of the gang would continue to make Pinkerton look bad, thanks to the Jackson County (also known as Southern Indiana) Vigilance Committee. They were among the best known and most effective regulators in Middle America. As Pinkerton's men brought the outlaws in for trial two and three at a time, the committee took them from custody and lynched them. Among them was Frank Sparks.

Frank Reno and Charlie Anderson escaped to Canada but were arrested in Ontario. In another bold, publicity-grabbing stunt, Allan Pinkerton glibly bragged that he brought them back from Canada. He was right about one thing. He went to Canada. But all he could do was wait and write letters until the pair were extradited in his custody.

When he got back, Pinkerton had to turn them over to an Indiana sheriff because they'd been arrested on warrants from Floyd County. That meant Frank and Charlie were locked up in the tiny New Albany jail, where Frank's brothers Sim and William were also housed, about sixty miles from Seymour, headquarters of the vigilance committee. And that sixty miles wasn't going to stop the committee. They'd already lynched most of the gang and had waited years for Frank.

Everybody knew it was coming. Pinkerton tried to convince the sheriff to send the gang to a more secure jail with more guards in another town, but the sheriff was determined to protect them right there in his little lockup. Sure enough, late one night a mob of fifty men slipped quietly up to the jail, disarmed and tied up the lone guard, and cut the telegraph lines. Then they broke into the sheriff's house, which was in the same building as the jail. His wife watched as the invaders demanded the keys to the cells, which the sheriff refused, then beat him, still demanding the keys, and still he refused. When they shot him in the arm, that was all his wife could stand, and she handed over the keys.

The mob took the gang out of their cells and up the iron stairway so they could get a nice drop on the lynch ropes. There on the second floor they hanged them all. Anderson's rope snapped, so with broken bones and in great pain, he was hanged a second time. The committee was back in Seymour by breakfast.

After John Reno confessed in Daviess County Court on January 18, he served a bit over ten years of a twenty-five-year sentence in the Missouri State Penitentiary. When he went home to Indiana, prosecutors did their best to get their pound of flesh but could only convict him of counterfeiting, for which he served another three years.

John went back on his promise to turn over the Daviess County cash. It was never recovered, so maybe Sparks got it all. Maybe John got his share and enjoyed it until he died at home at the age of fifty-seven. The notorious Indiana train robber never went back to Missouri. After all, that's where he was put away by a small-town sheriff who went outside the legal bounds of his office, not to mention across state lines, to enforce the law.

Martial law during the war set the stage for a too-powerful government in the postwar years. The mentality was there. The people were there. The methods had been practiced. So when the war was over, while most men were tired, battle weary, and homesick, there were others who were itching to keep on hunting at the behest of government.

High-profile cases like Sam Hildebrand and Jesse James weren't the only ones who had a price on their heads, and there was no place such men could settle down and return to civilian life. They were being hunted by such passionate men, even if they attempted to surrender to law enforcement authorities, they might walk right into a bounty hunter's rifle sights.

Law enforcement had discovered a handy tool in bounties. When the bounty hunter came around asking for information, the people of Missouri were loyal to one another, distrustful of the law, and of course tight-lipped. But cash was especially tempting in the era of postwar poverty, good at wiping away old loyalties. A prize of a few dollars could buy a lot of grain, and many's the farmer who sold out his friends, and even relations, in order to keep his children fed.

There were over 300,000 deserters on both sides in the course of the Civil War. Some returned to war after a trip home or enlisted under an alias to collect the enlistment bonus. Some ran away and enlisted in the enemy camp. However, hunting deserters was a business that seldom paid off. When a deserter was caught it was usually by accident, or by a little investigative work by local militia. Most deserters got away with it, and they were almost never executed, the prescribed punishment. But desertion was one more log on the fire, one more aspect of running, hiding, and hunting for Missourians after the war. There were lots of men who broke the law and had to live with that the rest of their lives. Lots of men hunting men.

Governor Thomas Fletcher, the first governor of the state who was born in Missouri, was a Union man and a veteran of the Enrolled Missouri Militia. He was a compassionate Republican who loved Missouri and his neighbors. Like Lincoln and Johnson, he was conscious of reconstructing the Union with healed feelings, brotherhood, hope, and progress. To him, bounties were the opposite of what he was trying to do. He didn't want men hunted—he wanted them invited back into society. So he walked lightly with bounties.

Governor Joseph McClurg, who took office in 1869, ventured a little further into bounties. After all, Fletcher had been only partly successful in healing the old wounds. McClurg was entering office facing a continuing reign of vigilantism, Civil War resentment, and men who couldn't go home. While Fletcher could afford the luxury of patience, the time for that was over. McClurg made a $300 bounty standard and used it time after time. He couldn't afford to go any higher. After all, there were so many fugitives from justice by that time, he couldn't offer too much for any one.

It was Governor Thomas Crittenden who turned bounty hunting into a hammer of government. He campaigned on a promise to bring Jesse James to justice. He posted extraordinary rewards for major criminals. He was a publicity hound who used the rewards, and the resulting captures or kills, to intimidate other criminals, as well as to boost his own reputation as a crime-busting governor.

By the time Crittenden came into office in 1881, the Pinkerton Agency had grown in expertise, power, and scope. One of the prizes they sought was the James-Younger gang, and the railroads and banks continued to fund that pursuit. In 1874 Pinkerton sent two men after the Youngers, acting on information that they were lying low near Roscoe, Missouri. Various Youngers were suspected of various crimes, and like the James boys, the Youngers had plenty of friends and relatives who were eager to hide them, feed them, lie for them, or do whatever they needed. Pinkerton sent Louis J. Lull, who went under the name W. J. Allen, along with James Wright, who took the alias of John Boyle. They needed somebody who knew the country and locals, so they enlisted the help of Deputy Sheriff Edwin B. Daniels from Osceola.

The night of March 16 the agents stayed at the Commercial Hotel in Osceola, drank in the bar, and tried to discreetly pry information out of the other customers. Somebody mentioned that maybe a farmer named Theodorick Snuffer knew something about the Youngers, so the next morning, Deputy Daniels led the agents out to the Snuffer place.

That morning the agents said they were cattle buyers, but to Snuffer they smelled like Yankees. Snuffer knew plenty but wasn't about to tell those three. Osceola had been the site of one of the most savage raids of the Border Wars when Jim Lane and his Kansas Red Legs burned and plundered the town and murdered civilians. The atrocity touched every family for miles around, and they had long memories.

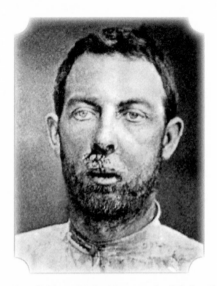 

Jim (left) and John Younger (right), brothers who robbed trains as part of the James-Younger gang.

Up in Snuffer's attic, Jim and John Younger listened to the whole thing. If they didn't do something, the agents and the deputy were likely to continue prowling around until they caught the Youngers by surprise. So when the three men rode out, Jim and John followed, overtaking them about three quarters of a mile up the road. The Youngers swung around and in front of them at a junction called the Corners. Wright (aka Boyle) panicked and galloped away, which of course gave away the other two. Lull (aka Allen) again brought out the cattle buyer story, and when Jim Younger didn't buy it, Lull drew his pistol and shot young John through the neck, then spurred his horse and galloped past the Youngers and into the woods. When the bullet hit John's neck, his adrenaline kicked in, instantly turning him into a reckless warrior. He couldn't even feel the wound, but he whirled his horse to give chase to his own murderer. With blood pouring down his shirt, he ran down Lull and ended his life with a shot to the back and another to the head as the agent lay on the damp spring ground. Meanwhile, Jim drew and fired, killing Daniels, whose dying shot sent a bullet grazing Jim's leg. John's horse eased out of the woods and back into the road, where John fell and died.

Both Youngers were wanted men. But Daniels was the only legal authority there that day, and he had no warrant. He, Lull, and Wright were acting on their own, doing what they thought should be done in the name of justice, without regard to what was legal. It was another Pinkerton vigilante blunder.

Perhaps the Pinkertons' best-known overzealous miscue was the visit to the home of Jesse James's mother and stepfather, Zerelda and Reuben Samuel, in 1875. That tragic night came after Pinkerton already had quite a history with Frank and Jesse. Agents had been sent at different times to spy, gather information, and set the stage for more agents to come and bust the gang. But each time a spy came, the James brothers discovered him and killed him. They pinned a note on one that read, "The same to all spies." Of course Pinkerton responded by sending another one.

Jack Ladd was a strapping Pinkerton agent who came into Clay County with complete secrecy and got a job as a hand working for Dan Askew, a farmer neighbor of the Samuels. Ladd was a good worker and was truly a good hand on the farm, but that probably didn't matter to Askew. He was a veteran of the Missouri State Militia and hated the James boys and their kind. Ladd's real mission was to find out when the brothers were coming to visit their mother. After a while, he heard they were coming, got word to Pinkerton, and the agency sent a special train to carry their best agents. The train made a special stop for them miles from the Samuel farm, in a stretch of railroad hidden by dense woods, where they met Ladd and another man with horses. It was January 27, a dark, blistering cold night, about 7:30 p.m.

Arriving at the Samuel farm about midnight, they called for Frank and Jesse to come out. They had no way of knowing that Ladd's information was all wrong and the boys weren't in the house. Huddled around the fire in the living room were the James boys' mother, Zerel-da, her husband, Reuben Samuel, their mentally disabled son, Archie, and a maid. When they ignored the posse's calls, one of the agents went to the next step. He had a bomb, a hollow iron sphere filled with a mixture of combustible materials—maybe some gunpowder, lamp oil, and other chemicals. Nobody knows exactly what was in it, but because it was tightly packed inside the ball, it was bound to explode, not burn, if ignited. The agent walked up on the porch, lit the fuse, heaved the ball through a window, then ran back to his companions. Of course the breaking window startled everyone inside. When they recovered their composure they saw a sizzling ball lying on the living room floor.

Zerelda Samuel didn't know exactly what it was, but she was the first to respond. After all, Reuben hadn't been mentally alert since he was hanged repeatedly by the Kansas Jayhawkers in 1863. Mrs. Samuel intended to heave the ball back outside, but it was so heavy she couldn't lift it. So Mr. Samuel took the ash shovel and rolled it into the fireplace. There, it exploded instantly, sending iron shrapnel spraying across the room. It ripped Archie's stomach wide open, and he would die later in the night. The maid was badly wounded, with a gash across her head. Reuben, who was closest, was injured only slightly. But the flying hot metal chunks shredded Zerelda's forearm, and it would have to be amputated.

The agents fled the farm that night not knowing exactly what damage they'd done inside the house. But they knew it was bad, and they soon found out exactly how bad. As news of the attack spread across the nation, it became the worst publicity disaster in Pinkerton's history. It galvanized opinion in favor of the James boys, especially in northwest Missouri. In retaliation, Jesse and Frank killed the neighbor Askew, then two agents. The others were long gone back to Chicago, leaving behind another chapter in James brothers vigilantism that a lot of Missourians considered good justice. People were happy to support the James family, and that helped keep them alive.

Jesse and Frank James's mother, Zerelda James Samuel, after the Pinkerton attack that mutilated her right arm.

In the spring of 1882, Governor Crittenden announced a reward of $10,000, an astonishing sum at the time, for the capture of Jesse and Frank. About the same time, Bob and Charlie Ford, who sometimes claimed to be kin to the James boys, but weren't, grew tired of being shunned by Jesse. He tolerated them and included them in some scouting rides, as well as some family gatherings. But he never did trust their loyalty, nor their backbone for work outside the law. So Bob Ford had a face-to-face meeting with the governor and made a deal to bring Jesse in.

The plan to get Jesse was Ford's own, a mixture of premeditation and opportunity. Charlie and brother Bob joined Jesse, his wife, Zee,

*This portrait of Jesse James was taken some-
time after the war, as he pursued a criminal
career and life as Mr. Howard, husband and
father. He was right to be afraid of being
lynched.*

and their children for a meal at the home in St. Joseph where the couple lived peacefully as Mr. and Mrs. Howard. After leaving the table,
Zee was in the kitchen, the children went out to play, and the men
eased into the parlor. Jesse took off his gun belt, then stepped on a
stool to straighten a sampler that hung above the door. That was Bob's
chance. He pulled his .44 caliber Smith & Wesson New Model revolver
and put one slug into the back of Jesse's head, ending his life, along
with the James-gang era.

The cowardly traitor Ford was Crittenden's own personal lone vigilante. And he was treated as such by the law. After running through

Robert Ford was officially pardoned of murder in the first degree by Governor Crittenden on April 17, 1882, following the killing of Jesse James on April 3.

the streets shouting that he'd killed Jesse James, he was arrested, tried, and found guilty of murder. His co-conspirator Crittenden pardoned him the same day.

A couple of years later Crittenden overplayed his hand in the case of "Omaha Charlie" Stevens. Stevens had been sent to prison on a murder conviction. But while he was there he made and mailed trinkets to Crittenden's daughter, who was terminally ill. As she lay dying, she begged her father to pardon her imprisoned admirer, and of course the governor couldn't refuse. In fact, Crittenden didn't think it was a lot to ask, pardoning Stevens. After all, he pardoned a convicted felon, including many murderers, about once every three days.

No sooner was Stevens out of prison than he was back in his old stomping grounds of Maryville, drinking and picking fights. One night when he was liquored up in a saloon, he pulled a pistol and shot a man dead at point-blank range. The murder was witnessed by dozens of men, so he was arrested and jailed. But people talked about how Crittenden pardoned Stevens once and might pardon him again.

On December 9, before Stevens could get to trial, a tall man, a stranger in Maryville, appeared on the street talking up a lynching. The crowd was easy to arouse, especially after many of them had patronized the local bars past midnight. Around 2:00 a.m. a group of about sixty men, most of them with kerchiefs over their faces and led by the tall stranger, approached the jail and called to the sheriff. He stepped out and refused to give them his prisoner, so they retreated. When they came a second time, the sheriff shouted and fired over their heads, but that didn't stop them. They marched right up to the jail, knowing the sheriff wouldn't really fire into the crowd. The mob became quiet and orderly, and in just a little while Stevens dangled from the railroad bridge outside of town. The tall stranger was never identified, but it was rumored that Crittenden sent him, just to be sure he never had to face the question of whether to pardon Stevens a second time.

CHAPTER TWELVE

WYATT EARP AND THE VIGILANTES

Lamar, Missouri, was just getting started, a hopeful community growing up around a sawmill, when the Civil War came along. It was burned twice, once by Quantrill and his raiders, and once by the evacuating Federals. Then everybody left when Order No. 11 forced all the civilians to move out of Missouri's border counties. By the time it was over, Lamar was a ghost town. People trickled back in, mostly from the east and north, looking for cheap land and a new start. The town was finally incorporated in 1867. Officials were elected. Laws were passed. Things were looking up.

Still, when the Earp family moved to town in 1868 there was little to attract a new wave of immigrants. No rail service for miles around. The roads were nothing more than game trails. The nearest market for livestock, dairy, groceries, and tools was a hundred miles away. And worst of all, Barton County, like all the land along the border, was a highway for former guerrillas of the Union and Confederacy and all kinds of bandits who passed through on their way to and from Indian Territory. "The Nations," as Indian Territory was called, was supposed to be home only to the Native Americans who'd been relocated there, a couple of army posts, and a few white men authorized to be there as

Wyatt's parents, Virginia and Nicholas Earp.

traders, Indian agents, and such. Of course, that made it a magnet for every skunk, lowlife, and hard case who wasn't supposed to be there.

On the other hand, the country around Lamar was suitably flat and clear for farming, and it was nestled in a gentle bend of the north fork of the Spring River. There were picturesque swamps along the river, but overall, the county was well drained. From a purely aesthetic viewpoint, it was certainly prettier and more wooded, with more rolling hills, than Kansas, which stretched like a griddle beyond the state line twelve miles away. Farmers who settled along the border were beginning to understand that there was a rough tree line in that part of the country. It was as if God had scratched a mark in the dirt, saying everything to the east was going to have abundant forests, and land to the west, basically Kansas Territory and Nebraska Territory, would be grassland. Lamar was on the edge of that tree line, with enough trees for wood and beauty, and enough prairie to give farmers an easy start.

Nicholas Porter Earp was an opportunistic man, bent on acquiring land or making money or both, so he brought his family to Lamar, where his brother Jonathan Douglas Earp was the local Methodist minister. Nicholas was a veteran of the Mexican-American War and furnished two sons to the Union cause in the Civil War. He appreciated the prestige that gave the family and was happy to talk about it any time he could use it to his advantage. Further, he understood the benefits that come with owning multiple businesses while holding public office.

Years before, Nicholas got himself in trouble for selling whiskey in Iowa, where there was a local prohibition law. The arrest was particularly unseemly since he was a town constable. After paying his fines, he ended up unable to pay his taxes and lost his property to foreclosure. Clearly, the vision Nicholas had of establishing himself at the top of the social and political order just wasn't working out.

The family had already moved several times, so it was completely in character when he signed them onto a wagon train and moved to California after the gold rush of 1849. Out there, people could walk out the front door and make money. All they had to do was find a way to get it out of the miners' pockets. Nicholas began to set aside some savings. However, it was a hard and expensive place to live, so once again he packed up the family and returned to the heartland. The sleepy postwar town of Lamar offered the Earps a chance to start again.

By the fall of 1869, Nicholas owned a sizable farm and a combination grocery store and café. He became a confidant of the city leaders, talking freely about his law enforcement experience in Iowa, conveniently leaving out the part about his arrest and financial collapse. Thus, he was able to get himself appointed Lamar's town constable. His duties consisted primarily of collecting fees for building permits and business licenses. The tiny town had no jail and no justice of the peace, which left Earp virtually powerless to enforce the law. Even if he arrested someone, what was he going to do with a prisoner? He assessed such fines as he could, but it was barely legal, and certainly would not provide any sort of threat to serious criminals. Then Nicholas saw an opportunity to make the town more civilized while extending the family's influence. He convinced his friends that they must have a justice of the peace—and hinted that he'd be willing to serve if called upon. The deal was made, he resigned as constable, and he accepted an appointment as justice, although he had no formal training or experience to qualify him for the position. At that time, it was not unusual for a man to become a justice with no legal training. It amounted to a sort of local judgeship, a job often tendered to older men who had experience with law enforcement or government.

When Nicholas brought the family back from California to Lamar, sons Wyatt and Virgil wanted to see a bit more of the West. They worked as teamsters, hauling supplies for the crews building the railroads. Driving the heavy, over-laden wagons was an education in courage, brawn, and resourcefulness. Of course, the job also offered an education in the rowdy culture of the railroad camps, which included prostitution, gambling, and consumption of alcohol.

After the boys joined the family in Lamar, older son Virgil was happy to settle into farming with his father. Wyatt, on the other hand, had little patience with his job waiting tables in Nicholas's café. In Wyatt's mind, he had come to Missouri as a twenty-one-year-old man of some stature. He had been to the West. The great, wild, mysterious West. Any man who had been there carried a certain legendary status, and while Virgil cared nothing for such attention, Wyatt wore it like a badge. That, plus his father's endorsement, made it easy for him to win the confidence of the city council, and they appointed him constable, replacing his father.

The most eligible girl in Lamar was Urilla Sutherland, whose parents owned the Exchange Hotel, a magnificent three-story enterprise

Wyatt Earp at the age of twenty-one, when he was the constable in Lamar.

that dominated the sleepy town. Wyatt was about her age and just as eligible, a handsome man with dark, short hair, who carried himself upright. After meeting in December he and Urilla were married at the hotel in early January, with Justice Nicholas Earp officiating. They lived at the hotel until August, when they bought a little house for $50. After all, they were expecting a baby soon and needed to have a place of their own.

But fate had other plans for the young Earps. Typhus was a common enemy of the time, sweeping across Missouri in epidemics, as well as appearing in isolated cases. Urilla was one of those cases. The girl could not fight the disease and nourish her baby too, and she slipped

Top: Urilla Sutherland Earp. Bottom: The home in which Wyatt Earp and his bride lived for only a short time before her death.

into the arms of death that autumn. In November, after knowing his bride for less than a year, Wyatt sold the little house, and that chapter of his life was at an end.

He was not afforded much time to mourn, because the election was coming up. Nicholas and others in the town were under considerable pressure from a group of storekeepers who were up in arms about pigs running loose in the community. Nicholas was a hog farmer himself. The animals were easy to keep, rarely straying far from home, and if there weren't enough food scraps for their slop, they could forage and feed themselves on roots and acorns. In that era, most of the farmers just let them roam unfenced. But when they wandered into town, some folks took exception and wanted the constable to round them up and fine the owners. Wyatt was no hog wrangler—and didn't intend to become one. But the Earps could see that civilization was coming to bear. The people who wielded influence, the people who would bring jobs and money and opportunity to Lamar, wanted the streets free of hogs. If Nicholas Earp was to climb the political-social ladder, he and his kin had to throw in with the Republican city fathers, bankers, and of course his brother's flock of Methodists, against the flock of hogs.

But as the November elections approached, Wyatt decided he didn't want to run for re-election. Urilla had just died, and it was hard to focus his attention on being constable, much less running for election. So his oldest half-brother, Newton, announced himself as a candidate for constable at their father's insistence. Nicholas needed an Earp in that job. But Newton was a quiet farmhand, and Nicholas had no confidence he could win, so he continued to push Wyatt to run. At last, just before the election, Nicholas prevailed, convincing Wyatt to run for the job. The charismatic Wyatt announced himself as a write-in candidate on the penned-up-hogs platform. He won easily over Newton, who'd had enough family drama and moved on to homestead in Kansas. In the same election, Nicholas was elected to Lamar's board of trustees. He was beginning to get the kind of power base of which he had dreamed.

But there was another faction in Lamar, the people who wanted the hogs to run free and eat whatever they found. After all, penned hogs were more expensive to keep and feed. Those folks were former Southerners and people who'd lived in Missouri since before the war, many of them Confederate veterans or sympathizers. To them, the Earps would always be Yankee immigrants.

And there was another unsettling bump in the Earps' road. The Sutherland family, in their grief over losing Urilla, blamed Wyatt for failing to summon doctors until it was too late. One night, when Wyatt and his brothers Virgil and Morgan emerged from dinner at their father's café, they found themselves face to face with Urilla's brothers Fred and Bert, and their friends Granville, Lloyd, and Jordan Brummett. The gang of five had been drinking and were more than ready to insult the town policeman, whose job it was to keep pigs out of the street. Wyatt could almost ignore that kind of teasing, but he couldn't ignore their accusations about Urilla. The drunks said he cared nothing for his beloved wife's passing, and that he didn't take care of her because he was too busy running for office.

A word became a shove, a shove became a punch, and the fight was on. The Earps were outnumbered, but alcohol had taken the edge off their opponents, and the Earps had family loyalty on their side. They stood with their backs together, so one of them saw every approach of the Sutherlands and Brummetts. The fight went on, up and down the street, for a full twenty minutes, finally ending with all the men bloodied, but all three Earps still standing. It was a sign of not only the mixed feelings with which Wyatt was viewed in the community, but of the dark days into which he was descending.

The Sutherland boys hadn't been too far off the mark, and that's part of the reason their words carried such a sting. Indeed, Wyatt had postponed his own grief to follow his father's plans. He was still angry that during the war, his father chased him down repeatedly to stop him from enlisting in the Union army. He hated Nicholas's manipulation of position and power, always working toward using the family to help poke his own fingers into every aspect of the community. And yet, that's exactly the personality Wyatt would take on in his later years, controlling law enforcement and gambling in every town where he lived, sliding himself and his brothers into the jobs where they could be the most valuable.

In late 1870, with the election past and his wife gone, Wyatt was alone, restless, and tempted. He was discredited as a policeman for having a fistfight on Main Street. Plus, his job amounted to nothing more than collecting taxes and getting the occasional drunks off the street, then locking them up in an abandoned stone house because there was still no jail. That was not how he wanted to live.

And there was more trouble coming for him. In the middle of March 1871, the county leaders demanded that Lamar make its annual contribution to the school fund. In fact, the city didn't have the money to contribute, because Constable Wyatt hadn't turned in any of his collections for months. When an audit was conducted, there were questions and a lot of stammering around, with the upshot that Wyatt had properly collected the money but didn't turn it in to the city. Worse, he no longer had it. The county filed suit against Wyatt, along with his father, Uncle J. D., and a family friend named Maupin. Those three were dragged into Wyatt's legal problems because they were his sureties. When he took the job of constable, somebody had to guarantee that he would take good care of the town's money, and they did that in good faith. Then, when he couldn't produce the money he collected, they became liable, and the anger, embarrassment, and accusations flew. So what does a scallywag do when trouble's brewing? He leaves town and gets drunk.

Wyatt drifted south and fell into the company of Ed Kennedy, a man who had a lot more experience than Wyatt at getting into trouble. They crossed the border into Indian Territory and found a tavern, where they got good and drunk with one of the locals, John Shown, a man who had a wagon and a team, but not a riding horse. Shown knew who had some nice ones: Jim and William Keys, over by Fort Gibson. The more the men drank, the better stealing horses sounded. Wyatt and Kennedy would help Shown steal a horse, sell it to get rid of the evidence, and then buy one to keep. In their stupor it sounded like a great plan.

That very night they slipped away into the darkness with two of the Keyses' horses and headed for the Kansas state line to sell them. Then Wyatt and Kennedy planned to travel on, while Shown rode back home with a bill of sale for his new Kansas horse. But when it was getting near dawn, Shown realized that his wife would be worried about him. The trio didn't dare stop with the stolen horses because somebody could come along chasing them at any minute. Shown didn't dare trust Earp and Kennedy to travel on with the horses while he fetched his wife, because after all, they stole them for him. So the plan they concocted was for Shown to hightail it north with the horses. Earp and Kennedy would go get the wife in the Shown wagon. Drunks make odd plans.

In the morning Anna Shown found two strange men in her yard, saying her husband was traveling north with some horses and they were to bring her along. She didn't have much choice but to get in the wagon and go with them. They met Shown and the horses at the place they'd decided on, then Earp headed off at a canter with the horses, and Kennedy, Shown, and Anna followed at a slower pace in the wagon. So far, so good.

That night the three stopped to sleep in a camp along the road, and Jim Keys, owner of the horses, got the drop on them. Anna put on quite a performance, saying thank goodness Keys was there to save them from Kennedy. Her husband and Kennedy listened in wonder as she unfolded a tale of how Kennedy and Earp got poor John drunk and tricked him into stealing the horses, then threatened to shoot him if he tried to tell the law. Kennedy could see that she might get John out of the whole deal, with him, Kennedy, hanging for stealing the horses. So

Kennedy smiled and suggested that they settle the whole thing right there. Keys could take Shown's wagon team, and that would be the end of it, no harm done. But Keys was having none of that and kept his Winchester leveled at the horse thieves.

While Jim Keys was on the chase, his father, William, had gone to Fort Smith to get the law. Since the only law enforcement in Indian Territory was the Indians' own police and courts, any white men breaking the law there were the responsibility of U.S. marshals who were assigned out of the Fort Smith court. Deputy Marshal J. G. Owens heard Keys' story and filed a report with the court that Earp, Kennedy, and Shown, "white men and not Indians or members of any tribe of Indians by birth or marriage or adoption on the 28th day of March A.D. 1871 in the Indian Country in said District did feloniously and willfully steal, take away, carry away two horses each of the value of one hundred dollars, the property goods and chattels of one William Keys." A court commissioner issued a writ, and Deputy Owens was off to the Indian Territory.

Meanwhile, Wyatt sold the stolen animals to the first likely buyer he found across the Kansas line, then waited for Kennedy and the Showns. When his partners in crime didn't show up, he could have headed in any direction to save his own hide. But he revealed his underlying streak of duty and loyalty, returning back into the Territory to find them. Fortunately for him, he was a budding lawman and knew how to ask questions. It didn't take him long to learn that his accomplices were under arrest and there was a U.S. marshal after him. Wyatt took off, and it took Owens six days to find him. By mid-April Owens had him and the others all locked up in Fort Smith.

By that time Kennedy had sided with the Showns in painting Wyatt as the man who coerced him and John into stealing the horses. Anna Shown had perfected her version of the story, signed a sworn statement, and got her husband released, which helped Kennedy win an acquittal too.

Wyatt was arraigned with bond set at $500. But Wyatt Earp knew jails and he knew men, and two weeks later he busted out. A warrant was issued for his arrest, and it was fortunate for Wyatt that he was unknown in that country. Nobody knew where he lived, and the Fort Smith marshals had far too much to do to go look for him. Besides, the Keyses had their horses back. So in November, the warrant was returned unserved.

But in April, it must have been a long ride back to Lamar, with legal trouble on both ends of the journey. Wyatt was leaving a warrant for his arrest in Fort Smith and facing the school lawsuit in Lamar. In fact, he might not have gone back home at all if he'd known that more trouble had been brewing while he was gone. Farmer James Cromwell had filed suit against Wyatt.

Earlier in the year there had been a judgment against Cromwell that he couldn't pay, so Constable Wyatt confiscated a mowing machine from Cromwell's farm and sold it to pay the judgment. The records showed that Wyatt sold the mower for $38, which went toward the judgment, but Cromwell swore in his suit that the mower was worth every bit of $75 and that Wyatt must have pocketed the difference. Cromwell ranted and told everyone he met on the street. So Wyatt's reputation in Lamar was going downhill in a hurry.

It wasn't only the lawsuits and money that worried the Earps. The total of the money owed the school fund, plus the full price of the mower, was less than $300. Between Nicholas, Uncle J. D., and Maupin, they could have come up with that, borrowed it, or worked out a plan for Wyatt to pay it off. The real issue was that, along with the lawsuits, Wyatt should have been facing criminal charges of grand larceny for the funds and petty theft for the mower.

So far no criminal charges had been filed, thanks to Nicholas's influence. But the people of Lamar weren't blind. They knew what was going on, and they talked about it in taverns and on street corners. There were Sutherlands, farmers, taxpayers, parents of schoolchildren, and former Confederates, all talking loudly. If city trustee Nicholas could keep the law from prosecuting his son, then the people would find a way to prosecute Wyatt outside the law. They weren't going to put up with Wyatt stealing their town's money. So there's no question that Wyatt Earp was squirming between a jail sentence and the vigilante wrath of his fellow citizens.

Barton County remained one of the few counties along the Kansas border that never endured a reign of terror by a vigilante committee. But it came very close in the spring of 1871, when a lot of people were saying that was exactly what they needed to take care of the larcenous constable. Although many a quarrel in postwar Missouri boiled over under the pressure of war-time loyalties, the Lamar trouble was not so neatly divided along those lines. The Sutherlands were Yankees, like the Earps. Those out to get the Earps were of both blue and gray stripes. The Earps were still seen as outsiders, high-handed and self-righteous.

As the youngest in a family that swung on the pendulum of Nicholas Earp's ego, Wyatt craved respect and couldn't stand the wave of hatred he faced every day. His mood grew darker, and Nicholas's mood turned just as sour. In the school fund scandal, Nicholas stood to lose everything. His farm, grocery and café, and the keystone, his position as justice. There was no point in staying, being put to shame, and trying to start again in Lamar. Nicholas had run from trouble in Iowa years before, so it was easy for him to run from the Barton County trouble.

When he told Wyatt what he was going to do, the son had to choose for himself. His first concern was his brothers Virgil and Morgan. He didn't want them to stay in Lamar with their little brother in what they knew was a losing fight. There was nothing they could do to help in the legal battle. And did he really want them to risk their lives for him if the mob worked itself up as Wyatt feared? No, it was far better for his brothers to move on with their father. They agreed, and Wyatt wasn't about to stay and face the trouble alone. So it was that a county judge sent a new constable to seize the property of Nicholas Earp, and he found the property sold and abandoned. In the years to come, neither Wyatt nor any of the others in the family would speak of their time in Lamar. That's why they left few tracks for history to follow. After all, to the locals, the Earps were just a family who lived there a short time and ran away to escape their legal problems. Good riddance.

Wyatt was arrested for running a brothel in Illinois and later disappeared from history for a few years in Kansas. He surfaced in Wichita collecting some debts for a businessman, then the town marshal hired him as a policeman. Wyatt still hadn't learned from his mistakes, because just like in Lamar, he got into a fight when somebody insulted his family. In the spring of 1876, the *Wichita Beacon* reported that Wyatt was charged with assault, fined, and fired from the police force.

The marshal must have liked Wyatt's strong-arm tactics, because even though the city council wouldn't let him put Wyatt back on the police force, he put him back on the payroll. A month later the council relented and allowed Wyatt back on the force, and again he repeated one of his previous transgressions. Just like in Lamar, he was charged with collecting money for the city and not turning it in. That time, Wichita took it out of his paycheck.

Of course Wyatt went on to become a legendary lawman whose career rode into the sunset on dime novels and embellished biographies. There's no question that he was effective, or that he enforced the law with a minimum of violence, even declining to carry a gun. But he was always associated with the lowest elements of society. Community leaders detested him, even when they needed his services. And he tried to follow in his father's footsteps by combining public office with influence-peddling for personal gain. It worked better for Wyatt than it had for his father, but even the charismatic Wyatt was only able to manage that delicate balance for short periods of time.

In the years after Barton, Wyatt toughened like sun-baked saddle leather. In Tombstone, Arizona, he evolved into a full-fledged vigilante. He and his brothers repeatedly threatened and beat with pistols the members of an outlaw gang called the Cowboys, then rushed into the legendary gunfight at the O.K. Corral. Virgil was both a deputy U.S. marshal and Tombstone city marshal, and Morgan was a city policeman. Though later testimony would assert that Virgil legally deputized Wyatt and his friend Doc Holliday, Wyatt did not wear a badge that day. At the corral, they killed three of the Cowboys, and in the days that followed, the Cowboys killed Morgan and wounded Virgil. Then Wyatt took over Virgil's job as deputy U.S. marshal, but the badge was merely a mask of legality. He led a vengeance posse that wiped out every man remotely associated with the Cowboys. There was no doubt that the men he and his posse killed needed killing, but they never stood a chance of a trial.

One of the men who rode with Wyatt on that bloody quest was known as Turkey Creek Jack Johnson, a catchy enough assumed name. It replaced his previous assumed name, John William Blount, which replaced John William Blunt, the name he was born with back in Missouri. Jack was one of the Cowboys. He was not a pistolero, but simply a man who was willing to be led. When he and Wyatt met in Tombstone, they discovered their common roots in Missouri—Wyatt made him his friend and confidant in the Cowboys camp.

Wyatt wasn't the first to sway Jack's loyalties. Back in Jasper County, Missouri, Jack, who was then John, and his brother Bud fell under the spell of George Hudson. He was one of the most remarkably bad men to come out of Missouri, with a criminal career that ranged all the way to Colorado. Hudson was guilty of several murders and some creative thefts, including the capture of a whole wagon train load of silver ore. He controlled a gang in southwest Missouri, and in 1876 one of them was arrested for various crimes and lodged in the Webb City jail. George knew the gang could intimidate anyone who was thinking about testifying against the man, and he knew just how to do it. Every man was armed with a good repeating rifle, most of them the new Winchester Model 1873, and two or three revolvers. Their orders were to shoot up in the air to scare people, and keep shooting until they were down to one loaded revolver. That was just in case anyone was foolish enough to shoot back, and they had to shoot their way out. That night, they rode into Webb City, shooting as ordered. Of course, once a bunch of men start shooting, they usually find better targets than the air, such as store windows and signs. So by the time it was over, the town was badly shot up.

The intimidation worked, and nobody was found to testify against the prisoner. But in the course of shooting up the town, two men were killed by the wild spray of bullets and ricochets. That was murder, and the Webb City Riot, as it came to be called, was not going to go away. Hudson and his gang decided it was time to leave the state for a while, and young John Blunt decided it was time to get away from George. Good thing, too, or he might have ended up like his brother Bud. When Hudson's reign ended, Bud and the rest of the bunch made their way back home, Bud was arrested for murdering a railroad employee, and he spent the rest of his life in prison.

Out in Tombstone, John, who was at that time Jack, was never truly committed to the Cowboy gang's way of life. He liked crime's easy money better than he liked working for a living, but he couldn't stomach the Cowboys' terrorism, murders, beating, and preying on the weak. So it was easy for Wyatt to convert Jack. He originally recruited him as a sort of spy, and Jack freely told Wyatt who ran with the Cowboys and revealed such plans as he could learn. Then after the Cowboys ambushed Virgil and Morgan, Missouri roots proved to be stronger than Cowboys loyalty, and Turkey Creek Jack threw in with Wyatt. Of course, there was nobody the Cowboys were more eager to put in the ground, so Jack was incredibly brave to face their guns. But it was Wyatt Earp, the man who once ran from the threat of Missouri vigilantes—and became an Arizona vigilante himself—who rid the west of the Cowboys. And he did it with the help of fellow Missouri fugitive John William Blunt.

Chapter Thirteen

Doc Holladay and the Bounty-Hunting Preacher

Gadfly, Missouri, had its own Doc Holladay. He was not the consumptive dentist who became a famous companion of Wyatt Earp and joined him in the gunfight at the O.K. Corral. In fact, he was a kind, mild-mannered family doctor who grew up near St. Louis, married, and came west to settle in Barry County, northwest of Cassville. There he established his practice and enjoyed a wide circle of friends, counting among his patients most of the congregation of the Methodist church.

The pastor of that little white country church was a circuit rider who was as comfortable on a horse as he was in the pulpit. He was John A. Sartin, a man with deep, unflinching eyes, a man who was resolute in everything he undertook. Being an adventurous boy who loved a good fight, he left home at fifteen and lied about his age to join the 8th Missouri State Militia cavalry, July 1, 1863. In the daring 8th, he served under Captain John Kelso, an unrelenting Bushwhacker hunter.

The 8th rode patrols up and down the border counties, routing suspected secessionists, burning their homes and crops, and treating men, women, and children alike. The merciless militia rode with pistols in their hands and were ready to shoot at the slightest hint of resistance.

*An 1861 Navy Colt of the type
carried by Rev. Sartin.*

When William Larkins was captured and identified as one of a gang who murdered civilian Mark Harmon, Kelso was the officer who gave him an hour head start in exchange for the names of the other eighteen guerrillas in the slaying. Then Kelso's men tracked and killed every one of them. It was an experience from which Sartin would emerge with a hardhanded but clear view of the right, the law, the scripture, the Union, and of his personal responsibility to enforce them all.

In the army Sartin was mentored by an older preacher who told him he had a gift for the ministry. So after the war, with a little study and a few letters, he was ordained and sent into the field as a Methodist. With no single church to call his own, but rather making a circuit from one church to another, he was in the saddle and wearing a black frock coat, roaming some of the same country he'd seen while wearing his blue uniform. Some of those churches had a local pastor to fill in between his visits. Some just suspended services until he came around again. He settled down in Barry County in 1868 as the first one to ride the Shoal Creek circuit, and within a year he'd married pretty local girl Sarah J. Goodnight.

Everyone knew that Sartin carried a Navy Colt in a saddle holster. After all, he often left home on a Saturday night for Sunday services or rode all hours, day and night, to go minister to someone on his or her deathbed. It could be dangerous for a man traveling alone, and Barry County was a wild, barely settled place in the corner of the state bordering Kansas and Indian Territory.

Like any good man of the cloth, Sartin liked the idea of embracing the people of his church under his protective wings. He considered himself a protector of all good things in the wide-ranging circuit he rode. As he came around to each church for services, plus other visits for weddings, funerals, camp meetings, revivals, and baptisms, he took time to talk to people and get to know them. He'd find out what was going on in the community, and if he heard about any crime, he was not afraid to confront the suspects. Before long, Barry County was bubbling with stories about the preacher who rode over to so-and-so's cabin and asked him if he had stolen a hog, or failed to pay a debt, or been paid for a job he didn't finish. Many's the situation he righted just by showing up and talking in his no-nonsense way about who did what, and what needed to be done to set it right. He was a man whose manner and way with words meant he didn't need to pull a hog-leg from its holster to get results.

Being that sort of man, it wasn't surprising that Rev. Sartin became involved in the case of Doc Holladay. Doc was a good physician, and as soon as he set up practice, he started drawing patients from another doctor, Dr. George F. Perry, who maintained a dingy little office in Rocky Comfort. Perry was an ill-tempered drinker and gambler, and not the kind of person most people would want to trust with their health. But he was the only doctor in the area until Holladay came to Barry County.

There wasn't a lot of doctoring business to go around. Those were the days of home remedies, both real and imagined, and childbirth at home, sometimes with midwives. Travel was time-consuming and hard, especially in the wilds of sparsely populated Barry County. When all they had was the unpleasant Perry, folks tended to do it themselves. But when Doc Holladay opened a nice, clean office, made friends in the church and community, and was seen out with his devoted wife, he was a welcome improvement and quickly took patients from Perry.

It was inevitable that at some point the two docs would clash. When it came, it was in court in July 1876. One of Perry's patients sued him for malpractice, and the only expert legal testimony was that of Doc Holladay. Sure enough, he had to tell the truth, and he said on the witness stand that Perry wasn't a very good doctor. Well, Perry had enough. First the younger man came into town and stole his business, then he cost him the lawsuit, and at the same time ruined his reputation, which was going to mean even less business.

Perry had two things in his favor: money and plenty of acquaintances among the less savory element of the community. One of them was Thomas H. "Bud" Crawford, a man who never stayed in one place too long and who had a reputation for doing anything for money. He was just what Perry needed, so Perry went to see Crawford at a tavern in Pierce City, where Crawford was well known. After Perry bought a few rounds of drinks for the house, Crawford began raising his voice. He was able to convince the assembled crowd that an outsider, Dr. Holladay, had lied in court just to ruin poor, faithful Dr. Perry, who had taken such good care of all of them for so long. Crawford roused his friends into a mob that was willing to go ten miles from Pierce City to Gadfly and hang Holladay with a vigilante rope. Of course, the doctor paid Crawford a few bucks for stirring up the crowd and bringing the rope.

But Holladay was no easy mark, certainly not the kind of man to leave his happy home in the company of a bunch of drunken fools who wanted to hang him. When they arrived in his front yard after midnight he opened the door with his shotgun held casually at waist level. After a little conversation, the drunks determined that not one of them was interested enough in the Holladay-Perry feud to walk into the mouth of that scattergun.

Meanwhile, Perry was at home, happily thinking his competition was being eliminated. The next day, when he learned that his lynch mob didn't do its work, he was furious. His next step was to find a legal way to get Holladay in jail, hoping he could raise another mob to bust him out and string him up. He convinced his friend, Justice of the

Peace Amos N. Kelly, that Holladay had lied under oath about the malpractice. Kelly filed criminal perjury charges against Holladay; he had to be arrested. The sheriff and a deputy went to make the arrest, but Holladay was out seeing a patient. The next day, the Gadfly constable, John R. Montgomery, brought him in. It was July 10, 1876.

The day wore on, and as suppertime approached, Holladay's wife became increasingly worried. She sure didn't want to see night fall on their little house while she wondered what happened to Doc in town. So she and her young son walked to the home of the neighbors, the Halls, she left the boy with Mr. Hall and their children, and she walked with Mrs. Hall into town.

There they found that Doc had spent the entire afternoon with Justice Kelly, arguing the case and wrangling over whether Doc had to post an unheard-of bond of $400 on Perry's trumped-up charges. At last, after several wasted hours, Kelly convinced him that the charges had been filed, and there was enough evidence in Perry's affidavit that the charges had to be answered in court. Doc was fed up, and his wife was there waiting for him, so he posted his bond. By the time Doc, his wife, and Mrs. Hall left Justice Kelly's law office, it was near 9 p.m. and almost dark.

Meanwhile, Bud Crawford was still on Dr. Perry's payroll. All day he waited and watched Kelly's law office from a tavern on the opposite corner. The twenty-five-year-old Crawford was a beardless man of average height and weight. With his reddish hair and blue-gray eyes, he looked boyish. That is, until he smiled, revealing a missing front tooth, which, along with his permanent limp and the scratches on his face from a recent brawl, told of a darker side. As the day wore on into evening, he became more liquored up and more free with comments that he was going to kill Doc Holladay, one way or another. If Doc was lodged in jail that night, Crawford would raise a mob, get him out, and lynch him from the highest oak. But if Doc posted bond and walked out, Crawford planned to shoot him.

When Doc left the law office with the women, the evil Crawford was ready. He followed at a distance, so they weren't even aware of him until they were outside the town. Then he walked quickly until he caught up; they heard his footsteps and looked back to see who it was.

In a few steps Crawford covered the remaining distance and was upon them, passing, and blocking their progress toward home. He growled angrily that Doc was a fugitive, and he was taking Doc back to the constable. As he spoke, he pulled his .44 pistol and pointed it at Doc's chest, not more than a foot away.

"What are you doing with that pistol?" Doc demanded. Doc knew Crawford, had even sewed him up after one of his fights. Mrs. Hall took a step back, and the terrified wife threw her arms around her husband's chest, as if she could shield him from the big revolver.

"You're resisting arrest," Crawford clipped, clearly liquored up and on edge.

"Why, Bud, you must be a fool. You are not mad at me. I am your friend," Doc said, taking a step toward him with an outstretched hand.

Suddenly the Colt lurched, its boom shaking the woods along the road, its fire burning Mrs. Holladay's wrist, and the bullet entering at the point of Doc's collarbone. It ripped through his throat, and the women screamed. Mrs. Holladay tried to hold Doc, but he rotated slowly to his right and she let him gently to the ground, where he whispered, "I am shot. I am killed." In a matter of two minutes, his prognosis would be proven correct.

By that time Crawford was back in town. What he'd done had no legal standing. He wasn't a lawman, and Doc was free on bond. There was no open warrant for him. Crawford's drunken talk was all just a bluff to get Doc to resist, but in the end, it amounted to nothing more than cold-blooded murder.

The next morning an inquest was held, and Justice Kelly once more tried to help his friend Dr. Perry. After the coroner heard the story of the killing from the two women who witnessed it, Squire Kelley cross-examined them. He tried repeatedly to get them to tell more about how Crawford had been trying to bring Doc to a constable, and how Doc had resisted. But it got nowhere, and the jury clearly saw that Crawford was a murderer.

Even before the inquest verdict, the sheriff and his deputies had come from Cassville to look for Crawford; they came upon a camp he made, hidden below a little bluff deep in the woods. In fact, they were so close on his heels that their quarry had run off, leaving his blanket and a bag of fried chicken and boiled eggs. They pressed the hunt but lost the trail. Crawford disappeared. In his wake, Doc's friends posted a $1,000 reward for the killer, dead or alive. The reward got the attention of everybody in four counties. Men formed posses, asked questions, and checked vacant buildings, and still Crawford seemed to have vanished from the county.

The sad story might have ended that way. But there was one man who wouldn't let it rest. A man who was not bound by a sheriff's limits of county lines. It was Reverend Sartin. He was a shepherd, and someone had murdered one of his flock. There were two other motivating factors for the bounty-hunting pastor. One, with his experience in the bloody militia, he knew he could find Crawford and handle him. Second, he did not want to see his community descend into the chaos of mob justice. By serving as a lone vigilante he hoped to save the town from lynching Crawford. So he kissed Sarah goodbye and rode out, the old Navy Colt in the saddle holster and a new Smith & Wesson cartridge revolver on his belt.

Sartin preached and hunted, hunted and preached, for over a month. At last, the *Pierce City Empire* of September 16 reported that Sartin had brought Crawford in and collected his $1,000 reward. Crawford mounted a spirited defense, swearing that Justice Kelly assigned him to guard Holladay, but he was certainly not a legally sworn deputy, and nobody, including Kelly, would back him up. He was charged with murder, transferred to the Springfield jail, and died there while awaiting his trial.

Rev. John A. Sartin, vigilante pastor.

Sartin apparently liked the work, thought he was really good at it, and thought it was a valuable community service, plus a good way to supplement his meager preacher's wages. The April 28 edition of the *Empire* carried Sartin's advertisement headlined "Hunting Strays," offering to recover missing property, whether lost or stolen. He solved several minor cases, some for which he was hired and some that offered rewards. Then in October of 1881 some horses were stolen from Billy Withers. Other livestock had gone missing, and there were rumors that it was a gang of men doing the stealing, so Barry County posted a reward of fifty dollars a head for the thieves. That bounty was more than enough to motivate Sartin.

Within a couple of weeks he'd arrested two local men, but he knew there were more. Sartin convinced the two that there was no sense in suffering while their cohorts went free, so they told him whom he was looking for. There were three more, but they had left the area. Sartin tracked them over the line into Kansas and started making inquiries in Oswego. While talking with a man on the street he saw a man on the opposite corner whom Sartin thought was staring his way and acting suspicious. Sartin struck out with a purposeful stride, walking directly toward the man with his hand on the Smith & Wesson under his coat. Sure enough, the man was one of those Sartin was after, and he took off running. The preacher chased him at a dead run for a half mile, at which point the man ducked into a lumberyard and hid under a pile of slats. It didn't take Sartin long to find him and pull him out by his boots.

He squealed that there were two more who'd gone to Indian Territory. Sartin hired two deputies to haul the prisoner back into Missouri for him and took off, following the last two fugitives to Vinita in the Territory. He quickly apprehended one, then asked around town where he could find the last fellow. Armed with a tip, he proceeded to the man's house, knocked on the door, and asked to speak to the man of the house. The woman who answered the door refused to cooperate, so Sartin simply went up the street, located a justice, got a search warrant and hired two deputies, and was back in twenty minutes.

Though Sartin always went heeled, he didn't consider himself a pistolero. He preferred to put his trust in the power of his personality and a healthy helping of divine protection. Indeed, his self-confidence and powerful presence bested many an adversary. And that's how he planned to handle the last of his horse thieves.

He calmly showed the woman the warrant. Then, leaving the local deputies at the front door, he entered the house, looked around, and, finding nobody other than the woman, went on up the stairs. At the top he was met by a stout young man reaching for the pistol on his belt. Sartin didn't wait to exchange words but grabbed his prey by the shirt and crotch and in one smooth motion threw him headlong down the stairs.

There was one more thing to do before he could ride back to Missouri with his prisoners. When he had arrived in Vinita, in order to move the investigation along, he made it known that he'd happily pay twenty-five dollars for information on the man he wanted. He planned to pay as promised, and following the arrest Sartin returned to the man who'd pointed him to the last thief. He had to admit he didn't have the money. A man true to his word, Sartin waited in Vinita until the Barry County sheriff wired the money, then paid his informant before leaving town.

Back in Barry County he arrived to a hero's welcome. The two local men were still in jail, as was the one caught in Oswego and sent back on the train. Then Sartin rode in with the two he caught in the Territory, making a total of five. No doubt the publicity was excellent for attracting new members to his Methodist church.

Rev. John Sartin was a professional bounty hunter. He was paid, often handsomely, for bringing in bad guys, so perhaps he doesn't fit the mold of a true vigilante. And yet, Sartin was a man who hunted on principle, who took a case only when he believed in its merit. It's likely that even without the cash, he would have hunted the same men to set aright the scales of justice, trusting in the rewards of a life well lived.

CHAPTER FOURTEEN

THE BALD KNOBBERS

"Timber!" The woodsman's call of warning was the perfect metaphor for the trouble brewing in Taney County twenty years after the Civil War. It started slowly, picking up speed, grabbing, breaking, and tearing everything around it, until it finally came crashing down. That's the way the Bald Knobbers ripped through southwest Missouri.

A railroad tie is a mighty thing. Eight-and-a-half feet of stout, straight-grained oak, chestnut, or hickory. Most men can barely heft one end of a tie and drag it. But in the Ozarks, there were men who were known to work as tie hackers well past their sixtieth birthdays. Such a man could leave home in the morning with his wagon, fell a giant tree with a crosscut saw, clean the limbs with a double-bit ax, square it with a broad ax, and saw it to length. He looked for trees just over a foot in diameter and tall enough to yield two ties. He might sit down at midday to eat a hard-boiled egg, a biscuit, and a couple of persimmons. Then he'd lift the end of a tie on his mighty shoulder, set it into the wagon, grab the other end, and slide it up onto the stack. He'd repeat that for each one and be home before sundown with a dozen or more ties. In those days following the Civil War, the hill roads streamed with lone hackers and teams of hackers, all headed to market.

Tie rafters made rafts of railroad ties and floated them down Big Piney River to market. Disputes over timber land helped fuel the rise of the Bald Knobbers.

The railroads built steadily westward, arriving at Rolla during the war and connecting America coast to coast in 1869. They came to Springfield in 1870, then Pierce City, Neosho, and even Indian Territory by 1871. They brought families to the Ozarks, fanning out to settle the wilderness. The supplies they needed became available in little general stores, which were usually post offices too, and more tracks and depots meant more places to sell livestock, produce, and crafts.

Railroad ties continued to be needed for new construction all over the country, as well as for the never-ending work of maintenance on the existing lines. Tie hacking was big business in the scantily populated Ozarks, where land was painted with the brush of pine, poplar, cedar, oak, hickory, maple, and chestnut. A lot of the land belonged to absentee owners, corporations, railroads, mining companies, and banks. They neither knew nor cared who was cutting their trees, and that worked out well because most hackers didn't care whose land they worked on.

The Homestead Act was passed in 1862; after the war, people really started to take advantage of it. There were plenty of new folks moving onto government land, hardworking farm families who would own the land outright after they lived on it and worked it for five years. But Confederate war veterans were prohibited from homesteading, so the landowners were largely Republicans, and largely veterans of the Union army, or at least held Union sympathies.

Those settlers worked day and night to earn and maintain their little farms. And none of them could stand the thought of squatters, who also came to the Ozarks in droves after the war. They were people who had no money to buy land. Many of them Democrats, many of them Confederate veterans, and almost all Southern sympathizers. Squatters moved onto public land, or even in the deep hollows of someone else's property. If they were discovered and kicked off, they just moved on, with little worry about what they left behind, because their crude homes weren't much of a loss. Some of them were earnest, flat-broke people who had no other place to live. But some were the shiftless kind who expected to live free. Among them were the lazy ones, the ones looking for the unguarded chicken coop, and the ones who picked someone else's vegetables in the dark of night.

Worst of all, everybody hated taxes. So the ones who grudgingly paid their due truly detested the ones who paid none. People who owned nothing owed nothing. They drove on the roads and bridges, enjoyed the protection of law, and used the water, soil, and timber but did nothing to contribute. The Southern veterans weren't allowed to vote or run for office, so they had no interest in government. Banks wouldn't loan them money, and stores wouldn't extend credit. And to make matters even worse, the established members of the community sometimes learned that squatters were living together as husband and wife without the benefit of marriage. Stereotypes grew, along with lines dividing two classes of people who saw themselves and the other class quite differently.

The stereotypes were unfortunately all too accurate. Chances are, when a pig was stolen, it was done by the same man who squatted on government land, who beat his unmarried woman, who fought in the tavern, and who sent his children out to steal apples and potatoes from the neighboring farm. They were pretty safe in their mischief, too. Few laws were on the books, and most of the lawmen were only qualified to hold office because they were military veterans. When crimes were committed miles from the sheriff's office, he got the report when the trail was cold. He could go out and investigate, but roads were few and far between, and the crooks could hide in any of a thousand hollows, coves, and caves.

Into that divided society came a singular man who would change the history of Missouri. He was Captain Nate N. Kinney, a native of Virginia, a Union veteran of the Civil War who had served the army seven years in all. After the war he became a Post Office Department agent who tracked stagecoach robbers and other mail thieves. He had no patience if they resisted arrest, killing several of them. That approach to swift and decisive justice got the attention of the Atchison, Topeka and Santa Fe Railroad, which hired him as a detective.

When Kinney was ready for a break from law enforcement, he'd saved enough money to buy a saloon in Springfield, and that's where he made real money for the first time. So in 1883, at the age of forty-eight, he sold the place and moved to the country in high style, with his wife and children. In looking for a place to settle, Kinney focused his attention south, in Taney County, where he became instant friends with other wealthy Republicans. Kinney built a big home, then made it bigger, and he stocked his land with purebred hogs, cattle, and horses.

Kinney was a handsome giant, standing six feet, seven inches tall, with black hair and mustache, dark, languid eyes, and a granite chin, surmounting a physique that matched his frame. A man like that commanded attention wherever he went, and Kinney was a man who was happy to not only climb onto the pedestal, but to build it himself. At

*Captain Nate N. Kinney, founder and leader of
the Bald Knobbers.*

the nearby Oak Grove School he started the first of several Sunday schools, teaching there and leading the singing too. With his background, reputation, money, and appetite for leadership, people of all stripes naturally turned to him in everything from faith and family to politics, city development, and law enforcement.

One of the things that got Kinney's goat was that in the twenty years since the Civil War, Taney County had been the scene of more than three dozen murders, with not one suspect arrested. Of course the lack of prosecutions wasn't unusual in that era, when evidence was seldom found. If there were no witnesses, murder was a pretty safe crime. But prosecuted or not, the number of murders was unacceptable. There were other crimes too. Livestock disappeared. Houses were burglarized. Debts weren't paid. Animals were stolen or killed and crops burned in efforts to force families to abandon their land or sell at a cheap price. And for a variety of reasons, the law failed to provide any protection from the crooks who found their sanctuary among the remote hollows of the county. There were rumors that bribes had been paid to the sheriff, prosecutor, witnesses, and even judges. To a man of action like Kinney, something had to be done.

Kinney was not ambitious for political office. Rather, his interests lay in playing chess, moving the pieces around, trading favors and friendships, making connections. He saw himself as a power broker and a leader of leaders. Not the one in office, but the guiding star for those in office. And above all, he insisted on a lawful, godly place for his family to live.

So it was that on a half-moon night in January of 1885 he called a meeting of a dozen handpicked men in the side room of Yell Everett's store in Forsyth. Emotions ran high, just because of the meeting place. Only a couple of years before, Yell's brother Jim had been shot dead in front of the store by a known local ruffian, Al Layton, who was arrested, then acquitted for lack of evidence. There in the store, with Jim's spirit looking on, the staunch men of Taney County organized the Law and Order League. They agreed that Kinney would be the leader. Of course, that's exactly what he wanted, and he took on the job with the enthusiasm of the biblical David. They made it a secret society, and Kinney devised a secret vow and initiation ceremony. The group grew in number until the dramatic night later that year when they announced to the world that they were open for business.

Kinney called the next meeting on Snapp's Bald, a grassy, treeless hilltop above Oak Grove School. There in the darkness, a bonfire signaled that the meeting was starting, and men came from miles around. If they knew the password they were admitted into the circle above the trees, and if they wanted to join the league they were taken to one side to prepare for training and swearing-in. They stood and quietly repeated their oath, then sat on the ground as the granite-shouldered Kinney towered over them and spoke. He organized them into groups that could be called together quickly. The men's adrenaline must have been flowing from the minute they arrived, as the mystery and tension were all kindled into flames of righteous devotion. The Law and Order League was a mouthful of a name, so before long everybody called them the Bald Knobbers.

They soon had a chance to show their worth to the community. A local man named Newton Herrell was arrested and jailed for killing his widowed mother's boyfriend because he wouldn't marry her. A hundred Bald Knobbers, with kerchiefs tied around their faces, rode into

*James K. Polk McHaffie unlocked the
jail for the Bald Knobbers' first mission.*

Forsyth about 10:00 p.m., pulled Sheriff James McHaffie out of his house, and forced him to go unlock the jail for them. He begged them not to lynch Herrell, so whether it was his pleading or the fact that it was their first raid, Herrell was not lynched, just beaten bloody with ropes. Then the raiders made a couple of nooses with the blood-stained ropes and left them lying on the judge's bench in the courtroom.

Those nooses carried the message that the court had better take care of Herrell or the committee would. The raiders must have left feeling good, but they had not yet proven that they'd follow through with such threats. Herrell was acquitted, and—again—there were rumors that the judge or jury, or both, had been bribed.

Kinney and friends yearned to act more decisively, and they soon had a far bigger reason than the Herrell case. An old English couple, the Dickensons, had a large and beautiful general store in a settlement five miles north of Forsyth. Like all store owners of that era, they graciously extended credit to their customers, especially the hardworking farmers who barely scratched a living from their rocky hillside farms. Such families regularly bought on credit and cleared their account after railroad ties, crops, livestock, or crafted goods were sold.

Among the Dickensons' customers were the Taylor brothers, Frank and Tubal, as rough men as that country ever produced, and with no obvious means of earning a living. They had an old debt at the store, and when John Dickenson refused to extend Frank further credit for a pair of shoes, Frank became irate. He took the shoes under his arm and walked out without paying for them. Then he stormed across the street and bought a bullwhip, muttering under his breath, "I'm gonna wear this out on old man Dickenson."

That night the Taylor brothers and some others were in town drinking hard. When they were properly awash in corn liquor, they strode over to the Dickenson store, awakened the old couple, and when John Dickenson shuffled to the door, pushed their way in. Frank was beating Dickenson with the newly purchased bullwhip when Mrs. Dickenson

John Dickenson in front of his store, where he was beaten by thugs, an act that was later avenged by the Bald Knobbers.

ran in with a fireplace poker to defend her helpless husband. At that, the outlaws' pistols came out, and they fired point blank at the poor couple, hitting him in the mouth and shoulder, and her in the head. As they walked out triumphantly, Frank left the bloody bullwhip neatly coiled by the door.

Everybody was enraged. The sheriff was joined by his deputies, the Bald Knobbers, and others, all pouring over the hills to arrest the Taylor brothers. Ironically, the assailants thought they'd killed the old couple, and they hid out until they heard that the Dickensons survived. Once they found out they weren't murderers, the Taylor brothers figured they'd get out of the trouble pretty easily, so they came in to surrender. The men who rode with them in the Dickenson attack were never identified and may have left the county for good.

As Frank and Tubal sat in the Forsyth jail that night, they heard a thunder of hooves rolling up Main Street and knew what it meant. Vigilantes. When the deputies guarding the jail saw the Bald Knobbers riding in, they decided to take the night off, leaving the vigilantes to go about their job with no interference. The Taylors heard voices outside the jail, and before long there was a startling "wham," repeated over and over. That meant sledgehammers were being used to batter down the steel door of the jail. The Taylors moaned and cried for help, but there was none. Soon the door gave way, the brothers were hauled out, their hands tied, and they were put on horses for the short trip to a big oak tree about halfway between town and the Dickenson place. There, they were treated to a trial that lasted only a few seconds. The verdict was "guilty," and they were hanged from the oak.

Before the raiders rode out, one eased his horse over to the dangling corpse of Frank Taylor and slipped a note under his suspenders. Scrawled in pencil across the top of a shoebox it said, "This is the first, but it won't be the last."

That was the start the Bald Knobbers needed. They rode the hills waking people from their sleep, calling them from their dinner tables, and startling them in the fields. They whipped some men with switches. They left bundles of switches as a warning to others that they might be whipped if they didn't straighten up. Some people were punished, and some were told to get out of the county. Like the Slickers decades before, more than one Bald Knobber was known to buy a farm at a bargain price from a man who was dragged out of his home and whipped. A Bald Knobber might have a bill of sale already written out, and the beating victim, willing to do anything to save his life, would sign away his property for a few dollars. A few of the Bald Knobbers concealed their identity with kerchiefs or crude masks made from flour sacks. But as time went by they grew bolder, riding unafraid for anyone to know who was a member of their secret order.

Wild animals, or unpenned hogs or cattle, could get into a cornfield and ruin the crop. If a farmer killed such animals he was considered justified, and that was one of the Bald Knobbers' missions. They killed loose animals. Of course, like everything else they did, it led to praise

Although this scene of Bald Knobbers lying in wait beside a railroad track is from a 1919 motion picture entitled The Shepherd of the Hills, *the masks they're wearing accurately depict the ones worn by the original vigilantes.*

and damnation. In some cases, they were considered heroes for saving a man's crops. In other cases, they were accused of killing a farmer's stock so he'd go broke and have to sell out to them at a cheap price.

As vigilantes go, the Bald Knobbers were uniquely farsighted. They considered a broad section of law and morals to be under their jurisdiction. While other vigilantes acted after a crime in the interest of vengeance or punishment, Bald Knobbers were just as likely to work at crime prevention. More than any other long-standing vigilante group, they considered themselves moral guardians of the community. They were as much community planners as law enforcers.

On the law enforcement side of that equation, they were rough and ready. There was the case of Jim Brown, a Taney County man known as a career criminal, who had been living in Arkansas to avoid prosecution for what he'd done around Forsyth. Then in late August 1885, he decided to come home, and as he walked along, he stole a few things from a couple of farmhouses. The J. W. Nave family was home when Brown barged into their cabin near the town of Protem. Threatening them with a pistol, he quickly took some eggs and a nice quilt on which to bed down, and then left. Word spread, a few men tracked him, including the Naves' son Will, then a few Bald Knobbers joined the posse, and it grew to over fifty men.

Brown made it to his grandfather's house outside Forsyth, where he settled down with his quilt, feeling that he was safely home. But the vigilantes tracked him there, and when he saw them approaching up the hill, he slipped out and disappeared into a hollow. Knowing they were close to catching their man, the posse spread out in a line and moved steadily through the trees. Young John Manes happened to be the one descending a hill directly into Brown's hiding place in the hollow. With his pistol leveled, Brown watched Manes's approach, and when the boy was within about twenty feet, Brown fired once, blowing a fatal hole through his stomach. But young Manes was strong and had his Winchester cocked. The fugitive came up out of the brush snarling, "I got you with my pistol, and I'll get the rest of 'em with your rifle," and reached for the long gun. Just then Manes fired, tearing a gash along the length of Brown's forearm. Manes cocked and fired again, putting a round below Brown's shoulder.

The posse heard the shots and came running. By the time they congregated in the hollow, Manes was dying and Brown was out of sight. But they stayed on his blood trail and saw that he stopped in a farmer's springhouse for a drink of cold milk. Then they had to stop, because it was too dark to track. They only hoped that the wounded fugitive would stop for the night too. Sure enough, as the sun rose the next morning they saw Brown in the tall grass across an unmowed field, lying against the fence. He was weak from loss of blood, but still, none of the men was foolish enough to walk into his gun sights. The posse knelt about one hundred yards away and talked, joked, and wondered how they could get him. Then he made his mistake. When he rose and turned his back to make his getaway, one of the deadeye Taney County squirrel hunters put a rifle bullet through his heart, and Brown flopped headlong over the fence.

As the vigilantes congratulated one another on a successful hunt, they noticed that among them was John H. Haworth, a man who had stoutly refused to join the Bald Knobbers. One of them said, "Well, I guess now's the time we make a Bald Knobber out of John Haworth." They smiled and enticed him with membership in their band, but Haworth was against the whole idea. Even though he'd been a part of the Jim Brown posse, he said, "You'll never make a Bald Knobber out of me."

As a force for justice in the Brown chase, they'd been the law when no law was available. But the trouble remained that they were vigilantes. The regimented Captain Kinney couldn't possibly know what they

John H. Haworth, who refused to join the posse
and became a leading Anti-Bald Knobber.

did on their own, when they were away from his meetings and his sanctioned Bald Knobber rides. For that matter, if some of the members made a raid that they knew wouldn't meet with Kinney's approval, they'd just deny it to Kinney. Such was the case on the night twenty men rode to the farm of John Haworth, the man who wouldn't join after the Brown posse. They told him he had to join the Bald Knobbers or sell them his farm, and when he refused, they shot his roof full of holes. Haworth recognized John McGill, the man who did the talking, as a Bald Knobber. A couple of days later Kinney heard about the raid and immediately rode over to tell Haworth in person that his men had nothing to do with it. But Haworth wouldn't believe that Kinney didn't authorize the raid. He told Kinney to get off his place, saying, "If you stay here you're going to die, and you don't want to die here." Kinney had to ride away knowing he had made himself responsible for a constantly changing collection of men he couldn't possibly control.

By that time, almost every man in the county was going armed. Revolvers were plainly worn on belts, as much as a warning as for action. Winchester and Springfield rifles and all kinds of shotguns were a common sight. Then, as with any citizen vigilantism, enemies of the Bald Knobbers began to rise up. Some were upright members of the community who opposed the violence. Some were no-good hill people who opposed the imposition of law and order. One of those was Andrew Cogburn. He'd made himself a pest to Captain Kinney by sneaking into Bald Knobber meetings to spy, and by telling people on the street he was going to kill Kinney.

The animosity between the two came to a climax on a Sunday night as a crowd waited for worship services to start at Oak Grove School. The previous evening, Cogburn had started a brawl in town and caused some damage at a tavern, resulting in a warrant for his arrest on charges of public disturbance. Deputy Galba Branson went to church that Sunday night with the warrant, because Cogburn let it be known that he was going to be there. Everybody expected him to make trouble. And

Andrew Cogburn at about age eighteen, two years before he faced Captain Kinney in a gunfight.

foolish as it seems, since the warrant was for a minor offense, Cogburn had bragged loudly that he would never be taken alive.

The young Deputy Branson was no fool, and he thought it would be a good idea to ask Kinney if he'd like to handle Cogburn. Branson sent the warrant with a couple of riders up the hill to meet Kinney on the road before he got to church. They asked Kinney if he wanted the warrant, and warned him Cogburn was armed and itching for a fight. Captain Kinney put the warrant in his pocket, patted the Colt revolver that was buckled around his waist, and thanked the men for the warning. He would handle Cogburn just fine.

When Kinney rode in, the sun was settling behind the bald knob, and a crowd of men was gathered in the schoolyard. Some were Bald Knobbers, and some were friends of Cogburn. They all knew somebody was going to end up dead, but the action happened quicker than anyone expected. Kinney had no more dismounted his horse than Cogburn strode confidently around the corner of the building. Kinney pulled his pistol and announced clearly. "Andrew Cogburn, you're under arrest. Put your hands up." Cogburn threw up his left hand as a distraction and drew his pistol with his right hand. It wasn't surprising that he was able to draw against a man who already had a gun leveled at him. Many a lawman with pistol in hand has faced an armed criminal, only to have the outlaw draw and fire before the officer could react and fire his own weapon. So it was that Kinney saw Cogburn pull his big Colt and bring it up to level. Cogburn pulled the trigger, and Kinney should have been killed. But there was a click and a moment of hesitation. Then Kinney fired, striking Cogburn squarely in the heart, killing him instantly, and he fell still clutching his malfunctioning weapon.

The Bald Knobbers brought benches from the building, placed them around the dead man, and wouldn't let anyone near until the inquest the next morning. They wanted the coroner and sheriff to see that Cogburn's pistol was in his hand. By that time the crowd around the schoolhouse had grown to several hundred people, and the intimidation by the Bald Knobbers was complete. Kinney's men testified to the proper way he handled the arrest, and not one of Cogburn's friends stepped up to say a word to the coroner against Kinney. The official report said that it was a legal arrest and that Cogburn attempted to shoot first, but the cylinder of his revolver failed to turn. There were no charges filed.

In many of Cogburn's adventures, including spying on Bald Knobber meetings, he was accompanied by his friend Sam Snapp, who was at the schoolhouse and saw Kinney gun down Cogburn. After the inquest cleared Kinney of any charges in the killing, Snapp made it known that he intended to get revenge by killing Kinney. But Captain Kinney had a bodyguard named George Washington "Wash" Middleton who took it

Wash Middleton, bodyguard of Captain Kinney.

upon himself to make sure Snapp never got close enough to take a shot at Kinney. In fact, Wash thought the best way to protect Kinney was to get rid of Snapp permanently.

Middleton saw a chance to kill Snapp in Forsyth, and he really didn't care who was around. He was sure Snapp would be armed. Everybody was going armed. But Wash had no doubt he could get the drop on Snapp and kill him. As Snapp came down the sidewalk singing a song making fun of the Bald Knobbers, Middleton stepped out of John Kintry's store. He stopped Snapp short and told him he didn't like that song. Snapp had an impudent reply, and Middleton said he was "nothing but a low-down Bushwhacker," hoping Snapp would go for his gun. Snapp shot back an insult of his own but still wouldn't reach for a weapon, and Middleton was out of patience. He drew the pistol from beneath his coat and shot Snapp down in cold blood. Snapp fell in a heap.

Middleton knelt down, thinking to quickly pull out Snapp's pistol and put it in the dead man's hand so he could claim self-defense. Snapp had to be heeled. But no, there was no holster, and not one of the big sheath knives that so many men carried. Middleton checked every pocket in Snapp's clothes, there was a not a weapon on him, except a little pocketknife in the pocket of his overalls.

Middleton stood and ran, heading south. Shooting Snapp was one thing. But shooting him when he was unarmed was quite another. He'd done it right in the middle of town, so there were plenty of witnesses. Middleton had a brother in Arkansas and thought he could get there and be safe from the law. But after running through the woods, up and down hills, Middleton couldn't run another step. He collapsed, exhausted, and leaned against an outcrop where a steady drip of water gave him a nice, cool drink. Unfortunately for Middleton, his friend and fellow Bald Knobber Galba Branson, now the sheriff, knew where to look for him, and pretty soon Branson's horse came plodding up. The two men exchanged pleasantries, and Middleton went back with Branson to the Forsyth jail.

Middleton never seemed too worried as he waited in jail for his trial. When that day came, he was a little surprised, but still not worried, when he was found guilty of second-degree murder. The verdict meant the court found that he was provoked into the shooting, and it wasn't a premeditated act. The jury set a sentence of forty years, but the judge thought they were far too impassioned, reducing it to fifteen years. Middleton went back to the Forsyth jail to await his transfer to the Missouri State Penitentiary. But just after midnight everybody found out why he never was worried. The jail door was unlocked, and Wash Middleton walked out, thankful for his Bald Knobber friends. Again, he headed for his brother in Arkansas, and this time he made it.

CHAPTER FIFTEEN

THE BALD KNOBBERS ON TRIAL

The Cogburn and Snapp shootings increased resistance to the Bald Knobbers, and a countermovement, the Anti-Bald Knobbers, gained strength and new members every time the Bald Knobbers acted. Vigilantes rose up against the vigilantes. Yes, the Bald Knobbers were acting in the public interest, and yes, they were ridding the community of some bad people. But their violent methods almost always led to more violence. What began as Kinney's commitment to crusading, beneficent leadership descended into an era of terrorism and reprisal. In 1888 the Anti-Bald Knobbers had had enough, and they determined to end the reign of Captain Kinney.

The county was still offering a reward for the return of Wash Middleton, but the city fathers, who were all Bald Knobbers, considered that merely a matter of bookkeeping. In time they'd retract that reward. Meanwhile, the murdered Sam Snapp's family and other Anti-Bald Knobbers were thirsting for vengeance. They put up their own reward for Wash Middleton, in addition to the county's reward, and set about finding a man to collect it. They hired Jim Holt, a man with a dim past that involved hunting runaway slaves for the bounty money and, when that business ran out, calling himself a private investigator. He trailed Middleton to his brother's place in the Boston Mountains of Arkansas.

To get there he had to cut through the reeds along the Buffalo River, then wade through water up to his chin to cross. When he got there, he couldn't locate Middleton. So Holt set up a camp and started watching what was going on in the area. He heard about a July 4th picnic at Parthenon, Arkansas, and figured Middleton might show up there. Sure enough, when the 4th rolled around, Holt spotted his man there in the crowd and approached for what would prove to be a classic Western shoot-out. The crowd parted as Holt approached and, stopping not more than fifteen feet away, told Middleton he was under arrest. Middleton, who was not a man to be intimidated, squared around to Holt, growling, "I don't know that I am," and drew his revolver. But the experienced Holt was faster, drawing and killing Middleton with one shot to the chest.

Unfortunately for Holt, when he got back to Taney County expecting to collect a huge reward, he was disappointed to find that the county wouldn't pay its portion. The reward was for the return of a live Middleton to serve out his sentence. The Snapps, however, were happy to pay what they'd promised for Middleton's death.

Anti-Bald Knobbers were unorganized and seldom met. No individual ascended to lead them, which is partly because many were peaceful men who wanted nothing more than an end to the violence. And yet, the existence of the Anti-Bald Knobbers loaned credibility to anybody who wanted to speak out against Kinney and his men, or anybody who wanted to strike back at them. Such a person might be a hog rustler, horse thief, wife beater, or arsonist, but he only had to call himself an Anti-Bald Knobber and somebody was bound to listen to him. As a result, Bald Knobbers were blamed for many a crime to which they had no connection.

Kinney continued to stand tall as the voice of reason. The night-riding Bald Knobbers continued their meetings and raids, though a flogging was as far as they went, and the rides were more likely to end in a bundle of switches on a doorstep, not more corpses swinging from trees.

But their opponents grew more vocal, wrote letters to the newspapers, and spread outright lies, inventing stories of Bald Knobber terrorism. Then the Anti-Bald Knobbers held a mass meeting and elected three men to go to Governor John S. Marmaduke, using the Cogburn and Snapp killings as a platform, begging the governor to send in the state militia.

The governor wisely refused, but Kinney was concerned that the idea had been pitched to the seat of government, and might be pitched again. He knew if the militia descended on Taney County, outright warfare would erupt. There were people in the hills who'd love to shoot at the blue uniforms, and others who'd love to shoot at any outside authority who came to enforce the governor's will. Once the shooting started, it would be hard for anyone to tell who the enemy was. So he called a meeting of both sides, and to his credit, it was well attended by men from both camps. In one of his most brilliant moves, Kinney used the meeting to form a second delegation to visit the governor. It was a mixture of Bald Knobbers and their adversaries, and when they got to St. Joseph they told the governor everything was fine and they didn't need the militia.

Still, the concerned governor sent his own man, Adjutant General J. C. Jamison, a Confederate Civil War veteran who might command some respect from both groups in Taney County. Indeed, he met separately with Bald Knobbers and Anti-Bald Knobbers and told them both their causes were admirable, but illegal, and they had to quit completely and immediately. But both sides knew there was only one man who could make that happen: Kinney.

He called a meeting on the Forsyth square, in the broad daylight of a beautiful spring day, 1886, and told the Bald Knobbers they'd accomplished what they set out to do. Their era was finished. At his direction they adopted a new set of resolutions, stating that they stood ready to assist law enforcement if called upon, but that the authorities were qualified to do their jobs without them. Most important, they resolved to disband the "Citizens Committee."

Men still rode at night. But they weren't Kinney's men. He had such sway over them that they adhered to their promise to disband. So it was somebody else out terrifying citizens of the county, using the old Bald Knobber name. So people still thought it was Kinney's men, ill will continued to build against the former Bald Knobbers, and Kinney and other former leaders of the group continued to be threatened. So Kinney always went armed, and when he spoke at church he laid both his belt pistols, Long Tom and Short Tom, on the pulpit.

By 1888 there had been a series of lawsuits against a Forsyth store owner named J. S. B. Berry, and Kinney was one of those who testified against him. So the stage was set for trouble, and things got worse when Berry's store went into receivership. The sheriff was the receiver, but Berry spread the word that anybody who tried to liquidate the store would be killed. The worried sheriff, a former Bald Knobber, turned to Kinney, as so many had done for so long, and asked him to take over as receiver. The fearless captain was happy to help, not thinking he was really in any danger.

The Anti-Bald Knobbers thought Berry got a raw deal in the lawsuit, and there was talk of helping him get the store back at any cost. Among his friends Berry counted Bill Miles, a loudmouthed Anti-Bald Knobber from the old days. Miles and others had been busy gathering weapons, and on Saturday they met to store them away for an armory at the home of Tom Layton near Kirbyville. When news of the gathering reached Kinney, he was rightfully afraid Miles and friends would use those guns to seize Berry's store. So Kinney and his men rode into the Layton yard and interrupted the gathering. Layton, Miles, and their friends each picked up a rifle and walked out to meet the captain. Among them was Haworth, the man who'd threatened Kinney after his roof was shot full of holes. "We're here to disarm you," Kinney proclaimed.

Layton answered, "Well, we don't believe you'll do that."

Kinney said, "We are doing this in the interest of peace," to which Layton replied, "What you are doing is a pretty way to start a fuss and we will settle that right here. You might disarm us after we're dead, but not while we are living."

Seeing the possibility of serious bloodshed, Kinney backed down. "All right," he said. "But on Monday we'll be selling the goods from the store, and I'm warning all you men to stay away."

The parting shot was a comment by Layton, "You'll never live to sell those goods."

That night Berry, the one losing the store, hosted several men to a poker game at a remote Ozark cabin. Those at the table were all willing to take the life of Captain Kinney, and they agreed that the winner of the game would have the honor, as well as a nice-size purse to which several men had contributed. Bill Miles won. He scanned the table, studying the cards, cast his eyes around to each man at the table, and sighed. He was the chosen one, and the group drank into the night while they laid their plan.

On Sunday, Miles rode to Captain Kinney's house and extended a hand of friendship. He didn't want to join the men who followed Kinney, he said, but he didn't want to be enemies, either. Kinney said that was fine with him, but warned Miles to stay clear of the store in Forsyth until it was cleared out. Miles agreed and rode out. He smiled—it was all a trick to get Kinney to lower his guard.

The next day, Kinney was taking inventory of the store, getting ready for the liquidation sale, when Berry showed up and reported to him that there was a claim against some of the tobacco twists, which were stored in a back room. He asked Kinney to count those out to be returned to the owner. Kinney went deep into the store to work the tobacco, where it was extremely hot. He took off his coat and removed his pistol belt, placing it on a shelf. Various men drifted in to talk and get out of the sun, but Kinney told them to get out, he had work to do. After they left and the store was quiet again, Kinney heard a noise. He turned and realized that Bill Miles had come in with the group and was still in the store, standing on the other side of a counter.

"I told you to get out," Kinney snarled. Seeing he was alone with an armed Bill Miles, he knew he was in danger and reached for his pistol on the shelf. From the corner of his eye he saw Miles go for his gun. "I'll kill you," Kinney said, just as Miles cut loose with a shot that shattered Kinney's wrist. An inhuman cry came from the captain, and as he grabbed the wounded arm and fell to the floor, Miles reached over the counter and, without seeing Kinney, fired three more times in the direction of the struggling man on the floor, until there was only silence on the other side.

Miles cracked open his top-break Smith & Wesson and reloaded as he walked out the door saying loudly, "I've killed Kinney in self-defense." Indeed, the lone vigilante had avenged all Captain Nathan Kinney's lawful and unlawful acts in one squeeze of the trigger. He walked to the sheriff's office and surrendered. In the days to come, the captain was buried with military honors, and Miles went on to be acquitted at a heavily publicized trial.

Even then, the reign of vigilantism wasn't over in Taney County. Sheriff Galba Branson was one of the thirteen original Bald Knobbers, and he wanted Bill Miles dead. But he didn't want to mess with Miles's brothers Emanuel (called Manuel), Jim, and Elisha, and their father, Old Bill, back in the hills. So Branson thought to catch Bill by surprise at one of the upcoming 4th of July picnics. Kinney's widow also wanted revenge, going so far as to put up the money for Branson to hire Ed Funk, an Arkansas bounty hunter, to go with him. Funk had a reputation as a fearless man who had faced many a desperado, and Branson was happy to let him take the lead in arresting Miles.

Branson and Funk went from one store to another, and one 4th of July gathering to another, trying to find Miles, knowing that he'd be celebrating someplace. The sun was low in the sky when they finally found out where he was and hurried over to Kirbyville. All the Miles boys, Bill, Manuel, Jim, and Elisha, along with their friend Rufus Barker, were there having a good time at the Kirbyville picnic. Barker had warned Miles about the bounty hunter Funk. All day people came up to Miles and told him the same thing: Branson and a bounty hunter were gunning for him. So by the end of the day, Miles and his gang were plenty on edge.

They'd also been sipping on a whiskey jug they kept cool in the spring. As they prepared to go home, they went to the spring to retrieve the jug. Miles bent toward the spring, and in that moment heard an unknown voice from behind: "Are you Bill Miles?"

"I sure am," Miles said, skinning his revolver and whirling. The bounty hunter reached for his pistol, but Miles was faster, dropping Funk in his tracks. At the same instant, Jim Miles drew his pistol to protect his brother. As Funk fell, he shot and struck the sixteen-year-old Jim in the groin. Jim shot at the same time, his shot going wild. Branson started his draw, but Manuel's gun was already out, and he fired twice into Branson's belly just as Bill shot him in the heart. The dying Branson got off one shot that cut harmlessly through Manuel's coattail.

Then it was over, and the silence was louder than the gunshots. The brothers inventoried the situation, and Elisha hadn't pulled a gun, so he was sent home. Bill, Jim, and Manuel made their getaway. Their friend Barker hid Jim in a barn, fetched a doctor for him, and Jim lived to tell the tale. Manuel escaped in a woman's clothing, and he lived for many years in Virginia. Bill and Jim were finally jailed in Springfield. They were tried, claimed self-defense, and were acquitted in 1890. Fearing revenge by stragglers of the Bald Knobbers, they moved to Texas and never returned.

By that time, over twenty men had met their end by the rope, knife, or gun. For four years, vigilante justice had ridden through Taney County like Death on a black stallion, bringing a storm of fear, destruction, shattered spirits, and death.

But back when it all started in the mid-1880s there was plenty of good publicity about the Bald Knobbers, and the good people of Christian County thought such a vigilante group would also serve their community well. With a little help from a couple of Captain Kinney's top men, they organized a group, adapted the Taney County vows and secret signs, and went even farther, designing a costume. If the Christian County folks learned anything from Kinney and friends, it was that a good disguise might save a lot of trouble. Though the design was far from standard for all the men, it was basically a flour sack over the head, with holes cut out for eyes and mouth, and painted in red and black. Some had horns made by stuffing rags into two tops corners of the bag and tying them off. The horrible flopping heads had a terrifying effect, especially on the more superstitious people of the hills.

The Christian County bunch would prove to be not only far more colorful, but also far more dangerous. They became known for threatening, then beating, any of their own members who didn't go along with their leaders' orders. Liquor was illegal in the county, and of course liquor was the fire behind most of the county's crime, because there was a still in every hollow. It was secretly sold in stores and was served in warehouses and lean-tos, anyplace that had room for a table and a couple of chairs. So the Bald Knobbers kept busy smashing stills, burning backroom taverns, and laying the switch to the whiskey makers and peddlers.

Though nobody in Christian County yielded the power that Kinney did in Taney, war veteran David Walker was one of the first, and certainly the most consistent, leaders there. Bull Creek Dave, as he was known, was in charge of the eastern company of Bald Knobbers, the most active group. He was a tall, light-haired, and blue-eyed man, and a poor but honest and hard-working farmer. He and his wife had nine children, and the oldest, Bill, stood shoulder to shoulder with his father on the farm and in the Bald Knobbers. In fact, Bill was the most enthusiastic of all the gang and earned a reputation for short-tempered brutality, always ready to accuse, flog, and beat. No doubt he had the best intentions, to make the county a hospitable place for earnest families. But the boy took to marauding like a duck takes to water. He was

Hotheaded Bill Walker; his father, Dave Walker, leader of the Christian County Bald Knobbers; and John Matthews. The St. Louis Post-Dispatch *published these images when the three were hanged for murder.*

only seventeen when the night riding started, and he immediately saw himself as a crusader. Besides that, he wanted to please his father. He was an able hunter who was good with both livestock and crops, and the fact that he had a baby face and no whiskers may have compelled him to try harder than necessary to assert himself as one of the raiders.

On March 11, 1887, three companies of Christian County Bald Knobbers were to meet at Smelter Holler, near the Walker farm. It had been the site of a lead smelter, but after the lead mining business played out it became a sawmill, which was also later abandoned. The wooded slopes of the surrounding hills concealed dozens of limestone caves and provided plenty of hidden places to meet. That night three companies of masked men were meeting, but only two were there when a chill rain sent them under shelter in a cave. When it ended an hour later, they started a fire to warm themselves. And after all that, the last group never showed. The no-shows were supposed to be bringing information on whether a suspected moonshiner had indeed been making whiskey. But without their report, the men waiting around the fire didn't have a mission for the night.

While waiting, they initiated a new member. They talked of other mischief they could do but couldn't come to any agreement. Bud

Ray and some other men drifted home, and finally around 10:00 p.m. Bull Creek Dave adjourned the meeting. Some started one way, while Dave, Bill, and most of the others went the other way, along the ridge, carrying their masks. Those who rode over on horses or mules were leading them, and the group walked along together. But there was a lot of grumbling. Bill Walker and the other young bucks were simply not content with going home after a wasted evening.

The group was nearing the home of Bill Edens, an outspoken critic of the Bald Knobbers. It was just an opportunity too good to pass up, and the young Bald Knobbers saw a chance to end their night with some excitement. They determined to give Edens a good whipping. Bull Creek Dave, the leader, had by then become the follower, as he watched the young ones don their masks and bang on Bill Edens's door. When there was no response, Dave's firebrand son Bill announced that Edens and his family must be over at the home of Edens's father, James. The gang was suddenly energized with a destination and a purpose. Giving a whoop, Bill led the gang farther along the ridge, to the elder Edens's home. Just as Bill expected, that night James Edens and his wife happened to be playing host to their son Bill, his wife, Emma, Bill's sixteen-year-old sister, Melvina, her two babies, and her husband, Charles Green. Charles was known as a loudmouth smart aleck, and the hooded raiders hoped they'd find him there too.

Rev. C. O. Simmons had been a willing, but unhappy, member of the Bald Knobbers from the beginning. He repeatedly said that he joined to enforce the law, but they were doing illegal things. And he was repeatedly threatened in return, being told in no uncertain terms that he had to either pitch in or be beaten just like their enemies. As a result, rather than serving as the conscience of the gang, he was disrespected, and when he pleaded for them to give up the attack on the Edenses, nobody listened to him. By the time they got to the dark cabin the young bucks were at a fever pitch, hopping the fences, approaching both the front and back doors, and yelling curses to the family inside.

Simmons couldn't take it, so he turned and walked away. Bull Creek Dave knew Simmons was right, but his shouts for his men to stop were drowned out by their shouts at the cabin.

The family in the cabin awoke in terror, and the men tried to pull on their pants and face the trouble. Old Mrs. Edens handed James his pistol just as the vandals smashed in the glass of the cabin's only window beside the front door. It all happened so fast. As pistol shots zinged through the window, the first Bald Knobbers to the door slammed a railroad tie against it, knocking it from its hinges. At the same instant, the men behind the cabin splintered the back door with an ax.

Pouring into the sixteen-by-eighteen-foot house, the men came face to face and hand to hand with the family. The unarmed Bill Edens, standing in the middle of the room, was shot dead immediately. Someone saw the revolver in old James's hand and hollered, "He's got a pistol! Get him." The man with the ax obliged, bringing the weapon down across the old man's head. He fell on Emma, who was also shot. Charles Green had a gun too, and he shot Bill Walker in the leg. As Walker fell back into the fireplace, he shot, killing Charles with a bullet to the head. Melvina grabbed a shotgun barrel just as the weapon fired, taking off the end of her finger. Her nightshirt was set afire, either from a gunshot or from the scattering fireplace brands, and still she struggled, ripping one assailant's mask enough to get a good look at him.

The Bald Knobbers came out of the cabin smothering the fire on Bill Walker's clothes and helping him walk with the wound in his thigh. When Rev. Simmons heard the gunshots he came back, but stood helpless. All Bull Creek Dave could do at that point was herd his men away from the cabin, leaving the three women in the yard screaming for help. Dave invented alibis for the men and told them to go home, no more than two walking together. Then he put Bill on his horse and led him off to have his shot-up leg treated by relatives in Douglas County. Bull Creek Dave's dream of an orderly, law-abiding community had been annihilated in one bloody act of thoughtless murder.

Investigators found two of the red and black masks at the Edens cabin, and Emma was able to identify the one man she saw. She was wrong, but close enough. She said it was Bud Ray, a clean-shaven Bald Knobber, but in fact he was one who left the Smelter Holler meeting early. When he was arrested and questioned, he saved his own hide by telling who else was there, including the equally clean-shaven Bill Walker. That's whose mask Emma had ripped off.

People were questioned, and arrests were made. The Bald Knobbers were through with the whole business, so several of them told what they knew. Following a grand jury, sixteen men were charged with the murders, but dozens were arrested and charged with over 250 different crimes. Only four were tried for murder: Bull Creek Dave Walker, his son Bill Walker, John Matthews, and his nephew Wiley Matthews. Bald Knobber Joe Inman was there at the Edens cabin, and he was livid about the murders. Saying he got into the organization to enforce the law, not break it, he turned state's evidence and proved to be a key witness in the murder trial. All four were found guilty and sentenced to hang. That produced a rush of the others to confess in the hope of getting a lighter sentence. Some were merely fined for illegal assembly, while some received long prison terms. Among those, Rev. Simmons got the lightest sentence, twelve years, because he was not armed the night of the raid, and because he spoke so eloquently and wept so pitifully in his own defense.

Even after all that, a few hard men of the Christian County Bald Knobbers weren't ready to give up. One night, as the four convicted men awaited the hangman's noose in the Ozark jail, a trustee was the only guard on duty. The hardcore Bald Knobbers bribed the trustee to open the cells, bound and gagged him so he would have an alibi, and smashed a hole in the wall of the jail with sledgehammers so it would look like they broke in. Then, almost comically, Dave and Bill Walker refused to leave. They were going to take their medicine. The Matthews boys had no such scruples and certainly didn't want to their rescuers to think they didn't appreciate all the effort that went into breaking them out. So they took off into the woods. John was captured a few days later by a farmer, but nephew Wiley got clean away.

The Walkers' attorneys jumped at the events, thinking their clients' refusal to escape gave new hope for clemency. They made a motion to the court. They wrote a letter to the governor. But neither the courts nor Governor David R. Francis was impressed. The hanging of Dave and Bill Walker and John Matthews was scheduled.

Sheriff Zack Turner delayed as long as he could. He'd never hanged anybody before, and he couldn't find anybody who knew anything about building a scaffold. After all, it was the first legal hanging in the history of the county. Turner toyed with the idea of bringing in a professional, but the Walkers begged him not to, saying wistfully that they preferred to die at the hands of their neighbors. So Turner and his deputies built a gallows with one big trap door so Dave and Bill Walker and John Matthews could enter eternity together. The romance was thick enough to stir with a stick. The night before the hanging, Bill Walker was baptized in a washtub inside the jail as he sang "Nearer My God to Thee." That was only one part of the religious fervor that surrounded the execution, including confessions, all-night sermonizing and singing, Bible reading, and mournful promises through the jailhouse walls that the condemned and their families would reunite in heaven.

Finally, two years after the vigilantes murdered the Edens men, on May 10, 1889, the three Bald Knobbers walked to the gallows, their hands bound, wearing black robes. After more talk, promises, and prayers, black hoods were placed over their heads, and one of the most botched hangings in history took place. A good hanging is supposed to result in instant death by snapping the neck. But that morning in Ozark, Bill's noose came apart and he crashed to his knees on the ground below the scaffold with untold injuries and blood gurgling in his throat. The other two ropes stretched, leaving Matthews and Dave Walker slowly choking, their toes touching the ground. They were

In this 1896 photo from Carrollton, Missouri, an unknown man prepares to meet his maker quickly, the way hanging was intended. The sawhorses in the foreground are evidence that the men of the town have just finished building a proper gallows. The man to be hanged, flanked by a carpenter, executioner, and sheriff, is hooded, his legs are bound, and he wears a genuine hangman's noose. Hanging in Missouri wasn't always this tidy.

hanged again, this time on shorter ropes, but still died from strangulation, not broken necks. At last they were pronounced dead and cut down. During all that, the injured Bill was lying on the ground under the gallows. At last, he was brought up through the hole and the trap door repositioned. Then he was dropped and strangled. In all, it took the county over thirty minutes to kill the men.

The escaped nephew, Wiley Matthews, made his way to Oklahoma near Fort Gibson, where he lived the rest of his life under the name of Charlie Jones.

Vigilante justice has a hard time finding a stopping point. Back in Taney County, where the Bald Knobbers started, there was one more chapter in the unrelenting series of retributions. Reuben Isaacs was a

Bald Knobber who was appointed sheriff to fill out the term of Galba Branson after he was killed by the Miles boys in the 4th of July picnic shootout. Isaacs wasn't a lawman, so a few months later, after the election, he was happy to hand over the jail keys to the next sheriff. But during the brief time he was in office, he had the unpleasant duty of bringing the Miles brothers back for trial.

Bill and Jim Miles had been captured in Springfield after the shootout with Sheriff Branson and bounty hunter Funk. Reuben Isaacs returned them to Forsyth to stand trial for the two killings. That simple duty was enough to make him a marked man among the Anti-Bald Knobbers, and he knew it.

Isaacs fled with his family to Indian Territory. Rumors followed that even there Anti-Bald Knobber bounty hunters were looking for him. So in 1895, tiring of the difficult life on the plains, and still worried that the night riders could come at any time, Isaacs sent his wife and children back to his family in North Carolina on the train, intending to follow. He wanted to travel alone and anonymously, just in case there really was someone coming after him.

Isaacs left Indian Territory with the family's belongings in a covered wagon, with a traveling companion, seventeen-year-old William T. Dial. What Isaacs didn't know is that the young man had been sent to Indian Territory from Taney County, specifically to find Isaacs and make friends with him. The Anti-Bald Knobbers had prepared him for the mission.

The two men set out in their covered wagon and made it to Texas County, Missouri, where young Dial had an uncle who was a county judge. They camped near Cabool, on the Big Piney River. At a beautiful spot beneath the trees they put some meat on the fire, and the horses grazed quietly. After supper, young Dial walked a couple of miles to spend the night at his uncle's house. The next morning, rather than returning to the camp he made with Isaacs, his uncle took him to the depot, where he boarded a train headed east.

As the day passed, the horses wandered over to a neighboring farm, and people came to check on the unknown wagon by the river. Inside, they found Isaacs's body with an Anti-Bald Knobber's bullet in his head. Investigators found out that Dial had been traveling with him, and Dial was charged with the murder. Of course, he was nowhere to be found. After learning that he had other family in Bowling Green, Kentucky, detectives went there. They couldn't find Dial, but they did turn up a blood-spattered pistol he left in a repair shop and never retrieved. Then suddenly he surfaced again when he was jailed for other crimes seven years later, in 1902, and the Missouri murder charges came to light. However, the other charges took precedence, he was convicted and jailed, and he never returned to face the courts of Texas County. The murder of Reuben Isaacs, the final act of Anti-Bald Knobber vigilance, went unpunished.

Chapter Sixteen

Mob Mentality

The men swarmed out of the hotel where they'd been meeting, into the street, and out to the fringe of the town where the shanties clung desperately to the ground as if the next Missouri thunderstorm might dissolve them into the mud. The mob of fifty men were quiet enough as they walked through the darkness, but when they got to the hastily built structure they had targeted for the night, their murmurs grew louder. Even then, the man inside didn't hear them. He was dead drunk and passed out across his little table. When the crowd kicked in the door he fell off his vegetable crate chair. Neighbors awoke at the commotion and cowered under their covers, praying that the mob wasn't coming for them. The men dragged their victim, groggy and panic stricken, into the street and proceeded to take turns beating him with leather straps, hickory switches, and brooms, until he lay bleeding and moaning in the dust. His crime: laziness.

That was in St. Charles in 1858, and that's the sort of situation in which some Missouri vigilantes found themselves. If they couldn't find a law to enforce, they turned to enforcing the moral code of the mob. The violence surprised and unnerved folks. Sometimes it was extreme. Sometimes instant.

Even Jesse James, who considered himself a hero of the people, was terrified of being lynched. In June 1870, James was charged with robbing the bank at Gallatin and wrote to the editor of the *Liberty Tribune:*

> I can prove, by some of the best men in Missouri, where I was the day of the robbery and the day previous to it, but I well know if I was to submit to an arrest, that I would be mobbed and hanged without a trial. The past is sufficient to show that <u>bushwhackers</u> have been arrested in Missouri since <u>the war</u>, charged with bank robbery, and they most all have been mobbed without trials.

He goes on to cite the case of Thomas Little:

> A few days after the bank was robbed at Richmond, in 1867, Mr. Little was charged with being one of the party who perpetrated the deed. He was sent from St. Louis to Warrensburg under a heavy guard. As soon as the parties arrived there, they found out that he [Mr. Little] could prove, by the citizens of Dover, that he was innocent of the charge -- as soon as these scoundrels found out that he was innocent -- a mob was raised, broke in the jail, took him out and hanged him.

James was right to fear the might of the mob. A man alone, or two or three, might share a vision of right, wrong, and what should be done. One might emerge as a clear leader. But mob vigilantism is a living beast. Or a volcano, with an emotional core fueled by backroom whiskey, sparked by rhetoric, until it explodes and spills out over the community. Everybody brings their collective store of memories, morals, traditions, ceremonies, ideals of punishment, and methods of violence. Their collective consciousness grows as the people feed on one another, and emotion overtakes reason. It can become impossible for anyone to control the mob. Nobody can be sure how it's going to turn out. After it's all over, people wonder how it happened the way it did.

Some mobs grew to hundreds of men, a mix of rough farmers and townsmen in bowlers. Sometimes they milled about the street for days, discussing their success.

Mobs sometimes lynched a man to squeeze the life out of him. But sometimes they squeezed information out of him. In 1858, the same year the mob beat that one man for being lazy, Ozark County was building a road along the White River. Among the men who worked on the road was a drifter from Arkansas named J. Hue Green. About the time he joined the crew, pigs started disappearing from nearby farms, so Green was suspected. People talked, rumors increased, and finally a mob formed, bent on getting information out of Green. They were sure that if he wasn't stealing the stock, he knew who was. They put a noose around his neck and hauled him up to a maple limb, then let him down to see if he'd talk. They did that three times, after which he was brain damaged and almost dead, and as he lay on the ground gasping for breath, they finally decided he didn't know anything.

Sometimes that method of getting information could even inspire a man to incriminate his own father. When thieves had been working around Corsicana in September 1874, the *Neosho Journal* reported:

> On Saturday night a party went out and arrested Tom Davis, a suspicious character living nearby, and taking him to the woods stretched his neck with a halter until he confessed not only to his own crimes but to those of a considerable gang in Barry, Newton and McDonald counties. Aaron Davis, his father, was arrested and parties are on the hunt for more of the gang.

Jefferson County, bordering St. Louis County on the south, was home to many veterans of the Revolution and War of 1812 who moved there to settle on their land grants. Earnest pioneers came across the Mississippi for cheap farms in the hills. There were rough lead miners who worked hard and fought hard. And there was a stream of vagrants, petty thieves, and desperate outlaws on their way to and from St. Louis, with its money, its vice, and all the adventure that inhabited its waterfront.

The people of Jefferson County knew if they were going to have decent lives, they'd have to be on their guard and, if needed, put their shoulders to the wheels of justice. That's just what they did in 1840. A farmer named Yeider was away to market, leaving his wife at home on their farm near Potosi, when a neighbor took it as a chance to sexually assault Mrs. Yeider. Then he decided to conceal the crime by killing her, and to make sure the Yeiders' son didn't testify against him, he killed him too.

When Mr. Yeider came home to the horrible scene, he spread the alarm, and the sheriff easily tracked the murderer to his nearby home. He was taken to the county jail in Hillsboro, but not for long. Legend has it that every man in the county assembled that night, a mob too big for any jailer to resist. The lynchers took the prisoner back to Yeider's farm and hanged him from the tree in the front yard until dead.

That was good experience, and the people of Jefferson County were ready for their next chance at vigilantism just two years later. A Pevely farmer named Herman Juede was killed, along with his wife, by an ax-wielding hired hand, just so he could steal a few dollars. Living nearby was Herman's brother Louis, Pevely's first blacksmith. Suspecting the hired man, Louis organized a gang to go to the man's cabin. There they found him with the stolen money, and as the newspaper put it, "[He] was not annoyed with a trial." They hanged him on the spot. It was one of those times when a whole mob was just sure of the right thing to do.

In 1862, Samuel Parker Eoff, a fifty-two-year-old German from St. Louis who farmed 140 acres on Big River, got so mad at his oldest son, William C. Eoff, that he shot and killed him at the breakfast table, to the screams of the boy's mother, Mamie. William's sixteen-year-old twin brothers Jasper and John ran to the home of their married brother, Thomas, and together the boys summoned some neighbors.

Instead of becoming a lynch mob, they kept their heads and tried to do the right thing. They bound Samuel hand and foot, put him in a wagon, and took him to Hillsboro, where they expected to turn him over to the sheriff, who would file murder charges. But in town they only became frustrated by the red tape of law enforcement. The sheriff wasn't available, deputies wanted to wait for him, and the justice of the peace wouldn't do anything in a criminal matter without a written report from a lawman.

The frustrated gang of neighbors took Samuel back to his home on Big River. By that time a small crowd had gathered, a crowd aghast at the killing by the father of eight, a crowd big enough to descend into mob mentality. What's more, the whole family was part of the mob. The older boys were there, and the youngest children, Lewis (fourteen) and Kate (nine) cradled their traumatized mother. With William laid out on the kitchen table, the mob decided to do what needed to be done. They held court right there on the porch, with testimony by the sobbing Mamie and her children. Even Samuel testified that he was guilty and needed to hang. The court decided to oblige him, but they couldn't find a suitable rope on the place. So the second son, Francis, jumped on his horse and rode to Bates Mill, where they had plenty of good ropes in the store. Mr. Bates told the kid the mob needed to let the law handle it, and Francis replied that they already tried that. Thanks for the advice, he said, but their father really needed to hang. Francis rode home at a canter and came into the yard waving the rope to the waiting crowd. As darkness fell, Samuel Eoff's family and neighbors stretched his neck right there in the walnut tree in his own front yard.

Jefferson County was also the setting of one of the West's most extraordinary stories of vigilantism. It was the culmination of two tales of murder coming together over a period of years to climax in a single night of vigilante justice. Charles H. Bickford and Alexander Walker did a lot of business together, but in 1868 they had a disagreement that led to a lawsuit. Walker won, and in the weeks that followed, Bickford just couldn't forget about it. One November night he went to Walker's remote cabin near Vineland, stood in the yard, and called for Walker to come out, saying he wanted to talk and make things right. But when Walker opened the door, Bickford had his rifle in his hand and blew a neat .50 caliber hole through Walker's chest and back.

He was promptly arrested by Sheriff Fred Luchtemeyer and lodged in the Hillsboro jail, a stout new two-story building of native stone and brick. The cells were downstairs, on both sides of an aisle, which was entered by a steel door. Living quarters were upstairs for the sheriff and a couple of deputies, and the whole structure was protected by a twelve-foot-high wall. Bickford sat down on his jail cot and introduced himself to the man in the neighboring cell. He was Andrew Quick, who said his story began a few years earlier, before that jail was built, when the people of Missouri were immersed in the fear, distrust, and unpredictable violence of the Civil War.

George Higginbotham, a successful Washington County farmer, and his wife were sleeping in their impressive home, and their grown daughter slept another room. Suddenly they were awakened by pistol

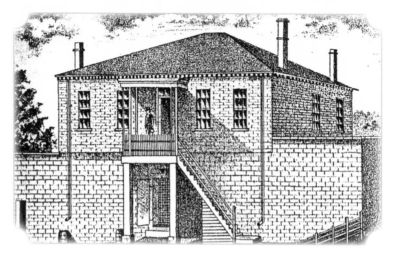

The Hillsboro jail, from which two men were taken and lynched.

shots and the pounding of horses' hooves in the yard. "George Higginbotham, Union soldiers are here. Come out and report," the men shouted. The farmer had little choice but to step outside, where he saw three men in Union uniforms. Union patrols were operating throughout the state all the time, so he had no way of knowing that these three were not truly soldiers. They were Southern Bushwhackers using the blue uniforms as a disguise to travel through the country and earn the trust of people like Higginbotham just long enough to get them to open their door. As George walked out onto his porch, three pistol shots rang out, and he fell dead.

The soldiers dismounted and stormed into the house, dragging the women into the sitting room and demanding the family's money. The terrified mother and daughter were too afraid to speak, even if they wanted to give up the cash. But the men weren't wasting any time. They already had a rope, and they dragged the women roughly down the front steps, past the dead farmer's bloody body, and out under a spreading walnut. There they slipped a crude noose around the daughter's neck and pulled her up to a stout branch. Of course Mrs. Higginbotham wasn't going to sacrifice the girl's life for any amount of money, and though she still feared the men would kill them, she revealed where George kept his money hidden. The thieves took $800 from the house and disappeared into the night, leaving the battered, grieving women to their misery.

The mother and daughter were able to mount a horse and ride to the nearby home of the Higginbothams' son. After burying his father and caring for his mother and sister, the son wasn't about to let the callous murder, beatings, and theft go unpunished. And he knew if he didn't take the law into his own hands, nothing would be done. After all, that kind of thing happened almost every day in Missouri during the war. With no lawman or military body to correct all the crimes, hundreds of them went unpunished. The son was no man hunter, so he determined to find one. It took him months, but he finally found a man willing to track the criminals down. He was a man experienced in hunting Bushwhackers and other sympathizers who supplied information and goods to the Confederates, and he thought he could do the job. So the Higginbotham boy gave him some money to start, with a price on each man's head, and it didn't matter how long it took. It's a good thing he included that last part in the deal because it took a very, very long time.

At last, after the war was over, in 1867, the bounty hunter brought in one of the men, who confessed in return for a reduced sentence. He agreed to a prison sentence of twenty years, which was a long sentence, but still better than the gallows, and then he named his two accomplices. One was never found. But the other, Andrew Quick, was said to be the one who fired the three slugs into the old man. After another year, in 1868, the bounty hunter tracked Quick to Hillsboro, where he was found drinking in the Old Stone Tavern. Thanks to the first raider's confession, the bounty hunter had a valid warrant for Quick. He arrested him and put him in the Hillsboro jail, where he was would wait for someone from Washington County to come and get him. And that's how Quick just happened to be there in the jail when the sheriff locked Bickford into the next cell for killing Walker over their lawsuit.

That was Quick's great misfortune. Back at the Old Stone Tavern men were getting riled up over Walker's murder. Walker was well known and well liked, and besides, it was postwar Missouri, and people just preferred to see their justice handled quickly and decisively. It took a while to work up the courage, but a little past 1:30 a.m. a few men climbed the stairs to the sheriff's office and knocked on the door. When Deputy William Clark opened it, the leader of the mob invited him out on the balcony to look at the swarm of over a hundred men. The deputy was duly impressed and happy to cooperate. They then roused Sheriff Luchtemeyer and the other deputy, Vollmaehre. The sheriff didn't want anyone taken from his jail, but neither did he want to argue with that big bunch of armed, though polite, drunks. He got his keys and accompanied them downstairs to get Bickford.

Hillsboro's Old Stone Tavern, where Andrew Quick was arrested, across the street from the courthouse.

The terrified Bickford was still healing from being shot in the leg during a completely unrelated fight a couple of weeks before, so he wasn't putting up any resistance. The mob was escorting Bickford out when they noticed Quick in the next cell and asked Luchtemeyer what he was in there for. He said Quick was a murdering Bushwhacker, and everybody agreed the sheriff needed to unlock his cell too. The mob leaders told Quick not to worry, they were just going to take him back to Washington County to face his charges, and he had nothing to fear there in Hillsboro. Though he wasn't sure about that, he had little choice but to cooperate. The vigilantes put the sheriff's own handcuffs on the men and helped them into the bed of a wagon. Then, leaving the sheriff to fret away a sleepless night, they walked with the wagon up to Main Street and west to the big maple on the edge of town, where they quietly hanged both murderers from the same branch. After all, they figured, it would have been a lot of trouble to get Quick back to Washington County, and the result would have been the same.

It was that sort of genteel decorum among later mobs that helped sustain vigilantism. Such mobs relied on great numbers, one hundred to three hundred people, who, though armed, went quickly and quietly about their business. A jailer or sheriff might be awakened in the middle of the night to find the jail surrounded by so many resolute men that he couldn't defeat them. There was no need for shouting, shooting, or unduly upsetting the sleeping citizenry. They simply overwhelmed the sheriff with numbers. Besides, he often found himself talking with some of the community's leading citizens.

Such was the case with Robert Hepler, who was a tenant farmer on the property of Joseph Goodley outside Lamar, in Barton County. In the depths of winter 1892, the Heplers ran out of food and money. With no regular work and no way to feed his wife and children, Robert Hepler grew increasingly desperate. Still, he found enough money for corn liquor, and the more he drank, the darker his thoughts. Finally, one day when he knew his landlord Goodley was away on a business trip, Hepler went to Mrs. Goodley and demanded some money. He'd pay her back in the fall, he said, but she had to help his family get through the winter. When she told him she had no money, he picked up the fireplace poker and killed her and her seven-year-old son. He took a few whacks at a daughter, but he felt sorry for her because she was paralyzed, so he didn't kill her. She was the one who would be able to tell the sheriff who did the horrible deed. After all that, Hepler had to slip back home a murderer, and with no money to show for it.

Two more Goodley daughters who had been ice skating returned home to the gruesome sight. They alerted neighbors, and the seriously wounded, paralyzed daughter whispered to them that the killer was Hepler. The neighbors swarmed over to his house and found him still wearing the same clothes, stained with Goodley family blood.

They did what they should have done, took him to jail in Lamar. But the murder of a helpless wife and child was too much for the people to bear, and a mob began to form the night of Hepler's arrest. The sheriff, following the example of many others who had been successful in preventing lynchings, took his prisoner all the way to Vernon County, where he was locked up in the Nevada jail, forty miles away. But it was no use, as word spread quickly of where he was taken. There were about two hundred men gathered in Lamar, and half of them got on the train for Nevada. When they got there they told the jailer he really didn't want to face that mob for a lousy murderer who really wasn't his prisoner anyway.

Their logic prevailed, and they got Hepler. He screamed and moaned as they walked to the train, waking half the population of Nevada, but by the time the train rolled into Lamar, he had resolved himself to his fate. Walking from the depot to the town square, Hepler enjoyed a fresh red apple and gave a full confession. He left instructions for his wife to take their children back to North Carolina and thanked his killers for bringing him back to Lamar to die in his hometown. Somebody said a prayer. Then with his hands and feet still untied, and the group assembled under a big maple on the courthouse square, a dozen men pulled on the rope and hoisted Hepler up to his slow death, choking, kicking, and swinging at the end of the squeaking rope. Everybody nodded and talked about how brave he was.

Although hiding Hepler in a distant jail didn't help him, it sometimes worked for prisoners. On November 19, 1870, at Potosi in Washington County, an elderly miner, David Lepine, and his young wife and baby were enjoying a visit by his wife's sister, Mary Christopher, and her baby. That night fellow miners Charles Jolly Jr. and John Armstrong were on a relentless drinking binge. Their route took them near the remote Lepine cabin, which got them talking about how David was too old to have such a pretty young wife. Worked up over that issue and in a state of complete drunkenness, they stopped at the Lepine cabin about 9:00 p.m. They rolled off the wagon and hollered for David—then barged on in without giving him a chance to open the door.

Waiting outside on the wagon was their designated driver, Jolly's twelve-year-old brother, Leon. They brought him along because they planned on being too drunk to drive. Leon heard loud voices and wondered what was going on inside, so he jumped down and peeked through a chink in the cabin wall. What he saw was Armstrong's failed attempt to rape the sister, Mary. When David Lepine tried to pull him away from the woman, Armstrong pulled his revolver and shot the old man four times. Mary tried to stop him, so he also shot her dead. Jolly then killed Mrs. Lepine with an ax, and the two men killed both children with the ax, hacked all the victims to pieces, and set the cabin on fire.

Nobody saw the isolated cabin burning, so it was the morning of the second day that a passing neighbor came upon the ashes of the cabin with the dismembered corpses. Citizens poured out through the countryside to help the sheriff find the men who committed the horrid crime. They arrested several people, but there was no evidence against any of them. Jolly and Armstrong were found sleeping off their binge at Jolly's cabin. As deputies got them in handcuffs, Sheriff John T. Clark approached young Leon, sitting on a stump, nervously watching the posse go in and come out with the two murderers. The sheriff knelt and asked if he knew anything, and the terrified boy was ready to "tell it all" if the sheriff would just protect him from his big brother.

News of the boy's story spread quickly. That night, with the two thugs lodged in the Potosi jail, a small mob gathered in the street. It was almost to be expected, in the face of such an atrocity, that the citizens would take it upon themselves to render justice. But Sheriff Clark told the mob he was not about to let that happen, and everyone went home. Nobody knew it at the time, but that would prove to be the beginning of the longest-running lynch mob in Missouri history.

The next night was Saturday, when alcohol loosened tongues and enhanced courage in the saloons of Potosi. The mob grew much bigger, and as it was approaching the boiling point, a city councilman ran over and warned the sheriff. Clark had been anticipating that kind of trouble, and quickly assembled six deputies in the jail, each one with a shotgun and a pistol. At last the liquored-up and self-righteous vigilantes pulled their pistols from their belts, retrieved their long guns from their saddles, and approached the jail. With the deputies backing him up, Clark calmly opened the jail door and stepped out in the lantern light to face the crowd of about one hundred armed men striding purposefully down the street. When they were no more than sixty feet away, he raised his shotgun and fired one barrel into the air to stop their advance. According to *The Missouri Democrat*, "The sheriff was then informed that unless the murderers were instantly delivered an attack would be made on the jail, when, the sheriff, all of his men, and the whole of the prisoners would be killed." But Clark had already given them his answer with his shotgun. Refusing to give up the prisoners, he further said he would defend his jail to the death. Any man who wanted to join him in the cemetery was welcome to advance on the jail. With that, he disappeared inside.

Nobody wanted a shoot-out, and nobody really thought it would come to that. The guards were certain they could face down the mob. But the vigilantes were confident they'd get the prisoners if they pressed the issue. After all, everybody knew Jolly and Armstrong were guilty. Some of the gang began to edge forward toward the closed door, just as others grew less brave and edged back. As the alcohol-fueled men bunched up and jostled one another, one foolishly had his finger on the trigger of his pistol, and as he was bumped, he accidentally fired the weapon. The deputies' response to the shot was instant. They all fired at once, wounding the mob leaders before the horrified men could run for cover. The shooting became general and then gradually lessened over the course of about ten minutes. When it was over, the sheriff and his deputies were fine, but thirty of their fellow townsmen were nursing wounds, and one man lay dead, a stone's throw from the door of the jail.

In the aftermath it was also discovered that an eight-year-old boy had wandered into the street to see what was happening and had been seriously wounded by a pistol bullet in his left lung. The following night, the third night of the trouble, the mob re-formed at the other end of the street. They still wanted the prisoners, and they were madder than ever over the sheriff's trigger-happy army and the wounding of the little boy. Clark sent two deputies with the prisoners Jolly and Armstrong in chains out the back door of the jail, where a wagon was waiting. They got the prisoners to the train and took them to the St. Louis jail, safely away from the Potosi vigilantes. That night Clark again bravely faced the mob alone, and since there were no murderers for them to lynch, they went home peacefully.

Within two months, Jolly and Armstrong were tried, convicted, and executed. Though justice was served, with the killing of a citizen and wounding of a little boy, the three-day rampage remained one of the great shames of Missouri vigilante history. It reminded lawmen that shoot-outs usually end badly. If Clark had sent his prisoners to St. Louis two days earlier, all that trouble could have been avoided.

The men of Cuba, Missouri, were not only lynchers, but also level-headed investigators when the whole Logan family was murdered in the fall of 1886. The Logans had just sold their farm, preparing to move west, and the killer had the idea that it was a prime time to steal the $1,400 they got for the place. R. P. Wallace was a drifter, an unsavory sort who'd been suspected and charged in a list of crimes. He was immediately a suspect in the Logan murders, and thanks to the telegraph, he was arrested in St. Louis. Sheriff Taylor went up there and brought him back to the stout, stone county jail at Steelville. No sooner was he there than a mob of fifty men showed up from Cuba. They got the jail keys and the prisoner, but as they moved down the street to hang him, the sheriff kept pleading, and that slowed them down. Then well-liked local judge S. J. Seay stepped up on a barrel and harangued the crowd with unparalleled eloquence that gave some of them pause. The sheriff seized the moment to grab the prisoner and slip him back in jail. Meanwhile, the crowd fussed among themselves, half wanting to proceed, and half convinced that they shouldn't.

But Wallace's stay of execution was brief. The would-be lynchers decided they should go back to Cuba and set about proving their case. After all, it was only about eight miles, and they could come back if they decided they still wanted to hang Wallace. When Wallace lit out for St. Louis he had left his suitcase in a hotel room. The vigilantes simply went there, opened the case, and found his clothes splattered with Logan family blood. That was all they needed, so they mounted up and made the return trip to Steelville. They didn't need the sheriff's approval or keys, as several were armed with sledgehammers and other tools. They battered their way through two steel doors, while Wallace moaned and went crazy with fear, listening to the battering and knowing where it would lead. The last steel door gave way, and about that time the sheriff showed up and unlocked the cell door. He wasn't going to let them destroy that too.

Wallace was bound and hauled out of town. The mob formed a makeshift court, where they tried and tried to get him to confess, but he never did. It didn't matter much. They were going to hang him any-way. Then he made one slip that was confession enough for the leaders. As they paused under the railroad trestle on the bank of the Meramec River, where they planned to string him up, the victim asked for time to pray. "Did you give that little girl time to pray?" a voice in the crowd demanded. Without thinking, Wallace replied, "No." And that was all the admission of guilt they needed. "Then you'll have to pray while you hang," was the response, and within the minute the scoundrel had a chance to do just that, as he strangled, dangling from the trestle.

Around 1852, livestock started disappearing from the farms around Smithville. One stolen mule was traced to St. Joseph, and the sheriff found out that the man who sold it there was John W. Callaway. Calla-way was promptly arrested and promptly posted bond, but that didn't stop the stealing. It became so bad that a grand jury looked into it and found that the rustlers were Callaway and the Shackelford brothers, William and Sam.

Some of the town's leading citizens organized one hundred men to ride and out and pay the Shackelfords a visit. When they thundered up in the yard, John W. Douglas, the spokesman for the group, calmly told the Shackelfords they were fingered by the grand jury, there were sure to be arrests and trials, and it would help everybody if they would just move away from Clay County. It seemed civil enough. No violence. Just a firm visit from one hundred neighbors, in an effort to end the trouble without more trouble. But the Shackelfords didn't take it well, telling the mob to get off their land. A few days later they sent word that they'd be in town on the following Election Day, when everybody else was in town too. They were coming armed, and the good citizens who tried to chase them out better tell their friends where they wanted to be buried. Sam Shackelford wanted Douglas to know he'd be the first to die.

Sure enough, on Election Day the Shackelfords and Callaway came to town, each armed with a Navy Colt revolver, a stout fighting knife, and a smaller dagger. Sam Shackelford didn't waste any time in locating

John Douglas, the man who led the delegation out to the farm, standing on the corner talking to William Ross. Sam approached with his brother William and insulted both men. Just when all four were coiled like rattlesnakes, another man walked between them, and that gave Sam the edge he hoped for. Behind the distraction of the passing stranger he drew his big Colt, firing twice into Ross, twice into Douglas, then whirling and emptying the revolver into another man.

Guns were illegal in town. So Douglas was the only man besides the thieves who came to town armed, and he did it simply because of Sam Shackelford's threats. Though hit badly in the torso, Douglas was able to pull his own weapon and put two slugs into Sam. By that time William Shackelford was on him with a Bowie knife, making a slash as he seized away the revolver. Then, turning it on its owner, he shot Douglas in the head, pivoted, and shot at other men on the street. Callaway, standing some distance away, drew his pistol and joined in the firing, wounding at least one townsman. Though he'd been shot twice, Sam started in on other men with his knives, killing one.

Though the citizens were unarmed, they were at least one hundred strong against the three invaders, whose cap-and-ball pistols were empty by then. The townsmen fell on the desperadoes in droves, pummeling them with clubs and rocks. There were so many of them that the three culprits, all wounded, had to shuffle themselves together and face outward like a pack of cornered wolves, in an effort to slow the assault. All they could do was retreat into the nearest store and slam the door.

The standoff continued for about an hour while the crowd milled up and down outside the store. People went home for rifles and shotguns, and soon almost everyone on the street was armed. The three wounded men in the store knew they couldn't fight their way out, and shouts for their surrender alternated with threats that the place would be set afire around them. At last they opened the door, threw their revolvers and knives out on the boardwalk, and emerged with their hands lifted in the air.

Necessary Evil

The sheriff watched it all, powerless in the face of the mob, and could only plead for them to wait and process the men through the courts. But seeing Douglas mutilated and the other men murdered on the streets of Smithville was too much for the mob. They set up their own street-corner court, and Callaway spilled the beans. He said they wouldn't have even come to town that day if it weren't for Sam. He said Sam wouldn't stop talking about it until he'd badgered his brother and Callaway into going with him. Callaway told who stole the livestock, and who sold it, and where, and generally confessed for all three. So about dusk they were all loaded into a wagon, taken to a sugar maple outside of town, and one at a time strung up from the same limb.

Were such vigilantes ever punished? Virtually never. In the Wallace hanging in Steelville, all fifty men went masked. Sometimes only the leaders were masked. Other times, they all flaunted their identity, unafraid of prosecution. Vigilantism was a crime, for sure, and yet it was very difficult to prosecute. The question was always, "Who did what?" The leader was not necessarily the one guilty of murder. Complicity, maybe. But then, was it worth the time and expense to prosecute a well-known citizen for that, when most people wanted the thug hanged anyway? After all, the law usually had plenty of other criminals, all more dangerous than a civic-minded mob leader. Then there was the matter of practicality. When almost every man in the neighborhood helped with the lynching, who was going to testify? Who would serve on the jury and convict them? Nobody.

CHAPTER SEVENTEEN

THE REGULATORS

In parts of the state where crime was the worst, leading citizens determined that something had to be done to stop a crime wave or to prevent crime before it happened. Something more dependable. Something more permanent. They needed a vigilante committee, a band of regulators, men sworn to defend each other, their homes, their town, and the public good.

In some cases, regulators were highly effective. After all, crime prevention is largely based on the threat of punishment. Sheriffs, marshals, constables, and policemen provide a consistent, visible threat to criminals. Vigilantes, on the other hand, were clerking in stores and plowing in fields, so they only reacted after a crime was committed. But when they were organized in a long-standing vigilance committee, with the names of the men they punished printed in the local newspaper, regulators could be very effective in preventing crime. They could be so scary that the criminal element would move on to easier pickings somewhere else.

Take, for example, the "Honest Men's League" of Greene County. It was forged into existence in 1866 to clean up the scourge of post–Civil War crime. The men were commonly called the Regulators, and somehow it became their conviction that virtually any serious crime should be punished with death by hanging. They executed Green B. Phillips, and nobody seemed to be able to say exactly why.

Phillips was a farmer and a well-known man around Cave Springs, having served as captain of the 74th Enrolled Missouri Militia. He was credited with the defense of Springfield when Confederates under General John S. Marmaduke threatened to take the big Union supply depot there in 1863. Even though the militia were farmers and shopkeepers—not regular soldiers—the men of the 74th held their position when the Rebel cavalry charged. So Phillips had been resting on those laurels for a few years.

The Regulators met in their usual secret session and discussed allegations that Phillips was associated with known thieves who were operating in the area. Later, whispered reports of the meeting to outsiders were never clear about whether Phillips actually helped the criminals, or shared their profits, or was merely friends with them. He may have only been guilty by association.

In any case, the Regulators sentenced him to death. The three men assigned to carry out the sentence waited for Phillips to go out to his corncrib at sunrise on May 23. Two of them poked their pistol barrels between the slats on opposite sides of the shed, while the third stepped into the doorway and ordered the unarmed Phillips out. They marched him toward the woods, where he could see no good outcome, so he ran. As quick as that, three pistols fired, and Phillips was dead before he hit the ground.

That went well, so the Regulators were ready for more. Three days after Phillips's demise, they happened to be meeting at Rice Schoolhouse outside Walnut Grove when word came that Charles Gorsuch and John Rush were irate about the killing of Phillips and were in the town ranting about it at that very minute. Gorsuch was married to Rush's daughter, they served with Phillips in the militia, and Gorsuch had even been in Phillips's Company C. Steaming over his murder, they made threats to find out who was in the Regulators and punish those responsible.

When word came to the meeting about the threats, the Regulators quickly decided the best way to protect themselves was a death sentence. They rode over to Walnut Grove, entering the town from four directions and trapping their prey in a store. They told the pair exactly why they were being executed, for theft, even though their (supposed) crimes would not have brought the death penalty in a court of law. Then the two men were taken about a mile out of town and lynched.

It's hard to say how many members the Regulators had, but one of their meetings at Springfield drew a crowd of 280. That got them so excited, they left the meeting and rode all the way into Christian County, past Ozark, to catch the fugitive John Edwards, who was wanted in Greene County. He also got the noose for stealing. The Regulators were a perfect example of the principle that an established, organized mob becomes its own law, and that the larger society's questions of right and wrong often fall by the wayside. Reports of groups like the Regulators always seem to raise the question of whether they were effective— apparently they were in Greene County, because the wave of thefts ended.

Johnson County was another area that suffered from lawlessness after the Civil War. The tipping point came on February 27, 1867, a stormy night of freezing rain and sleet. Tom Younger and his wife were staying warm at the farm home of Mr. and Mrs. David Sweitzer and their five children, eight miles north of Warrensburg. Suddenly, the door burst open and two men came in, apparently very drunk, begging for a place to stay the night. Just as Younger told them there was no room in the house, Sweitzer entered the room. He was their target.

Sweitzer had made a deal to buy another farm, and the robbers knew he would have the money, ready to pay for the farm the next day. They drew their pistols, seemed to suddenly sober up, and said, "We want your money," then fired. Both shots missed their mark, and Sweitzer dived at them. As they fell across the bed, each gunman got free enough to shoot, one bullet striking Sweitzer in the head and the

*Senator Francis M. Cockrell, Civil War colonel,
U.S. senator, and inspiring speaker at the found-
ing of the Johnson County vigilance committee.*

other in the stomach. As he lay dead, they rifled his pockets and found $130, then fled into the chill night.

Along the road they met another farmer, Jack Redford. Knowing he could identify them, they fired. It was hard to hit anything in that storm, and they killed Redford's horse. It was pointless to attack him anyway, as everyone in the Sweitzer house already knew who they were. The next morning the victims reported the murder, and the reaction was immediate. A crime wave had already terrorized the community for too long, and everybody from the preachers to the county judges was more than ready to act.

At 1:00 that afternoon a meeting started in the courthouse that grew steadily to a crowd of four hundred men. Leading citizens of the town and county spoke, including lawyer Francis M. Cockrell, a respected former Confederate colonel who would go on to become Senator Cockrell and a candidate for president. Professor Bigger of the local normal school gave the speech that was quoted in the introduction of this book, saying, "Vigilantism was but a case of the people exercising their sovereign power." They exercised their sovereign power that night by drafting articles to form a vigilance committee. By 9:00 p.m. it was written, read, and voted on, with officers duly elected. It also didn't hurt the cause that many of the men had taken breaks from the meeting to wet their whistles at the tavern across the street.

The committee's first order of business was to send one hundred men to arrest Dick Sanders. Everybody knew Dick and his brother Brackett were behind all the crime in the county, but until then, nobody had the nerve to stand up to them. The huge group was ready to ride, most with the group's weapon of choice, the shotgun. But nobody knew exactly where to find the Sanderses, so the riders went to the home of their sister, who was married to another desperado. The mob took him into custody, then forced the wife to lead them to Dick and Brackett. She took them to their mother's home, and sure enough the two criminals were there. Seeing the house surrounded, they didn't have much choice but to surrender.

The group and their prisoners, hands bound behind them, rode quietly about a mile north to where hundreds more citizens waited among the trees along Honey Creek. Men stood, leaned, and sat quietly on downed trees. There were calm greetings and respectful nods. And the only light was the glow of a full moon. It may have been the most pastoral lynching in Missouri history.

The tranquil scene was soon disrupted with the pointed accusations of the vigilante leader, who served as judge. The list of Dick's crimes was long, and every charge had a witness's name attached to it. Dick denied every charge and angrily asserted that everyone who said he was guilty was lying. But he could have saved his breath, because the judge sentenced him to death, pointing out that hanging was suitable for several of the things Dick and his cohorts had done, from murder to horse stealing. Innocence of one or two charges would have still left him with several death sentences. He added that they were doing Dick a big favor by saving him and his mother "the embarrassment of the gallows."

They put Dick up on his horse, there in the moonlight, and there was a little more talk, until someone suggested loudly that it was time to get on with it. Someone whipped the horse out from under him, and Dick Sanders strangled, turning slowly while the rope creaked against the oak limb above.

The crowd had no more stomach for hanging, so they let Brackett and the brother-in-law go. But those two were far from repentant, and the next night they met at the home of Bill Stephens. Stephens had also ridden with Dick Sanders as second-in-command during their crime spree, and now he was the leader of the bunch. Nobody knows how many gang members were there that night, but it was said to be a big group, and each one was heavily armed. Stephens was smart, or scared, or both, and told the bunch that they'd have to let the heat die down before they got into any more mischief, and they disbanded for the night.

Meanwhile, the committee was deciding what to do next. They did enough investigating to determine that the gang was still intact and ready to ride with Stephens. And so the Regulators decided to cut off the head of the snake again. March 4, before dawn, twenty committee members crept through the woods to Stephens's farm, each one armed with a revolver and a double-barreled shotgun. They hid along the fence and woodpile and behind the corners of the barn and shed. As morning broke, the door opened and Stephens stepped out, bent to scratch his dog's ears, then stood and stretched as he took a deep breath of the brisk morning air. Boom! The stunning sound of twenty shotguns broke the stillness, and Stephens fell, riddled with buckshot. Somebody dragged him inside, and the posse waited around until he died, about noon.

That was the end of it. The rest of the gang disappeared from the county, and some from the state.

The committee's confidence was growing to match their digni-
fied manner. Perhaps no other vigilante group in Missouri matched
them for the businesslike way they went about their work. Even more
remarkable was the fact that they were such a mix of Republicans,
Democrats, and men from all walks of life who saw eye to eye on
vigilantism.

The next target was Jeff Collins, another outlaw who made his home
in Warrensburg. Somehow he heard that he was next on the list. Then
word got back to the committee that he planned to leave town before
they could get around to him, so they hurried to execute their plan.
Some men of the committee located Collins and spent the afternoon
drinking with him while others set up guard posts to be sure he didn't
escape. Men with binoculars set up an observation post on the fourth
floor of the Ming Hotel across the street from where the men were
drinking, and they were watching when Collins finally left the tavern
about 4:00 p.m. They watched him all the way up the street, then using
hand signals, they let the men on the street know Collins had entered
a house. The arresting posse immediately moved into position. Well
after dark, when Collins came out with a bag packed, ready to bolt,
he found himself looking into a circle of more than a dozen shotguns.

"Surrender!" the leader commanded. Collins knew when he was
licked, and said so. When he was ordered to drop his twin pistols, he
reached for them, then the leader of the group hollered, "Stop. Loosen
your belt and drop the whole rig," and he complied. A livery stable
courtroom was waiting for Collins, who protested his complete innocence when he was accused of being a member of the band of robbers.
But the verdict was a foregone conclusion, and he was sentenced to
hang for robbery. The group quietly took him out of town to a blackjack oak with a limb overhanging the road, and there he uttered his
last words, "Tell my mother I died a brave, but innocent boy" (Ewing Cockrell, *History of Johnson County, Missouri*, Historical Publishing
Company, Topeka, KS, 1918). Several men were already on the rope,

and they hauled him up to kick and strangle. Somebody cut him down the next night.

It wasn't that the Johnson County sheriff, Thomas W. Williams, wasn't trying to do his part. Bill Stephens, the outlaw who was gunned down at his front door, had a son, Thomas. He and Morgan Andrews were teenage members of the gang who had fled the state to save their hides, but were arrested in Lawrence, Kansas. Sheriff Williams needed to salvage a little dignity for his office while the committee was doing his job for him, so he got the two young men extradited. When he and a couple of deputies brought them in on the train about 11:00 one moonless night, the committee was waiting with fifty men at the head of the train and fifty more at the back. The sheriff and his deputies had to give up their prisoners, and to add to their embarrassment, the committee tied their hands behind them and sent them on their way home. That night the two returning teenage prisoners swung from the committee's nooses. Though it was probably little comfort to them, they weren't the last ones hanged. *The New York Times* later reported that thirty men were lynched by the committee in Johnson and neighboring Pettis counties over the course of about six months.

The vigilance committee in Jefferson County in 1883 may have been the most politically connected one in Missouri history. It was organized by the newspaper publisher and editor specifically to stop a string of livestock thefts and arsons, which had led to two murders. All those crimes were the work of a gang, and the vigilantes hatched a perfect plan to turn the accused men against each other. It involved the sheriff, the prosecuting attorney, a local judge, and even a promised pardon from the crime-busting Governor Crittenden. After the whole gang had been arrested, and all begged to turn state's evidence against the others, they were all back out on bail. The leader of the bunch was reported in newspapers as far away as *The New York Times* to be Mack Marsden, who had pled innocent all along, and was more than ready to testify against the others.

The plan worked, culminating in the ambush slaying of Marsden and his sidekick Allen Hensley by three of the gang. The gang member who led the assassination was charged only with hog stealing, and after serving a small fraction of his sentence, Crittenden turned him loose. The gang fled the state, the crime wave stopped, and there was no more need for the vigilance committee.

While the Jackson County, Indiana, vigilance committee that wiped out the Reno gang may have been the nation's most effective regulators, America's biggest organization of regulators was started by David Mc-Kee, a farmer and rancher, and a few of his friends in Clark County, Missouri. There, where Missouri, Illinois, and Iowa came together, horse thieves were busy stealing stock and moving them quickly across state lines for sale where they knew local lawmen couldn't pursue them. McKee started the Anti-Horse Thief Association (AHTA) in 1854, but it became inactive when most of the men and a lot of the horses went to the Civil War. Of course horse thievery worsened during the war, so when McKee came home in 1863 after serving as a Union major, he rekindled the association.

What made them different from other similar groups is that they weren't intended to be vigilantes in the strictest sense. They set out to protect property, especially horses, by observing and tracking criminals. Rather than arresting people and dishing out punishment themselves, they intended to help lawmen gather evidence, locate criminals, and bring them to justice through the courts.

Dues were minimal, about twenty cents. Their motto was "Protect the Innocent, Bring the Guilty to Justice." They learned how to help the law, and lawmen learned to depend on them. Members were organized into pursuing committees, so when there was a theft, men were ready to ride and track the crooks, no matter how long it took or where the chase led, until they were caught or the trail ran out. Captured thieves were turned over to the vigilance committee, who gathered evidence, took the rustlers to the law, and continued to work with the prosecution of the case. The AHTA had success right from the beginning. As its reputation spread, stockmen in other counties and other states started their own chapters.

The AHTA could be as tenacious as any law enforcement agency and could respond with gunfire when they had to. The association functioned well into the 1900s, and at its peak it boasted membership of some forty thousand members in Missouri, Oklahoma, Texas, New Mexico, Colorado, South Dakota, Illinois, Nebraska, Iowa, and Kansas. They were unique in all of American history in their longevity and size, as a vigilante group that abided by written law and not their own, declined to call themselves vigilantes, and generally stopped short of taking the law into their own hands. In later years, many AHTA chapters evolved into civic clubs and served their communities in other ways.

CHAPTER EIGHTEEN

PERSONAL JUSTICE

A crook might escape the law. Or a crook might be caught and tried, then beat the charge. So in some respects, vigilantism was a matter of practicality, and the mob wasn't always the most practical situation. Sometimes the do-it-yourself approach was best. Take, for example, the 1880 case of Jefferson County's Andrew Wilson.

Wilson was thirty and married to Sarah R. Huskey, the thirty-three-year-old daughter of pioneer farmer Elias Huskey. Andrew and Sarah worked a little farm on Dry Creek, in the northern part of the county, and had three children. They took twenty-two-year-old Martha Schultz into their home because she needed a place to live, and they needed help with the housework. But before long, Andrew and Martha became romantically involved. When Sarah complained, Andrew beat her, which quieted her until the next time. Finally, when Sarah caught them in a position that a married man and a housekeeper shouldn't be in, she decreed it was her or the maid, and Sarah prevailed.

Martha moved out and was working for her room and board in DeSoto but had to quit her job when she found out she was pregnant. Andrew decided he had no choice but to do the right thing by her, which of course was the wrong thing by his devoted young wife and children. He found a place for the pregnant girl to live for a couple of

Elias Millard Huskey, pictured on his wedding day in 1874 with his second wife, Clara. If he was guilty, he must have been one vigilante who had a clear conscience, as he enjoyed a long and productive life as a farmer and family man. He and Clara eventually had seven children, and he lived until 1924.

weeks with a Mrs. McAnally. Then he made a longer-term arrangement with another Dry Creek farmer, Mr. Drennan, who didn't care a lick about the morality of the matter and was happy to rent the room.

After giving Martha all that attention and paying her rent, Andrew the rat told his poor wife and some other people exactly what he was going to do: leave Sarah and take up with Martha. One sunny day, as promised, Andrew put his clothes and extra pair of shoes in a feed sack and drove his wagon down to get Martha from Mrs. McAnally's house. Martha packed up her meager belongings, loaded them into Andrew's wagon, and they started toward Drennan's place, where they planned to move in together.

As soon as Andrew left home in the wagon, Sarah saddled up the riding horse and rode over to tell her daddy Elias that Andrew skedaddled, just as Andrew said he would. Elias was an old-line settler who took care of his own business. He could have sent the law after Andrew, but there was a good chance Andrew and his girlfriend might just move away and never be found again. And even if the law caught them, even if he was sent to jail, the law wasn't going to be able to get any money out of him for his wife and children. Even worse, there was nothing the law could do to repair the shame Andrew had already brought upon Sarah, not to mention her broken heart. She and the children would likely have to move in with Elias, and then how would she ever find another husband? There was no good outcome, as far as Elias could see.

So Elias took his son Millard and his shotgun loaded with buckshot, and they waited among the cornstalks lining the road where they knew Andrew and Martha would pass on the way to Drennan's place. The seventy-year-old Elias wasn't sure he trusted his hand with a gun anymore, but Millard was an excellent shot. There was no need to face the romantic couple, no need to speak. When the wagon went by, the men simply stepped into the road behind it and blew Andrew and Martha to eternity. And that was that. A coroner's inquest determined that it was Elias and Millard who did the shooting, and father and son were arrested. But later, both were acquitted for lack of evidence, not to mention lack of anyone thinking they'd done anything wrong.

Ah, romance. Bradley B. Byrd took an interest in Louise, wife of Jefferson County farmer Jack Kevens of Plattin. One day Byrd caught her alone and forced himself upon her. The Kevenses filed charges against Byrd, but that was an era when a crime of rape wasn't pursued with great vigor, and it even carried some suspicion of the victimized woman. It was a tragic scenario for the husband and wife, and one in which Byrd had a pretty fair chance of beating the charge.

On May 12, 1886, there was a hearing in Judge John Thomas's chambers, upstairs from the courtroom, in the Jefferson County Courthouse. Byrd, the accused, showed up and waited, but neither Jack nor Louise Kevens appeared. After a while, the judge continued the case, and people started to leave. As the bailiff, guard, and attorneys chatted, Byrd was the first to leave. He descended the empty stairwell, and there

Judge John Thomas was waiting to hear the Byrd case when gunfire erupted in the stairwell of the courthouse.

The Jefferson County Courthouse in Hillsboro, site of the stairwell shootout.

waiting for him on the landing was Jack Kevens, who pulled a revolver from under his coat and started firing. He missed.

Byrd ran back up the stairs and down the hall with Kevens hot on his heels. By that time he'd pulled a pistol from his own coat pocket, and when he turned to fire, he tripped and fell. There, the two men emptied their revolvers, with only one bullet hitting anything human. Nobody was sure which man fired the shot, but it put a painful hole in Byrd's thigh. Kevens ran from the courthouse and was later arrested. Both men came to trial for their crimes of passion. Byrd the rapist went to prison. Kevens the irate husband was acquitted. After all, he did nothing but start a little gunfight in the courthouse.

During the Civil War, Jim Ingram led a band of horrific Bushwhackers out of northwest Arkansas, harassing Union troops and Unionist families on both sides of the border with Missouri. In 1864 he and his gang stopped at the home of thirty-five-year-old William Stone near Mount Vernon. Stone was a father of eight, whose second son was killed in the Union army in 1862. That was more than enough war for Stone. But a law passed that same year required every able-bodied man to serve in the Enrolled Missouri Militia. Stone's service amounted to little more than guarding a railroad bridge. But to Ingram it was a crime against the Confederacy. He and his gang galloped into the yard and called out. When Stone opened the door, Ingram shot him dead.

Stone's thirteen-year-old son, John, knelt beside his murdered father in anguish, then looked up fearlessly at the armed raiders and demanded to know who they were. "This is Jim Ingram, fighter for state's rights and against Yankee oppression," hollered back one of the band, a trace of irony in his voice.

"I'm going to kill you," the boy cried, tears streaming down his face. "No matter how long it takes, I'll find you and kill you." The boy's threat brought laughter from the Bushwhackers, who turned their horses and rode calmly out into the night.

After the war, Ingram moved to Texas for his health, of which he would have had none if he had stayed around the Missouri border. And the Stone boy stayed true to his promise. He made repeated trips to Ingram's home base near Fayetteville, Arkansas, and made it known that he'd pay a handsome reward to the person who told him when Ingram returned. Then after a few years, in 1870, Ingram figured it was safe to move back to Fayetteville. But in those days, in those hills, everybody needed money more than they needed loyalty to a Bushwhacker. So the day after Ingram returned, someone rode all the way into Missouri, about fifty miles, to tell John Stone and collect the reward. Stone paid and gratefully shook the informant's hand.

Stone saddled up and rode hard for Fayetteville. He had a little cash and he laid a plan. With a few dollars per man, he established a guard for himself at the Roberts School House, where Ingram would be attending church services that Sunday. The men stood in the yard outside, each one sporting a pistol in his belt. When Ingram arrived in a wagon and started toward the church, Stone stepped out from the circle of men and fired without warning. He missed. The former ruffian didn't have a gun. There was nothing he could do except run for cover behind a horse team, and Stone ran straight at him. Ingram then broke cover and ran for the church, thinking he could make it inside, but Stone put a bullet squarely through his back and into his black heart. Mr. Roberts, the schoolteacher and preacher, came outside at the sound of gunfire, and seeing Ingram fall to the ground, grabbed Stone and held him. That's where the armed guard came in. They faced Roberts and told him to let Stone go. After checking the man on the ground to make sure the job was finished, Stone mounted up and rode back to Missouri, a satisfied lone vigilante whose patience finally paid off.

There was a similar case of a patient tracker from Ozark, in McDonald County. During the war, that was Southern territory. And that was also Union territory. Above all, it was Bushwhacker territory. A man was almost forced to align with one side or another, and whichever he chose, he was going to be in danger. William H. Larkins was a tough man who signed up with the 4th Regiment Volunteers, Confederate, but soon found that he couldn't stand the discipline. After just two months, he decided he'd rather run roughshod as a Bushwhacker, so he deserted.

In no time at all he was riding with a band of Bushwhackers who targeted Mark Harmon, an outspoken Union loyalist in Neosho who was running for office. One night as he rode home, nineteen Bushwhackers approached him on the road, ready to end his political career. Harmon drew his pistol and ran his horse for cover behind a tree. But there were too many assassins. As they surrounded him, he was no match for their rifles.

After the ambush killing, 1st Lieutenant John R. Kelso of the Union's 8th Regiment Cavalry, Missouri State Militia, was irate. Kelso vowed revenge for his friend Harmon. He and his men were Bushwhacker hunters; they patrolled that area with ruthless intensity and dispatched many a Rebel to his grave. Kelso's gang practiced a combination of hard riding and straight shooting heroics with a detective's patience and resourcefulness. They had their contacts, knew whom to talk to, and soon their inquiries in the neighborhood dug up the names of a few of the gang of nineteen, including William Larkins.

During the war, everybody needed guns. Regular soldiers were issued arms, but Bushwhackers had to get them where they could, which usually meant stealing the best. They went very well heeled with lots of revolvers. So William Larkins's next mission was to find and acquire more guns. He was acquainted with John A. Jackson, a prominent attorney and Union man in Ozark. He had money, and probably guns.

Larkins knocked on Jackson's door looking for work. Jackson had no work for him, but Larkins came back repeatedly over the next couple of days for various reasons, asking again about jobs and doing favors for Jackson. He kept up the friendly pressure until finally he saw enough of the house to know where Jackson kept his guns. Then Larkins made his brazen attack. In the middle of a day when he knew Jackson was home, Larkins kicked in the door and headed straight for the gun cabinet. When Jackson came into the room and lunged to stop him, Larkins put a pistol bullet through Jackson's leg. After all, Larkins had grown to like the fellow and didn't want to kill him. But it was a fool's raid. All of Missouri was under martial law at that time, and troops and militia patrolled everywhere. Jackson's screams quickly brought help, and Larkins was arrested before he got very far with his armful of rifles and revolvers.

When word of the arrest reached Colonel Kelso, the militia officer, he recognized the name Larkins as one of those from the Harmon killing. Immediately, he had Larkins brought to him and offered a one-time deal, yes or no. Larkins would die on the spot, or he could confess the names of the other eighteen men who killed Harmon. If he squealed, Kelso would set him free with a one-hour head start, after which he would turn the troops loose, and they would try to catch and kill him. It wasn't much of a choice: die or get a running start. But Larkins was a prudent man, took the deal, and dictated a list of the other murderers to Kelso's adjutant. The names were investigated, and Kelso was satisfied that the men were indeed a bunch of secessionist Bushwhackers. He handpicked a patrol and gave them the task of tracking down every man on the list, including Larkins.

Kelso lived up to his end of the deal and gave the informant an hour's head start. Larkins made good his escape, running by night, sleeping by day, and moving from one Southern sympathizer to the next. He didn't stop until he arrived in Jefferson County. It seemed a safe place, near St. Louis, but in the country, and a long way from Ozark. It was Union territory, and to blend in with his surroundings, Larkins enlisted in the local company of Enrolled Missouri Militia, which was inactive at the time. With any luck, he wouldn't even be called to report. He made a halfhearted effort to conceal his identity by dropping the "s" from his last name. He even went so far as to make sure a rumor circulated back around Ozark that he'd joined the Union army and been shot for insubordination. He knew the rumor would find its way to Kelso's men, and he hoped that would be the end of their pursuit. After all, Kelso's men had eighteen other secessionists to track.

Soon after arriving in Jefferson County, Larkins, aka Larkin, met Phillip Haverstick, a Union solider home on leave. Larkin visited his family, took a liking to Phillip's sister Julia, and married her in 1863. Their first child was born in 1865. After the war, the Larkins settled on a nice little farm near the Haversticks.

But Larkin's past was catching up with him. Before the end of the war, seventeen of the men who killed Mark Harmon were hunted down and killed. One named Adams made it to Texas and was never found. That left Larkin.

But Larkin was the coward of cowards, the man who saved his own skin by turning over the names of his friends. And one of the Union men in that handpicked patrol couldn't let that go. He was a man with a firm resolve and short patience with a coward. Or he may have been one of Harmon's three sons. John Harmon was an active guerrilla, and David Harmon served in the state militia. Both were arrested by General Jo Shelby's Confederates when they captured Neosho in 1863, and both escaped. David even got away by stealing and riding off on Shelby's horse. So either of them was capable of such a committed pursuit of Larkin. Whoever it was, he searched until he finally located Larkin in the spring of 1869, then watched for his opportunity. He'd been on Larkin's trail for seven years, so he didn't mind waiting a little longer for his chance. One day as Larkin was walking across his farm, he stepped from the trees into a field, a single rifle shot rang out from the woods, and Larkin fell dead, shot through the head.

The unseen assassin, a man with no name, returned home. Larkin was buried at the edge of the woods in a grave that was unmarked, never visited, and finally lost. He was a dark figure whose life was taken by a lone vigilante, for reasons that nobody in the Larkin family ever knew. And that's why his grandchildren were never taught to call him Grandpa, but "Grandma's husband."

One of the most colorful personal justice stories involves another man with no name. S. M. Brice was a man without a trade or purpose, a shiftless petty thief and heavy drinker who wandered from one ill-gotten dollar to the next. He had a wife and children in Cassville, Missouri, but he was rarely there. In the spring of 1874 he made a swing through northwest Arkansas to see what kind of trouble that state had to offer. Like many, he figured if he worked things right, he could always escape back into Missouri and the law couldn't follow him.

In the saloons of Fayetteville, Arkansas, he heard about a gray horse that won every quarter-mile race thereabouts. The quarter mile had become a popular race among the quick, stout breed of horses that were favored in the West, and the gray was reported to be the fastest in the world on that short, straight track. The next day, Brice showed up at the horse farm where the gray lived, pretending to be a Missouri horse trader. He admired the horse and inquired what the owner would take for him. Of course the price was a high one, so Brice said he'd think about it and rode away. But the next morning when the farmer went to feed, the gray was not in his stall.

The farmer gathered his son and a friend and set out in pursuit. From the tracks, they knew they were chasing one man, but there was no telling what they might find down the road. There could be a gang—could be an ambush. The trail led into Missouri and disappeared in the Ozarks between Cassville and Neosho. Still, the farmers, who had become hunters, didn't give up. They were patient, set up a camp, and started asking questions. Sooner or later, someone was going to notice a man on a fast gray horse, and the hunters would be ready when they heard about it.

Pretty soon Brice made a costly mistake. He passed a farm where he didn't see anyone out working, so he slipped into the barn and stole a horse collar and some blacksmithing tools. He took them down the road to Cassville and sold them, but the farmer from whom he stole them wasn't far behind. Brice was caught and jailed, but the constable knew him, considered him a nuisance, and just wanted to be rid of him. Brice was released on the condition that he leave town, and he figured he might as well go home, which was just outside of town. He spent Sunday night in a rare visit to his family.

Monday he was gone again to Pierce City, where he set about his new business, winning money racing the gray horse. He bought drinks and worked up bets. He was willing to take on all comers, and he was making bets up to $500 on the gray, which he couldn't possibly cover. Monday night he slept in the livery with the horse.

Two things happened that night. First, the hunters closed in on him. They heard about the man on a gray horse who had been arrested and released with the stolen goods. From the neighbors, from storekeepers and bartenders, from the Cassville constable, and from his family, they uncovered his every step until they ended up in Pierce City. Second, early Tuesday morning somebody shook Brice from his drunken slumber and told him some men had been asking around about him. Brice moaned and crawled out of his straw bed, saddled the gray, and eased out of the livery as the sun was breaking over the trees east of town. He headed up the road to Springfield, thinking to lose his pursuers in that bigger city and make a quick sale of the stolen horse.

But the hunters were waiting. They knew Brice wouldn't go back south, so they just had to watch along the north side of town. Brice only made it about a mile out of town before the three men circled around and kicked their horses out of the trees to block the Springfield Road. The owner of the gray called to him to stop, but instead of halting, Brice kicked the gray hard.

It was a good idea. The gray was built and trained for a rabbit-quick start. Brice knew it would only take a few seconds to put some distance between himself and the hunters. But the hunters also knew they couldn't catch the gray; they had no intention of a chase. Instead, the gray's owner leveled his .45 long 1870 Colt Single Action Army. His horse was steady as a table. The first shot was rushed and missed. With the second, the hunter took his time, let out a slow breath, and squeezed the trigger. The bullet tore into Brice's right leg. The hunter didn't want to take any more chance on hitting the precious gray, so he aimed higher, at a less valuable target, and put the third shot into the right rear of Brice's head, propelling him from the galloping horse to flop in the dust.

After a quarter mile, the gray horse ended his race, slowed, and stopped, and the hunters retrieved him. With him ponied alongside, the three men sauntered past the unconscious and dying Brice, but didn't stop to chat. They did, however, stop to eat and rest their horses in Cassville, where they suggested that the family might want to fetch their victim. The owner of the gray didn't give his name, but he did tell the constable not to let any more Missouri riff-raff come stealing Arkansas horses.

A crook just never knew who might come after him, but then sometimes the vigilantes didn't know who they were chasing. In Greene County in 1867, George Croson went out to feed his stock and found one of his horses and a saddle and bridle gone. He gathered a couple of neighbors and tracked the thief over the Texas County line. That's the kind of pursuit vigilantes could make, whereas sheriffs can't. The thief stopped at a blacksmith shop near Houston to get a horseshoe replaced, but when he saw Croson and the others approaching, he swung into the saddle and galloped away from the shop. The pursuers all drew their pistols and fired, hitting him in the side and thigh, and he tumbled into the dust.

Croson rode up, happy to nab the scoundrel and get his horse back. Then, as they talked, both sides were surprised. The wounded man grimaced in pain and admitted to killing Judge H. C. Christian in Springfield a couple of days before. He had escaped from jail there and thought the men who shot him were part of the Springfield posse that had been chasing him. Croson hired a wagon, loaded up the killer, and took him back to Greene County to hang for killing the judge. It was an arrest the sheriff couldn't have made, and Croson was hailed as a hero.

CHAPTER NINETEEN

DECENCY TAKES A HAND

Toward the end of the nineteenth century, clear-thinking, decent people began to understand that vigilante justice always left more to question than if the same crime went through the courts. Not that the courts always got it right, and not that they got it done quickly. But folks were too often left doubting by vigilante acts like the one in Ray County in the fall of 1896.

A couple of miners named Jesse Winner and James Nelson drank until about midnight at a Richmond tavern in Ray County. Winner, steamed up about his wife, had been bending Nelson's ear about it for hours. The previous night Winner had a terrible fight with his wife, Eva Sharp Winner, and he punched her square in the jaw, knocking her across the kitchen table. Eva had grown up an orphan, and she was a pretty tough lady. She wasn't going to put up with being treated that way, and told Jesse so. She shook her finger and said if he ever did it again, she'd tell what she knew and put her husband and his friends in the grave.

What she knew was that her husband and Nelson had robbed and killed a successful farmer named Clark over in Excelsior Springs, fifteen miles west of their little farm. And that's why Winner and Nelson were drinking: They were afraid Eva would send her abusive husband

and Nelson to the gallows. For that matter, Nelson's wife also knew what they did, and they figured she might talk too. In their drunken madness, they decided to kill both of their wives that very night.

As they left the tavern Nelson waved to another friend from the mines, Lon Lackey, asked him if he wanted to take a little ride in the moonlight, and Lackey came along. The three rode in Lackey's buggy to the gate leading into Winner's cabin. Lackey waited there while Winner and Nelson walked up to the house. When they came back ten minutes later, wringing wet with sweat, Nelson told Lackey that Winner killed his wife with an ax. In fact, that was an understatement. First, he hit her with a kitchen chair, and when she ran outside, he knocked her down with a fence rail. When the bloodied woman stood up, that's when he split her head wide open with the ax. And while all that was going on, Nelson slit the throats of the Winners' three-year-old girl and eighteen-month-old boy in their beds. There was an older daughter, deaf and mute, who slipped out unnoticed and hid in an empty barrel until the men left.

Winner said they were going to kill Nelson's wife next. But instead of taking them to Nelson's house, Lackey just took them to his place. They were so drunk and exhausted by that point, they forgot about the next murder and slept the rest of the night.

The day after the killings, neighbors noticed things weren't right at the Winner house, went to check on them, and discovered the atrocities. The deaf, mute girl was still there, but when questioned by authorities, they found she was so uneducated, she couldn't communicate at all. She proved to be a living witness who was no help in solving the crime.

That same day, a hungover Winner wandered into town and flopped onto a bench on the square. When someone came in with news of the murders, he seemed completely surprised. Sheriff-elect Green asked him where he was the night before, and he told the truth: He'd been drinking with Lackey and Nelson. Green went out to check on Nelson, who by that time was home with his wife. Green decided he wasn't

Neighbors gather around Jesse Winner's cabin, where his wife and children were found murdered.

involved in the murders but went to Lackey's house and arrested him before heading back to town to arrest Winner.

Of all the crimes, domestic killings, especially killings of children, were probably the hardest for the public to stomach. So all that day people talked, tempers rose, and little mobs gathered on street corners. Sheriff Holman and others spoke to the crowds. Among those begging the would-be vigilantes to let the law handle the case was John Sharp, Eva's brother. That carried a lot of weight, and everybody went home. For a while.

Sheriff Holman decided it was very likely that the people would make a run on the jail, so that night he slipped Winner and Lackey out, took them across the river in a boat to Lafayette County, and locked them up in the Lexington jail. The next day, as he continued his investigation, he interviewed Lackey's sister. She told the story Lackey told her, of Nelson and Winner committing the murders, and Lackey just being the innocent friend. So the sheriff arrested Nelson, took him to Lexington, where Winner was locked up, and brought Lackey back to the Richmond jail. Lackey was still charged with being an accomplice, but opinion was growing that the other two were the murderers.

In fact, taking the two men to Lexington might have worked against the sheriff, posing an enticing challenge to the developing mob. The idea of going over there was somehow appealing, and by about midnight, their number had grown to 250. It took several boats and a lot of trips, but they all got across. They were well organized and moved quietly to the jail, surprising the jailer. He never expected such a huge mob to come all the way across the river. Still, he stood his post and refused to open the cell. But the mob was ready with every tool they'd need to batter it down. They destroyed the cell door, got their men, tied them, and took them trembling and moaning in protest back to hang in Ray County. They only walked about a quarter mile from the river, where a burr oak proved just perfect for the purpose, and both men were hanged from the same limb. They were pulled up and tied off with their toes touching the earth, so they died an agonizing death by strangulation.

Sheriff Holman then took Lackey to Kansas City for safety. He was returned to face complicity charges in the murders, but since there were no witnesses or evidence, he was acquitted.

Across the river, prosecuting attorney Aull, of Lafayette County, pursued the lynchers hard. He did not want his county seat known as a place where vigilantes could storm the jail and take prisoners out for hanging. In fact, he came up with a completely different slant on the case. He contended that Winner and Nelson did not kill Winner's wife. Instead, the people who did the murders were the same ones who led the lynch mob. He believed they were also in on the Excelsior Springs murder, and they killed Winner's wife to keep her quiet about Excelsior. They were in a hurry to lynch Winner and Nelson so the truth didn't come out about any of the murders at a trial. But prosecutor Aull couldn't get anyone to believe his complex story.

And that was the shame of the whole scenario. The truth of the Excelsior Springs murder and the murders of Winner's family would never be known. Two men were hanged without evidence or witnesses of their crime. Lackey was off free. And there was a possibility that Aull was right, the real murderers were among the lynchers. So it ended with nobody knowing for sure who was guilty. That was too often a problem with vigilantism: Nobody knew for sure.

In Missouri's epic tale of crime versus punishment, it's important to remember that a third force persisted. For every act of violence, someone spoke against it. When we tell the stories now, those thoughtful voices are rarely heard above the din of angry threats, gunfire, and thundering hoof beats, but they were always there, pleading for reason and restraint. There was a heartbeat resounding, the rhythm of family love, babies in the cradle, vegetables in the garden, and prayers at sunrise. The more women, schools, churches, music halls, punch bowls, gravel roads, books, and newspapers spread across Missouri, the less people were willing to put up with violence by anybody. They demanded better lawmen, jails, and courts, and fewer night riders and corpses hanging under the bridges.

It wasn't that lawmen didn't want peace too. They were generally public-spirited folks who wanted to live in orderly, productive communities, just like anybody else. Of course, they also had selfish motives for wanting an end to vigilantism. When somebody else did their job, whether it was a bounty hunter or a vigilante gang, it made the lawmen look bad. And maybe worse, vigilantes could be more dangerous than outlaws. Every time a mob assembled, every time a sheriff had to protect a prisoner, the lawman's life was on the line.

There was a time when lawmen laid their lives on the line to protect criminals—and suspected criminals—from vigilantes just to keep their jobs. But lawmen increasingly came to see that they actually were risking their lives for a bigger ideal of peace and order. In 1899, Sheriff Ben Turner of Poplar Bluff was one who saw it clearly. He arrested E. B. Johnson, an unemployed black man, who was identified by two girls, aged eight and fifteen, who said Johnson stopped them as they walked along a country road and forced them into the woods at the point of a revolver. They escaped without harm, but that night, with Johnson under arrest, a mob formed and prepared to storm the jail. Sheriff Turner simply walked the handcuffed Johnson out a side door to a waiting wagon. It was none too soon, as within minutes the mob came storming in and found an empty cell. Turner deposited his prisoner in the cellar at the home of a deputy, where he rested comfortably under guard until his hearing. The girls admitted to the judge that they made the whole thing up, and Johnson was cleared—and prudently moved out of the county. Still, an innocent man was almost lynched. The case spoke clearly to the question of who was qualified to administer justice in Missouri.

When Sarah Graham's family in Indiana didn't hear from her around Christmastime, they got worried. Back in August she'd taken her two boys and joined her husband, George, in Brookline, Missouri, and there hadn't been a word since then. So her brother-in-law T. L. Breese went to find her.

Sarah had given up on her husband once. When they were living in Fort Wayne and he went to Missouri State Prison for horse theft, she divorced him. But he got out and swore he was going straight, so she married him again. After he went to prison again for forgery, her family wanted her to divorce him again, but she stood by her man. She and their two sons waited for him there in the bosom of her family.

Sarah didn't know that while he was in prison George attended a revival led by Emma Molloy, a nationally known evangelist and leader of the Woman's Christian Temperance Union. During the energetic services, George, age thirty-five, saw the light—and the light was in the shape of Emma's attractive twenty-three-year-old foster daughter, Cora Lee. He made it a point to get personally acquainted and line up a job for himself with Emma's crusade when he was released. Emma hired him to run her newspaper. That business failed, which is no surprise, because rather than managing it, George was like a hound dog fol-

Evangelist Emma Molloy.

lowing Emma and Cora as the ministry's operations moved to Illinois, then Kansas. Then they had a revival in Brookline, five miles west of Springfield, Missouri.

Emma thought the place and the people were so nice. But perhaps more important, nobody there knew her, Cora, or George personally. So she bought a little farm where she could relax, pray, and write her sermons in seclusion. George, Cora Lee, and a hired man all lived on the place, and the people of the area thought that was just wonderful, having such holy people living among them. Then in July 1885, George married young Cora Lee.

George continued to answer Sarah's letters and send her money to support the boys. But as time went on, her questions became more demanding. George suggested the boys come live with him, while she insisted that George come home to Indiana. At last, she cleverly agreed that the boys should go live with him in Missouri—and she would bring them.

The last thing George wanted was for his real wife to show up on his other wife's doorstep, so he insisted on meeting Sarah in St. Louis, saying he wanted to save her the trouble of traveling all the way to Brookline. So in September, Sarah met him at the St. Louis hotel as he suggested. But the next day, when he was ready to leave with the boys, she informed him that she was coming along. They argued, but George couldn't keep her from following him. So together they took the train to Springfield: George, Sarah, and the boys, age eleven and thirteen.

At Springfield, George again tried to send Sarah home, telling her it was a five-mile walk to the farm. She said that was just fine. So George insisted that the walk was too much for the boys, rented a hotel room for them, and made arrangements for the manager to look after them, saying he'd be back for them with a wagon. Then he and Sarah walked through the night while he decided what to do next. Of course by that time, Sarah knew something was going on at the farm that he didn't want her to see. When they got to the gate, George was at the end of his rope. He pulled out a .38 caliber pocket pistol and put one bullet in Sarah's heart, then stripped her clothes and threw her down an abandoned well. Why he took her clothes is unclear, because he ended up throwing them down the well too.

He loaded up Emma and Cora Lee, and together they drove a buggy into Springfield and fetched the boys out to the farm. George told them Sarah decided suddenly to move away to the West Coast. The boys must have been confused and heartbroken, but for five months George certainly enjoyed life. Then in January Sarah's brother-in-law Breese showed up, found out what was going on, and filed bigamy charges against George. George was arrested, and then the local constable tried to search the farm for Sarah, but Cora Lee wouldn't let him on the place without a warrant.

Vigilantes don't need a warrant. About fifty men went back with the constable and swarmed over the farm, completely disregarding Cora's ranting that they had to leave. They lowered a man down into the old well, and of course he found poor Sarah and her clothes. George was charged with killing his wife, and Emma and Cora Lee were arrested and charged as accessories.

At the preliminary hearing in March, the older boy, Charlie, testified that he'd seen his father in bed with both women many times. That was the frosting on the cake. The town was scandalized. And yet, the citizens of Greene County were trying to let the law handle things. It was a new era of decency. They helped search the property, but that was as far as they wanted to go. It was up to the law to prosecute and punish George. Emma, the evasive evangelist, bailed out of the Polk County jail but left Cora Lee there.

While George sat in the Greene County jail, he issued a confession that was full of lies, generally intended to clear the women. He said they didn't know he was still married to Sarah and had no part in the crime. Of course he also said he stabbed Sarah in the neck and didn't shoot her, implying that someone else might have done that. And he also bragged in great detail to several jailers, attorneys, and reporters that Charlie was telling the truth. He'd been in an unbridled sexual relationship with both Emma and Cora for years.

By April there still was no indictment, and people had been decent long enough. One night 150 men rode into town and awakened the sheriff, marched him to the jail, and forced him to unlock it. They took George out to the edge of town and stood him up in the bed of a wagon with a noose around his neck, tossed the rope over an oak, and tied it off. Then they pulled the wagon away and watched George strangle. He spent twenty minutes dying.

The people left Emma and Cora in the hands of the law. They endured several trials, but in the end were both acquitted. Perhaps they were guilty of complicity in the murder or the cover-up. Perhaps not. That was okay, because the vigilantes of Greene County drew the line where there was doubt. It was a huge step toward decency.

There's no better place to witness the decline of vigilantism than the place where it reached such a pinnacle, in Taney County, where the Bald Knobbers once reigned. It was March 1, 1892, when John Wesley Bright and his wife, Matilda Gideon Bright, walked down to the spring one morning with a milk pail. He returned to the house alone, loaded his pockets with boiled eggs, and told the children to stay in the house. Then he left. After a while the kids went to the spring to see why mother hadn't come back, and found her face down in the sparkling spring water with the milk pail in her hand and a bullet hole in her heart.

Bright was caught the next day and jailed in Forsyth. All he had to say in his defense was that his wife had been too friendly with their neighbor, Mr. Jones, and he just couldn't control his jealousy. But nobody believed his accusations against her. Especially not Matilda's many relatives who lived in the area. After a hearing on March 12, a mob gathered in town, growing louder and more threatening, intent on taking the prisoner and lynching him. Sheriff John L. Cook sat on a porch across the square, smoking his pipe, visiting with passersby, and watching the drama unfold.

The story really began a few years back, in the Bald Knobber days. Before he was sheriff, Cook was a Bald Knobber, and Matilda Bright's uncle, J. J. Gideon, was one of the Bald Knobbers' favorite attorneys. If a Bald Knobber was arrested for beating or hanging some no-account criminal, he could count on Gideon to defend him. So that evening Cook knew most of the men in the street, some of them from the old days. About dark, the mob was looking pretty serious, so Cook decided it was time to take action, and the action he decided on was to go home. As he rose from his rocker, he advised his young deputy, George L. Williams, to do the same.

But the conscientious Williams wouldn't leave his post. He continued to watch the throng in the street concentrate into about twenty-five hooded figures who approached the jail with sledgehammers and started battering the steel door. Williams was unarmed. But believing a gun might just provoke more violence, he bravely strode across the gravel street and waded into the midst of the mob, shouting orders, and pulling the masks off of two. The scuffle was brief. Two pistols shots from opposite sides hit Williams, and he was dead when he hit the ground. The mob destroyed the steel door, dragged Bright out screaming, tied him, and put him up on a horse. It truly was a spontaneous group, and at that critical moment, when everything was going so well for them, they realized they didn't have a rope. So two men ran to the town well and cut the rope from the bucket. The vigilantes then took Bright to a big oak in the cemetery, where they hanged him until he was dead.

Sheriff Cook cut the body down the next morning and dropped it on the courthouse steps with the noose still around Bright's neck. Cook's disdain for the killer was so intense, he made sure nobody moved the body for several days, while loose hogs wandered up and fed on it.

The lynching of Bright was one thing. The killing of the deputy was quite another. That got the attention of the governor, who offered a reward for the conviction of each man in the lynch mob. Some said it was Bald Knobber action, but that's not precisely true. It was true that some of the men involved had been early-day Bald Knobbers, including Reuben Isaacs, the temporary sheriff who would be ambushed by his young traveling companion three years later in Texas County. But some had been Anti-Bald Knobbers. The more important link among the men who lynched Bright is that almost all of them were related in some way to Bright's dead wife, Matilda Gideon Bright. They included Matilda's cousins Abraham Lincoln "Link" Weatherman, Samuel W. Weatherman, Martin Weatherman, Luther Keithley, and James Stewart.

Sheriff Cook really didn't care to take the deputy's killing any further. After all, he told the kid to go home. But Cook had a nice public relations move up his sleeve. The *St. Louis Post-Dispatch* reported that he had asked all able-bodied men to join his deputized army against the vigilantes. They'd been lynching people with frightening consistency, and the sheriff was determined to end it with an invasion of lawmen. Of course that was all hot air.

With the governor involved, the prosecuting attorney couldn't overlook the case. He knew the identities of the lynchers and had to bring sixteen of them to trial. But there was a plan afoot. One of the imprisoned vigilantes, George Friend, turned state's evidence—and still the rest of them knew they had nothing to fear.

The trial became a joke. The accused men included Link, who was justice of the peace, along with an attorney, the county coroner, an ex-deputy, the assessor, and a judge's son. It was easy for Sheriff Cook to handpick the jury, because every man in the county was eager to help acquit the prisoners. If the prosecutor had wanted to win the case he would have forced George Friend, his star witness, to testify in return for promises of freedom. Instead, the prosecutor dropped the charges in return for a promise to testify. Later, when he took the stand at the trial, Friend simply refused to say who did what at the lynching. The prosecutor, who had no case, explained to the judge that he had to drop the charges against the other members of the mob. Friend had transformed himself into a local hero. The legal wrangling dragged on, but in the eyes of most folks, justice had been served when Bright was lynched.

Still, the fact remained that vigilante justice had run up against the law and found it to be a tenacious enemy. The men who escaped punishment for the lynching could smirk as they told they story, but they knew things had changed since the old days when they rode unfettered throughout the county with nobody daring to stand in their way. From that time on, there would be an increase in the number of constables, coroners, sheriffs, prosecutors, and judges who could not be bought, bullied, or influenced to leave the straight and narrow.

There was a new counterforce, an undercurrent of decency, not just among lawmen, but among all people. It comes with civilization. The public finally began to see that the law didn't always get it right, but that the vigilantes were worse. All things considered, law enforcement was better left in the hands of the pros.

It was another good lesson when lynchers missed a chance to get the bad guys in Carrollton. The Taylor brothers were mixed up with Gus Meeks in a bunch of stealing, arson, selling stolen goods, and other crimes. Meeks was caught, tried, and sent to prison, then released in return for his testimony against the others. As soon as he got back home, he went directly to the Taylors and boldly told them not to worry, he'd lead the law up a dead end road. Laughing, he said of course he wasn't going to testify against his friends. But the Taylors weren't laughing. They killed Gus, his wife, an unborn child, and their youngest daughter. Somehow they left a seven-year-old girl, Nellie, unconscious but alive, and they put the whole family in a shallow mass grave. After a while the little girl woke up, clawed her way out of the grave, and tattled on the Taylors.

Nellie Meeks, who survived being buried alive in the Taylor brothers' attack.

They were jailed, their trial went on for days, and every night mobs milled about the street. Actually, the Taylors had as much to fear from a legal hanging as an illegal one. They were bound to swing, either way. But the vigilantes had a special concern in the case, because it was rumored that the Taylors had spent $1,500 on buying two jurors to make sure there was a hung jury. The mob was ready, and still somehow they never quite made that shift from talk to action. They left the Taylors in the hands of the court.

Meanwhile, the Taylors got to thinking that maybe $1,500 wasn't enough to guarantee a hung jury. Maybe they should get on out of there. So that same night they made a break by sawing a bolt, removing a bar, and getting out on top of the cage that was their cell. From there it was a climb to the roof and a slide down a water hose. But a guard in the jail yard caught Bill Taylor and another man who slipped out with them. George escaped and was never caught. A month later, at Bill's totally legal hanging, many an onlooker shook his head and wished they had hanged both of the Taylors vigilante-style when they had the chance.

Of course as time went by, law enforcement got better at its job, more people were sickened by the extremes of vigilante justice, and mobs were more often foiled one way or another. In the Jefferson County town of Eureka, in April 1872, four men enjoyed playing cards at a quiet little tavern. Playing in pairs, they started one last game to decide who would pay the tab for their drinks. Chris Cooper and his brother lost that game and suggested one more, best two out of three. But John Stoker, of the other pair, was a mean drunk who laid his pistol on the table and said the weapon would decide who'd pay. Stoker's partner laughed, slapped Stoker on the back, and good-naturedly said he'd pay for the drinks. Three of the men walked to the bar, but Stoker lagged behind, still fuming over nothing at all. Before they could order a beer, Stoker walked up, shot Cooper point-blank in the chest, and killed him outright.

Everybody in the bar piled onto Stoker and pinned his arms. He had brought a bloody end to their pleasant evening and they were mad enough and drunk enough to hang him. But as they pushed Stoker toward the door and a lynching at the corner oak, the dead man's brother blocked the door and pleaded for Stoker's life. The room was full of witnesses, he said. Let the law take its course, and surely the courts would deliver Stoker to a legal gallows. With that, the mob awakened the sheriff and handed over Stoker. It was one vigilante mob that voluntarily relinquished its prisoner.

In 1897 Erastus Brown, of Union, lived to see his trial because of one brave, anti-vigilante citizen. Brown jumped a young woman as she walked home from the grocery store on a remote country road, hit her in the head with a rock, and raped her. She knew Brown and named him as the assailant while she was still recovering at the home of her neighbors, the Sweets. Soon, three hundred men gathered, divided into patrols, and fanned out to find Brown. He was tracked and captured, hiding in the woods in neighboring Franklin County.

A farmer named Louis Smith was the one who found Brown. He and a handful of friends tied him into a buggy and took him to the Sweet farm, where the girl rose from her bed long enough to identify him. The three hundred had gathered there, ready to take the prisoner into the woods to dispense justice with a rope. But Brown was in Smith's buggy, and Smith was determined to get Brown to jail, and not to a limb. Without fear, and with his hand on the revolver at his waist, he faced the mob and told them that was what he was going to do. Then he and his friends started off to town by a back route.

Meanwhile, word of the attack on the girl reached Union. A deputy rode quickly out to the Sweet farm and learned that the suspect had already been taken to town by Smith. The brave deputy jumped on his horse and galloped after the buggy, hoping he wasn't too late. He fully expected that Smith was really going to take the man into the woods and lynch him with fewer witnesses, rather than take him to town.

A couple of hours later the deputy rode slowly into Union alone. Word spread that Brown was dead in the woods, hanged by Smith and friends. But the whole thing was an elaborate hoax to protect Brown and make sure he was properly tried. After the deputy rode in alone and the lie of a lynching spread, Smith slipped Brown into the jail after dark. There he quietly awaited his trial, and nobody knew he was there. It was a strange case of reverse vigilantism.

The entire time vigilantes were running loose across Missouri, lawmen weren't just sitting idly by and collecting their $60 a month plus room. They talked about vigilantism, read newspapers about it, fortified their jails against it, and planned ahead for what they'd do when it was their turn to face a mob. Aside from the numbers involved, for a sheriff facing a mob, the biggest problem was the vigilantes' own innocence. The lawmen weren't up against people who needed to be punished for a crime. The idea was to stop them from turning themselves into criminals. The next problem was familiarity. It wasn't like chasing down a stranger. Lawmen came toe to toe with vigilantes they knew, sometimes their best friends, sometimes the city fathers. Above all, the lawman had to find a nonviolent solution to violence. No sheriff wanted to shake the foundations of his hometown by getting into a gun battle with his neighbors.

While law enforcement jobs once went to military veterans, rough men who needed a job, and men who could handle guns, increasingly it was a position sought out by men with ideals of peace and community. By men with education, who saw that vigilantism was a short-term solution to long-term problems. The sheriff, marshal, and constable needed the courage of Daniel, not only against criminals, but also against vigilantes. They had to be the law when nobody else wanted law. When the jail held a man who was caught red-handed, a man the courts might turn loose, one who would strike again if turned loose, the lawman had to be sure the public put its trust in due process of the law, and not in the vigilante noose.

Chapter Twenty

Technology Takes a Hand

The families of nineteenth-century Missouri were always impatient with trouble. Self-sufficient and resourceful, they developed a predisposition to say, "I'll take care of it." They knew if they didn't do it, usually nobody would. They had faith in God and themselves. If it was a breech-born calf, an injured horse, a snake in the cellar, or a raccoon in the henhouse, they could handle it. Their medicine was in the fields, their labor supply was at the neighboring farm, and their money was in a mason jar. So it's no wonder that the attitude with which they approached every phase of their lives extended to law enforcement.

But as more people lived in town and adhered to town customs, they depended on other people to do things for them. Somebody turned on the gas lights. Somebody stocked the store shelves. Somebody cleaned the horse manure from the streets. And lawmen enforced the law. As revolution and secession faded into history, people increasingly trusted their government, even to the extent of trusting it to prosecute the guilty.

Around that time, vigilantism met technology. The changes were gradual, stretching over the decades after the Civil War. Lawmen had some of those technological advances available to them for a long time before they figured out how to use them. A perfect example is the telegram. Inventors, investors, and progressive thinkers of every stripe saw the potential for communicating at the speed of electricity. But ordinary people, including small-town lawmen, had other things on their minds. Besides, telegraph wires were originally strung haphazardly in small pockets across America, because by mid-century there were about five dozen telegraph companies, all building their own little networks. Then almost overnight those little networks connected into one big network. And with just a little experience, lawmen began to see how the telegraph could help catch criminals.

In June 1871, a twenty-one-year-old black man, Bud Isbell, stopped at the home of a white man, Peter Christian, in Springfield to ask for a drink of water. Peter was away, so Mrs. Christian gave Isbell a cup with which to drink from the well. After he brought the cup back, he raped her, then fled as she raised the alarm.

An award was offered, and the Greene County sheriff sent telegrams to all the surrounding counties. In five days a couple of men from Newton County brought Isbell back to the Springfield square. To no one's surprise, a mob gathered. As soon as Mrs. Christian identified him as her attacker, Isbell was hauled out of town to a stout tree. There, the mayor gave an impassioned plea to wait for an investigation to prove Isbell's guilt or innocence, but with a great clatter several pistols were drawn and cocked, advising the mayor that his speech was over.

Then Isbell was strung up. When the horse was led from under him, the limb sagged and the rope stretched, and his feet hit the ground. So some men shortened the rope and hauled him up again. That time, as he strangled, kicking, a shot finally rang out, relieving his suffering. The racial implications of the case can't be ignored, because Isbell had been accused of the same crime with a young black girl a couple of years before, and nobody took any action, legal or extralegal, at that time. Still, it was a telegram that put Isbell in the noose, and it was one of the first cases to show lawmen how helpful the new technology could be.

There was a similar, but more spectacular case, the first week of March 1892, when John Perreton set out to work in his fields near Carrollton, leaving his wife busy about her housework. About midday, she heard a call from outside and opened the door to find a stranger standing at a respectable distance with a charming smile. Travelers stopped at farms all the time, so she was neither surprised nor worried about the visitor, knowing her husband was over the hill only a few hundred yards away.

The man in the yard was Lewis Gordon, who said he was from Independence, traveling home, and needed something to eat. Mrs. Perreton said she was sorry, but there was nothing cooked, so Gordon asked if he might at least get a drink of water. The trusting housewife, rather than sending him to the well, fetched drinking water from the barrel in the house. At that point, Gordon moved to the door, and after quenching his thirst, pushed the woman back inside, kicked the door shut, and grabbed her roughly. When she screamed, he pulled a pocket pistol from his dirty wool pants, brought it down hard across her scalp repeatedly, and told her he'd surely blow her brains out if she made another sound. With that, he raped her, and all she could reasonably do was stifle her anguished cries.

After Gordon left, the poor wife was able to crawl to the door and scream until her husband heard her and ran from the field. He washed her bloody scalp, then laid her on some quilts in the wagon, hitched it, and took her to the home of their neighbors. Leaving his wife in the care of that family, he and the neighbor man saddled two horses and rode out after Gordon. They also alerted the next neighbor, who took the report of the crime to the sheriff and the doctor.

From that point, Gordon was hunted in two directions. On the vigilante side, Perreton and his growing gang of friends and neighbors were riding, asking questions, and searching every barn, shed, gulley, and cave that could hide a man. On the side of the law, the sheriff sent a telegram to every other sheriff, police department, and town marshal for fifty miles around. The sheriff had been thinking about the telegraph. By then it had been used for all sorts of things for three decades, and he thought it might be useful for catching crooks. If it worked like he thought it would, he'd save a lot of time and energy, not to mention wear and tear on men and horses.

Sure enough, Perreton and friends were scattered across two counties, following four different trails. They were sure Gordon went north, where he could lose himself in the woodsy hills. But Gordon was eager to get home to Independence, so he had to go south to the Missouri River, ducking and dodging in the open country of farms and fields. That route also meant he had to pass through Wakenda, ten miles away from the Perreton farm. There, an alert constable read the telegram, saw Gordon, and thought he matched the description. He jailed the man and wired the sheriff in Carrollton, who sent two deputies to fetch the prisoner.

By noon, Gordon was lodged in the county jail. It wasn't long before the sheriff was notified that a mob was forming and he'd better make up his mind what he was going to do. John Perreton, husband of the assaulted woman, and his friends walked down the street to the jail about 9:00 that night. Of course the sheriff protested, but he wasn't about to risk his life to protect a man everyone knew was guilty. So Gordon was handed over to the vigilantes, who took him to a wooded area outside of town and ended his life at the end of a rope. It all took just a little over twenty-four hours, thanks to the telegram. Although the new technology could help catch the criminals, it couldn't protect them from vigilantes.

The rapid spread of information from one lawman to another was one of the worst things that ever happened to criminals in America. Besides the telegraph, there were more trains on more tracks. And more people living in more places, meaning farms and homes weren't as isolated, and neighbors could keep an eye on each other. Then the law started getting telephones. Though there were only a few telephones in rural Missouri in 1906, there were enough of them to play a vital role in catching one murderer, and then preventing his lynching.

When Jodie Hamilton was a boy, a mule kicked him in the head, another mule knocked him cold with a kick to the chest, and a tree fell on him. A lot of folks thought Jodie suffered lasting psychological effects from those injuries. His father Jim was an eccentric pseudo-preacher who was known for a terrible temper that combined violence with scripture. He was given to carrying a Bible while he worked his cattle and firing a shotgun into their hind parts when they didn't do what he wanted.

Jodie's schoolmate John Platter was at the Hamilton home singing hymns one evening when he began to shuffle his feet in time to the music. Jim Hamilton grabbed John by the collar, interrupting the song long enough to scold the frightened boy, "There's no dancin' in this house." Jodie adopted his father's high-handed religiosity with the other children at Ellsworth School, causing many a confrontation. In a fight between him and the Platter boy when they were teens, Jodie almost beat his friend to death. By the age of twenty-one, although he had a boyish face and was known as a pleasant sort, he exhibited a fuse as short as his father's.

Jim Hamilton and his second wife moved with the children to Kansas, but Jodie returned to Texas County. There, he found work with sharecropping farmer Edward Carney Parsons, who lived with his wife, Minnie, and three little boys on a farm west of the Big Piney River, about nine miles north of Houston, the county seat. When Minnie became pregnant with her fourth child, she wanted to return to her family in Miller County, so Parsons sold his half of the corn crop to the hired hand Hamilton and started packing.

Shortly before the move, Hamilton had come home with a nice horse carrying an even nicer saddle, and he told his partner he found the horse wandering loose. Hamilton and Parsons both knew the sheriff would be looking for the horse, and keeping it amounted to stealing it. So on the morning the Parsons family loaded their wagon to leave, Parsons offered to trade for the nice saddle. He told Hamilton he'd give him an old single-barrel shotgun and $25 for that nice saddle. Hamilton doubted that the rusty old gun would fire. Parsons honestly didn't know either, but he was ready to leave, and that was his offer. Though Hamilton refused, Parsons virtually blackmailed him, throwing the saddle onto the wagon, and telling him he knew the saddle was stolen, and the sheriff would sure like to know where to find it. So Hamilton grudgingly gave in and took the deal.

The Parsons wagon pulled out just before noon. The more Hamilton thought about the saddle, and the more he studied the rusty old shotgun that might not shoot, the more he decided he'd been snookered into a bad deal. He loaded the shotgun, struck out on foot, and caught up with the family in Steam Mill Hollow, just before it opens into bottom land along the Big Piney River. He demanded another $10 for the saddle, and Parsons refused. Hamilton continued to argue, but Parsons whipped up the team and went on with the family's trip.

That made Hamilton even madder, and he caught up with the wagon a second time as they cut across a field to catch the Boiling Spring Road to Success. The words grew more heated; Parsons could see Hamilton's anger spiraling out of control, and he reached for a knife on his belt. Hamilton raised the old shotgun and pulled the trigger. It fired, all right. It exploded. But the shot also blew Parsons's knee to pieces. When the younger man recovered from the explosion, Parsons was writhing in horrible pain. So Hamilton took the barrel of the gun and knocked Parsons a savage blow to the head, sending him to the ground. The pregnant Minnie jumped down from the wagon and grabbed the barrel to stop the beating, so Hamilton clobbered her too. Then to silence the screaming children, he knocked them off the wagon and cut their throats with their father's knife. By then the farmer had bled to death, but Mrs. Parsons clung to life, so Hamilton looked around in the wagon for something to finish her off. He found a double-bit ax, covered her with a blanket, and hacked her to death. He piled the bodies in the wagon, drove it into the woods, and left it hidden there.

Then he had to leave for a date. He tied one mule so it could graze, put the nice saddle on the other, rode to his girlfriend's house, and calmly went with her family to a revival. After church that night, Hamilton became the busiest man in Texas County. He returned to the wagon around 1:30 in the morning and found that the tied mule had wandered off. So he rode to a nearby farm, woke the farmer, borrowed a horse, led it back to the wagon, and harnessed it with the mule he'd been riding. But the horse and mule wouldn't pull together. There was nothing Hamilton could do but ride to another farm to borrow another mule. By the time he got that mule hitched, it was near daybreak, and he had to hurry. He drove the wagon, with its grisly cargo, down to

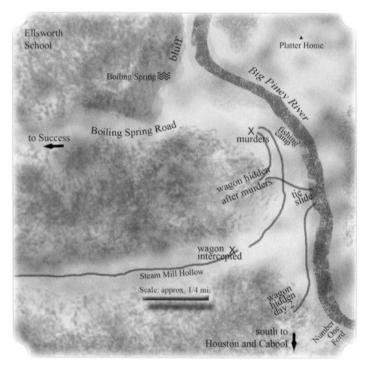

Jodie Hamilton's travels before and after the Parsons family murders.

Tie hackers slid their railroad ties into the river at slides like this one. Jodie Hamilton found a smaller one to be a convenient place to get the Parsons family into the river.

the river between the Boiling Springs and Platter's Mill. There at the tie slide, where tie hackers put their railroad ties into the river, he slid each body across the muddy bank and into the water. Then he drove the wagon into the next hollow and left it in the trees, returned the borrowed horse, returned the borrowed mule, and rode away on the dead family's mule. What a night.

From that point on, citizens got involved in an ongoing dance of vigilantism and cooperation that both helped and hindered the progress of the investigation. Ironically, while he was doing his dirty work, Hamilton had been dangerously close to county prosecutor Bill Hiett and attorneys Jim Hodges and Clark Dooley, who were camping on the river in preparation for fishing the next day. That morning, when Hiett rose early to cut firewood, he heard the sound of a wagon and team. The noise was eerily out of place, he thought, because there was no road in that direction. Later, after the men had been fishing for a while, they found the bodies of two of the Parsons children hung up in brush and weeds on the west side of the river. Remembering the sound of the wagon, Hiett thought there might be a connection.

The fishermen called out to John Platter, the childhood friend that Hamilton had beat up, who was out plowing his family's field on the east side of the river. He and his sister Alta brought their boat over to the fishermen, ferried the bodies across, and laid them out on the bank. Dooley went to the county seat of Houston for Sheriff Aaron Wood. Unfortunately, on his way to town, Dooley told everyone he met about the gruesome discovery, and long before the sheriff could get to the river, an angry crowd had gathered. Among them was the murderer Jodie Hamilton, posing theories on who could have done such a thing. He was sure the children were those of Ada Burton, a pretty widow who lived nearby. In fact, Hamilton said, she'd been threatened by a neighbor of hers. Come to think of it, he said, he'd seen that man carrying a heavy sack toward the river.

Acting on Hamilton's accusations, the crowd became a vigilante mob and headed for the neighbor's house. Hiett tried to get them to

John Platter in 1916 and Alta Platter in 1901.

wait for the sheriff, but they had seen the children with their throats cut and were ready to dispense justice themselves. So the resourceful Hiett ran to fetch Grandma Kimrey, the pretty widow Ada Burton's mother, who lived over by Ellsworth School. She came over to see the bodies and said they were definitely not her grandchildren. Hiett then ran after the mob as fast as he could—catching them just in time to stop them from hanging Ada Burton's innocent neighbor.

While they were all on their way back to the river, fourteen-year-old Harrison "Bo" Platter, John and Alta's little brother, returned from an early morning trip to the mill, about a mile south. He reported that when he crossed the river at Number One Ford he noticed an abandoned wagon in the woods. By that time, Sheriff Wood was on the scene, a deputy went to examine the blood-spattered wagon, and they found tracks leading from the murder scene in the field. The case was coming together.

That night Hamilton was again attending revival services with his girlfriend when the bodies of Edward Carney Parsons, Minnie, and the third child were found on the river bottom. The news made it to the church, and Hamilton acted as shocked as everyone else. However, he knew he was in trouble, told his girlfriend goodbye, and left the services. He rode into Houston with the nice saddle on Parsons's mule, left it at Bob Williams's livery, and hired Vinny Roberts to drive him south in his wagon to the train station at Cabool. There, he intended to catch a train west and leave it all behind him. In fact, Hamilton thought, it was his father's fault he had such a temper, so he'd just take the train back to Kansas and kill him. But close on Hamilton's heels was former sheriff James W. Cantrell. When he came to the livery not long after Hamilton left, Bob Williams verified that Hamilton left the mule with the nice saddle, and Cantrell figured the mule was the one missing from Parsons's team.

Cantrell ran to the sheriff's office and wired Deputy John Upton in the little town of Simmons. Upton immediately telephoned Jim Simmons, owner of the general merchandise store on the road to Cabool, and begged him to watch for Hamilton coming along in Roberts's wagon and do whatever he had to do to stop him. Simmons settled into his porch rocker, and when the wagon finally came down the road about 10:00 p.m., he called out. Hamilton said he was in a hurry and couldn't stop, but Simmons insisted Hamilton and Roberts come in for some coffee. The three men were still sitting inside, huddled over steaming cups, when Deputy Upton and Cantrell came quietly in the back door, revolvers leveled at the kid. Upton said simply, "It's all over now," and the escaping murderer was arrested, thanks to the telephone.

By morning a vigilante mob had assembled outside the jail in Houston, guns everywhere, and they wanted Hamilton. Sheriff Wood deputized twenty men, armed them heavily, and stationed them around the jail. Wood didn't think the mob could take his prisoner, but he sure didn't want the scene to descend into violence. So as soon as it was dark that night, he put handcuffs on Hamilton, put a hat on him and pulled it down low, and placed an empty rifle in his arms. Thus disguised as a deputy, Hamilton, along with Wood and a deputy, also carrying rifles, walked calmly from the jail to a wagon waiting on the next street. They drove to Cabool and put the prisoner on the train for Springfield over in Greene County. Although Wood had arranged for a curtained carriage to take Hamilton to the Springfield jail, the plan could be ruined if just one person saw him get off the train. After all, technology works both ways. Sure enough, news of the case had already reached Springfield ahead of them. Somebody saw the lawmen with Hamilton and made a telephone call back to Houston to report that the man the vigilantes wanted was there.

That was Sunday night. Monday night, fifty armed and mounted men from Texas County rode into Springfield, bristling with guns and claiming their right to hang the baby killer. But Hamilton was already gone, and the mob leaders were even allowed to come into the jail and look for themselves, just to be sure they didn't storm the place. While they were riding through the night, Sheriff Wood had used the telephone to line up another trick. He made sure he and some other men were seen getting off a train at Cabool and heading back to Houston. Of course vigilantes who were tracking the sheriff thought Hamilton was with him, so a phone call brought the fifty men galloping back to Houston, and again the mob surrounded the Texas County jail. But Hamilton wasn't with the sheriff. He had been taken in a curtained carriage to a different train, which took him to jail in yet another county. After a week went by, tempers cooled, and Hamilton was brought back, tried, and hanged. Postcards were sold bearing pictures of his hanging, and of the dead Parsons family laid out on a bed.

Hamilton's youthful picture in the newspaper had quite an effect on readers. That was no grizzly desperado gazing off the page, but a boy looking toward his future. He was a twisted youth, for sure, but the humanity of pictures like that turned people against vigilantism, just as the pictures of bodies on the battlefield had once turned people against the Civil War.

Jodie Hamilton, whose boyish countenance made it hard to believe he was a mass murderer.

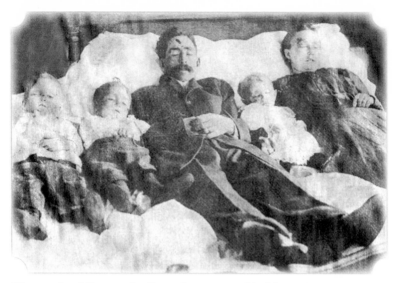

The murdered Parsons family, as they appeared in Missouri newspapers, inflaming sentiment against Jodie Hamilton.

Jodie Hamilton stands on the gallows waiting to hang. Among those with him is former sheriff Cantrell, who sent the wire that led to the phone call that resulted in Hamilton's arrest.

Photography came of age during the War Between the States, and yet, photographs could only be printed in the newspaper after they'd been rendered into lines by an engraver. Still, it was a vast improvement over an artist's ink sketch. The halftone was introduced in 1880, and though halftones were uncommon until after 1900, they allowed newspapers to turn photos into dot patterns that could be printed accurately. Criminals did not want their pictures in the papers, but the lawmen started to love seeing them there.

At the same time, governments and lawmen learned to be creative in their use of technology. In 1901, when Albert Shenkle raped a sixteen-year-old in Carrollton, Illinois, his description was telegraphed far and wide, and he was arrested in faraway Springfield, Missouri. Then the Illinois governor ordered the strictest secrecy around Shenkle's transfer. People had been talking about a lynching and milling about the streets of Carrollton, and all they needed was Shenkle. So the governor sent a special train with four companies of militia into Missouri and back to Illinois with Shenkle. When the train arrived, the soldiers formed a hedge around Shenkle and walked him safely to court, where he was convicted and sentenced, then back to the train and to prison, all before a mob could form. It was later revealed that the governor was so concerned about secrecy because he was afraid Shenkle's movements would be printed in the *St. Louis Post-Dispatch*, which was widely circulated in Illinois, and any word of the transfer was likely to result in vigilantes waiting for the train. Lawmen were learning that the spread of information worked both ways.

Jails were improved, which not only kept the prisoners in but also kept the vigilantes out. Evidence was inventoried and kept under lock and key. Cases were better prepared, and the scales of justice began to hang a little more level. The legal system has always been flawed, and yet, like our schools, like science, like medicine, there's been a steady march toward betterment, toward marking the mistakes and learning from the successes. So it is that vigilantism found less and less to contribute to the legal fiber of America as the years marched on.

What did the vigilante do instead of hanging rapists and beating men for being lazy? He got a job. Fewer men were isolated in the countryside on farms. Instead, they worked in stores and factories, drove delivery wagons, and operated streetcars. They had to be at work on time for a full shift, after which they went home and minded their own business. Men came home from work tired. They were well fed and happy to pay someone else to risk their lives to enforce the law. Meanwhile, back on the farm, the livestock was safer behind better fences and was taken to market in train cars.

Then the automobile came along and changed everything again for both sides of the law. In 1911 a Greene County farmer named Fred Ball killed his wife with a shotgun. He got away to his brother's house in Christian County, but after a sheriff-to-sheriff phone call, he was arrested there. Before nightfall a mob was forming to break him from the jail and hang him. Why would the citizens of a neighboring county, who knew neither Ball nor his wife, care that much about lynching him? Because his father-in-law, Joe Inman, a resident of Christian County, was a former Bald Knobber. He was at the Edens cabin the night the young Bald Knobbers broke in and murdered the family. Inman was the one who turned state's evidence against Bull Creek Dave Walker, his son, Bill, and John Matthews, the three who were hanged in 1889 for the Green and Edens killings. Joe Inman was a law and order man who knew a thing or two about organizing and leading a vigilante mob. But the Greene County sheriff was quicker than the mob, which arrived with their hanging rope to find Ball gone. He'd been taken away at the amazing speed of forty miles per hour in a 1910 Ford Model T and lodged securely in the Springfield jail.

Chapter Twenty-One

The Myth

As the vigilante disappeared, he was replaced by his own legend. In books, stories, and motion pictures, he was most often portrayed as a villain. And yet, America yearns for the vigilante's sense of personal responsibility. For his quest after justice. For the lone avenger. For the one willing to risk himself for the greater good. For the person who can rally a gang of like-minded people in the interest of protecting public decency. That's why even as vigilantism was dying out, every once in a while an individual came along who rose above the law to defend the people. The Old West style of vigilante kept rearing his head.

Family feuds flared and died out throughout American history. West Virginia's famous Hatfield and McCoy feud, for example, was a conflict sustained by unforgiving and unlikable people with no regard for the public good, whose ideals were lost in one act of revenge after another. Near the end of the nineteenth century, Missouri's St. Francois County had the potential to develop into such a war, when a simple act of home defense, protecting a corncrib from a thief, escalated into the Dooley-Harris feud.

Doe Run was a lead-mining town with plenty of rough men, including some for whom trouble was their daily bread. The Harris and Dooley families were farmers as well as miners. Both families had lived peacefully around Doe Run for several years. Then in April 1899, the time of year when food supplies were running low and spring gardens had not yet started to produce, William Dooley stepped out on his porch after supper. It was just past dark, and as he pondered the starry sky, a noise came from the corncrib. Dooley reached back into the house, took down his repeating rifle from its place above the door, and strode out to the shed. Expecting to find a raccoon or some other critter scratching around the securely latched door, he was surprised to see the figure of a man emerge from the open doorway carrying a bag of his precious corn. Dooley shouted a curse and fired, and the man fell, apparently hit. Then he jumped up and ran for the woods. Dooley shot three more times before his target disappeared into the trees, and in the darkness it was impossible to know whether any more bullets found their mark.

Dooley found out whether he'd hit something when Henry Harris died three days later from gunshot wounds. That might have been the end of it. But early the following summer, Henry Harris's son, James, bought the farm the Dooleys were leasing and living on. He told the Dooleys he was taking possession and they had to move out. William Dooley went to court and pleaded that his family be allowed to stay on the land and harvest their crops, but he had no legal basis to keep Harris from moving into the place. The Dooleys were evicted and forced to leave their ripening crops, assuring them of an entire year ahead with little to eat.

James Harris and his family moved into the place, where they stood to enjoy the fruits of all the work the Dooleys put in to the garden, vines, and orchard. Still, they were bound to suffer too. First, their dogs were poisoned, then their livestock, and James Harris knew it was the Dooleys' doing. That fall the evicted William Dooley's son John became the local schoolteacher, and among his students were many Harris children, including those of James, the one who took over the farm. Teacher Dooley laid the hickory stick on the Harris children so hard that their parents filed criminal charges. Though the case never came to court, and nobody was ever charged in the killing of the Harris farm animals, the blood feud had begun.

Winters were so hard that they cooled tempers along with everything else. And so there were no newsworthy problems between the families until the following July 25, when they came face to face at the annual Flat Rock Picnic. Knowing they'd see each other there, both sides were itching for a fight. Sure enough, they met in a rolling, dusty brawl, a common-enough event among such hard men in a mining community. But two of the Harris men came to the picnic with brass knuckles, which was bad manners in hill country fighting. The Dooleys got cut up pretty badly. That was enough to prime the fuse for their next meeting, and they all walked away promising to "go dressed," meaning they'd be armed from that time on.

With those warnings issued, for two weeks the families stayed away from each other until the annual Doe Run Picnic on August 4. Actually, they stayed away except for one member of each family. The wife of William Dooley, the corncrib defender, had left him, moved in with her sister and brother-in-law, and found a new suitor: Frank Harris. It didn't take any time at all for the news to spread. Rather than the Dooley-Harris love healing the feud, the romance added fuel to the fire that burned between the two factions. And neither family was going to show itself cowardly by staying away from the next picnic.

It was a bright morning, and the day promised to be hot, in more ways than one. A few vendors opened up booths with food, toys, and games, and music came from a small stage under the trees along the river. Among the wagons pulling in before 9:00 a.m. was the one bearing William Dooley and his sons Joe, Les, Bill, and John, the schoolteacher accused of abuse. Everybody knew they were looking for trouble because they didn't bring their women or children. As they dismounted from the wagon, people could see that each one of them had a pistol in a pocket or holster, or tucked into his belt, with extra ammunition in their pockets. They also had their rifles hidden under a mat of straw in the wagon bed.

But the Harris men took a different approach. James and Les came in two wagons, bringing their mother, wives, and children, and baskets of fried chicken and vegetables, in effect telling the Dooleys they intended to enjoy a nice community picnic, and weren't afraid of anybody. Frank Harris even came in his buggy with Mrs. Dooley at his side. The Harris men were all unarmed, and if another fistfight with the Dooleys came up, well, so be it. But there was a lone Harris man who had a different idea. Wes Harris, who lived at Pilot Knob, came back home for the picnic. He must have come to fight, because he's the one who got it started.

Later in the afternoon, as people milled around, it was inevitable that William Dooley would come up against someone named Harris. Wes Harris interrupted a conversation that William and his son Bill were having with another man. Wes coolly remarked that he wasn't afraid of William or any other Dooley, or of their guns. When that didn't provoke a reaction, he continued to insult the elder Dooley, who finally had enough. If Wes wanted a fight, he was ready. Dooley walked to the trees by the river and found a stick that made a suitable club, then started back toward Wes.

Wes then showed why he wasn't afraid of any Dooley that day. He pulled a red bandanna from his pocket, and wrapped inside was a Colt pocket pistol. Seeing his father about to meet the Colt in Wes's hand, Joe Dooley drew his own revolver from its holster, as Les Dooley ran for the wagon and fetched one of the rifles from under the straw. Running back, Les heard two bangs from Wes Harris's Colt, and watched his father fall dead, a pair of bullets in his chest. Instantly, Joe Dooley fired his revolver almost point blank at Wes and missed. By then, the rifle was at Les's shoulder, and he put a bullet through Wes's head. Joe Dooley then turned to see Frank Harris nearby and put two into his torso. James Harris ran away from the picnic area and into a field, where Les

Dooley chased him. Les paused long enough to catch a deep breath, draw a bead with the rifle, and put a slug into James's back, then three more before he fell. Bill Dooley pulled his pistol, and the only Harris he could see was James Harris's wife, so he took a shot at her, but missed. When the firing was over, Bill Dooley was out of his mind with anger and grief. He picked up Wes's gun that had killed his father and emptied it into the head of Wes Harris, then stomped his face repeatedly until his brothers restrained him.

Amazingly, James Harris lived with his wounds from the four rifle slugs. The Dooleys were charged in Wes Harris's murder and posted their bond. The legal proceedings dragged on, and threats were made, while men of both families "went dressed," month after month. Finally, two years later, Bill Harris boarded a train at Doe Run, followed by Bill Dooley. Ironically, back in 1900, Bill Harris was late getting to the picnic, arriving after the gunfire. The Dooleys still had their guns in their hands, and when they saw Bill Harris ride up, they fired, but never hit him, and he rode away unharmed. He was never part of the action that day, and never even got a piece of fried chicken. But in 1902, after he settled into his seat on the train, Bill Dooley walked up behind him, revolver in hand, and put a bullet behind his ear, then walked closer and put two more in for good measure. Bill Dooley was clearly a man of overstatement. He was sent to the state mental hospital and died there after many years. Joe and Les Dooley finally stood trial in 1905, and when the defense proved that Wes Harris shot first at the picnic, the Dooley men were found not guilty.

In older days, one of those families might have rallied their neighbors into a vigilante committee. They might have punished not only the opposing family, but other wrongdoers in the neighborhood. They might have "owned" the sheriff and other county officials, as did the Slickers and Bald Knobbers. But by 1900, that was in the past. The men in the Dooley-Harris feud, who chose to carry guns, who were ready to fight rather than walk away, weren't vigilantes. They had no broader

NECESSARY EVIL

community-enriching motive. They were opportunists. Maybe even bullies. Egotists, itching for a fight. The Dooley-Harris feud was private business that simply died out.

Even as late as 1915, in Pleasant Hill, there was a rash of unsolved crimes that had people ready to take the law into their own hands. As policeman Charles Poindexter was out questioning vagrants one Saturday night, searching for the robbers of a train, he came upon W. F. Williams, who pulled a revolver. The two exchanged gunfire, leaving Officer Poindexter and another unidentified hobo killed, and the pistol-toting Williams badly wounded. That night, Williams was in jail suffering from his wounds under heavy guard because the sheriff was worried that a mob might try to take him. But about 4:00 a.m. the guards decided nothing was going to happen and they could go home and leave one man on duty, which was what a group of vigilantes was waiting for. They quietly came into the jail, threatened the lone jailer, and took Williams. Sunday morning, folks on their way to church were greeted by the site of the bloodied Williams hanging from the fire hall bell tower on the town square, and nobody bothered to cut him down until after church. Although detectives from Kansas City pretended to try to identify the members of the mob, they gave up and went home, figuring justice had been served.

It was an embarrassment. And to make matters worse, it was widely believed that the men who did the hanging were policemen avenging one of their own. Lawmen have always had the opportunity to do a little vigilante work on the side, and there's no question that it has happened. But with the hanging in Pleasant Hill, there were men within the police force who were livid over the lynching, and newspapers across the nation railed against it. It was a dying gasp for vigilantism.

In that era of the early twentieth century, people were trying hard to shake off the reputation that caused crusading newspapers to refer to Missouri and Kansas as "the lynching belt." Even in 1920, a Kansas lynch mob stole a locomotive to chase down a man and lynch him.

The *St. Louis Post-Dispatch* scolded, "To make the lynching habit not only exceedingly unpopular, but exceedingly risky, is always possible. Resourceful, courageous officials have it in their power to administer deterrents. . . ." And when the newspapers stood against vigilantism, that was the final pin in the latch that constrained it. With the broad view of the press, interpreting current events with an eye toward history, armed with a daily, pervasive voice, the reporters, editors, and publishers began to stand firm for law enforced by officials.

How many motion pictures have featured the hangman's noose around the neck of an innocent man or woman? How many times has there been a last-second rescue by a gallant hero? Even the twenty-first-century television show *Mythbusters* was enchanted enough to test whether a rifle bullet could cut the hangman's rope to stop a hanging. Charles Bronson played a modern-day vigilante in a long series of *Death Wish* films. In the motion picture *The Oxbow Incident*, a reluctant Jimmy Stewart and a couple dozen other people hang three thieves in a heart-wrenching battle of morality, only to find the men were innocent. In *Unforgiven*, Clint Eastwood portrays a bad man who kills a bunch of other bad men, along with a couple of not-quite-so-bad men. And the audience is left not quite knowing how to feel, because vigilante justice is always hollow justice.

The lessons were a long time coming. Way back in 1876 a little book, *A History of Pioneer Families of Missouri,* said, "It teaches a practical lesson that should not be forgotten: viz. that good men, with the best intentions, may be led into the commission of unjust, unlawful, and cruel deeds when they take the law into their own hands and attempt to punish criminals and allay crime by summary proceedings." And yet that's exactly what happened for another quarter of a century.

Americans still harken to the vigilante story. We love the democracy of it. We love the right of the people to do right. We love the confrontation between good and evil. But more than the story, we love the person who's brave enough to put his or her own life on the line for others. We don't love vengeance for its own sake. We love sacrifice for the greater good.

Maybe there's a hint of vigilante heritage in all of us. Every once in a while, somebody chases down a purse snatcher. Or follows a bank robber while talking to the police dispatcher on a cell phone. Not long ago, the case of Ken McElroy became internationally known. He was the town bully of tiny Skidmore, Missouri, tucked away among the corn and wheat fields. McElroy was arrested countless times and indicted, but never convicted, for serious crimes, including assault, rape, and burglary. Then he shot and nearly killed a seventy-year-old store-keeper, who was also a beloved minister. Even after the man recovered, McElroy threatened to kill him. So one afternoon as he sat in his truck with his wife in broad daylight, a crowd of about forty people gathered around, and McElroy, the town bully, was shot to death, with multiple bullets from multiple pistols. Nobody saw a thing and nobody was prosecuted. That was in 1981, and it incorporated elements of mob mentality, individual vigilance, community regulators, and even a hint of government cooperation.

We crave justice. That's just the way people are wired. When the evils of the world steal our joy and peace, we may let things go, forgive, and move on with our lives, but we still need to be reassured that we're protected. The thing about justice is that it can be a long time coming. And in the meanwhile, we wonder, we grow impatient, and we want resolution. We love vigilantes not because they're villains or heroes, and not because they're right or wrong. It's because we need to trust that the law will win more than it will lose, even if the people have to enforce it themselves.

Acknowledgments

My special thanks go to research assistant Carole Goggin, whose resourcefulness and insight added depth and breadth to the work. Also to Lisa Gendron, genealogist and historian, an inspiration, and my ongoing research partner.

Thanks to Dixie Zink, who generously shared the library and notes of her late husband, devoted researcher Wilbur A. Zink. Also to Jim Weaver, president, Benton County Historical Society.

Special thanks to David Bertram Stark, USA Ret., Daviess County historian and a descendant of the original settlers of Gallatin, Missouri, who so generously gave of his time, knowledge, and resources. Also to Jim Stout of the Daviess County Historical Society.

Thanks to Ruth Carver, Jan Hite, Robert L. Hildebrand, and Darryl Lawson, for Sam Hildebrand's story. Also, Bettye Warner, for her history of Sam Hildebrand and St. Francois County, which she has preserved and shared on ancestry.com.

Thanks to Rosanna Miller, cousin, librarian, and tireless researcher, for Texas County nuggets, and especially for details of the Parsons and Platter families, based in part on the recollections of her mother, Nancy Platter Pittman.

This work would not be possible without the many historical societies, museums, amateur genealogists, and devoted researchers throughout Missouri.

Above all, my deep gratitude to my editor, Lauren Mitchell, and Victoria Monks, Keri McBride, and the Missouri History Museum for their faithfulness, support, and dedication to keeping history alive.

Notable Sources by Topic

The Bald Knobbers

Cobb, Vicki Layton. *Taney County Missouri*. Mt. Pleasant, SC: Arcadia Publishing, 2001.

Hartman, Ingenthron. *Bald Knobbers: Vigilantes on the Ozarks Frontier*. Gretna, LA: Pelican Publishing, 1998.

The Border Wars

Beights, Ronald H. *Jesse James and the First Missouri Train Robbery*. Gretna, LA: Pelican Publishing, 2002.

Confederate Veteran 25, no. 4 (April 1917).

Miller, Merle. *Plain Speaking: An Oral Biography of Harry S. Truman*. New York: Berkley Books, 1974.

Neely, Jeremy. *The Border between Them: Violence and Reconciliation on the Kansas-Missouri Line*. Columbia: University of Missouri Press, 2007.

The Nevada Daily Mail (Nevada, MO). April 20, 1893.

Nichols, Bruce. *Guerrilla Warfare in Civil War Missouri, 1863*. Jefferson, NC: McFarland & Co., 2004.

Petersen, Paul R. *Quantrill of Missouri—The Making of a Guerrilla Warrior: The Man, the Myth, the Soldier*. Nashville: Cumberland House, 2003.

Schultz, Duane. *Quantrill's War: The Life and Times of William Clarke Quantrill, 1837–1865*. New York: St. Martin's Press, 1996.

Stiles, T. J. *Jesse James: Last Rebel of the Civil War*. New York: Knopf, 2002.

The Civil War

The War of the Rebellion: A Compilation of the Official Records of the Union and Confederate Armies. Washington, DC: Government Printing Office, 1880.

Government Vigilantes

Birdsall & Dean. *The History of Daviess County, Missouri.* Joplin, MO: Hearthstone Legacy Publications, 1882.

Zink, Wilbur A. *The Roscoe Gun Battle: Younger Brothers vs. Pinkerton Detectives.* Clinton, MO: Democrat, 1967[?].

James Butler Hickok

Rosa, Joseph G. *They Called Him Wild Bill.* Norman: University of Oklahoma Press, 1979.

Mob Mentality

Edwards, John N. *Noted Guerrillas.* New York: Morningside Bookshop, 1975.

The Granby Miner (Granby, MO), May 16, 1874.

The Heritage News, Jefferson Heritage and Landmark Society, July 1994.

History of Clay and Platte Counties, Missouri. St. Louis: National Historical Company, 1885.

The Mormon Wars

Bushman, Richard. *Joseph Smith: Rough Stone Rolling.* New York: Alfred A. Knopf, 2005.

Church of Jesus Christ of Latter-day Saints. *Latter Days: An Insider's Guide to Mormonism.* New York: Macmillan, 2001.

Encyclopedia of Mormonism. New York: Macmillan, 1992.

The History of Jackson County, Missouri. Kansas City, MO: Union Historical Company, 1881.

Scott, Latayne C. *The Mormon Mirage: A Former Mormon Looks at the Mormon Church Today*. Grand Rapids, MI: Zondervan, 2009.

Van Wagoner, Richard S., and Steven C. Walker. *A Book of Mormons*. Salt Lake City: Signature Books, 1982.

Personal Justice

Bishop, Albert Webb. *Loyalty on the Frontier: Or, Sketches of Union Men of the South-West; with Incidents and Adventures in Rebellion on the Border*. St. Louis: R. P. Studley, 1863.

Sam Hildebrand

Breihan, Carl W. *Sam Hildebrand, Guerilla*. Wauwatosa, WI: Leather Stocking Books, 1984.

Murdock, Gene. *Sam Hildebrand's Footprints*. Bonne Terre, MO: Murdock's Historical Publications, 2000.

Ross, Kirby, ed. *Autobiography of Samuel S. Hildebrand*. Fayetteville: University of Arkansas Press, 2005.

Thompson, Henry C. *Sam Hildebrand Rides Again*. Bonne Terre, MO: Bonne Terre Printing Co., 1967.

Wilke, Martha Sue DeClue. *Sam Hildebrand: Guerrilla Fighter*. Bonne Terre, MO: Stolle's Printing Services, 1984.

The Slicker Wars

History of Hickory, Polk, Cedar, Dade, and Barton Counties, Missouri. Chicago: Goodspeed, 1889.

The Northern Standard (Clarksville, TX). July 31, 1844.

Vincent, J. W. "The 'Slicker War' and Its Consequences." *Missouri Historical Review* 7 (April 1913).

Williams, Walter, ed. *A History of Northeast Missouri*. Vol. 1. New York: Lewis Publishing Company, 1913.

Wyatt Earp

Alvin Rucker files. Oklahoma Historical Society, Oklahoma City, OK.

Gatto, Steve. *The Real Wyatt Earp.* Silver City, NM: High Lonesome Books, 2000.

Urban, William. "Wyatt Earp's Father." *True West Magazine* (May 1989).

Various Topics

Culberson, William C. *Vigilantism: Political History of Private Power in America.* New York: Greenwood Press, 1990.

Civil Government and History of Missouri, Columbia, MO: E. M. Stephens, 1898.

Daughters of the Republic of Texas. Vol. 1. Nashville: Turner, 1995.

Duff, Michael, and Barry Foreman. "Hanged by the Neck until Dead… Dead…Dead." *Bittersweet* magazine 5, no. 3 (Spring 1978).

Goodspeed's History (various counties). Chicago: Goodspeed Publishing Co., 1888–1889.

Elsea, Albert, and Neil Moss. *Our Missouri.* New York: MacMillan, 1939.

Johnson, David D. *John Ringo, King of the Cowboys.* Denton: University of North Texas Press, 2008.

Missouri: A Guide to the "Show Me" State. St. Louis: Missouri Historical Society Press, 1998.

Reavis, L. U. *Saint Louis, the Future Great City of the World.* St. Louis: C. R. Barns, 1876.

Stevens, Walter B. *Cenntennial History of Missouri: One Hundred Years in the Union, 1820–1921.* Chicago: S. J. Clark, 1921.

Steward, Dick. *Duels and the Roots of Violence in Missouri.* Columbia, MO: University of Missouri Press, 2000.

Viles, Jonas. *A History of Missouri for High Schools.* New York: MacMillan, 1933.

Woodson, W. H. *History of Clay County.* Topeka, IN: Historical Publishing Co., 1920.

Newspaper Archives
> *The Democrat* (Jefferson County, MO), transcribed by Lisa Gendron
> *The Missouri Democrat*
> *The New York Times*
> *The St. Louis Globe-Democrat*
> *The St. Louis Post-Dispatch*

INDEX

ABOUT THE AUTHOR

Joe Johnston, whose articles have appeared widely in history magazines, is a native of Missouri and the author of *The Mack Marsden rder Mystery: Vigilantism or Justice?*, also published by the Missouri ry Museum as part of its Missouri Vigilante series. He's a frequent tor to such magazines as *Wild West*, *True West*, *America's Civil aval History*. He's a writer, artist, songwriter, and inventor of us McDonald's Happy Meal.